Maverick Heart

Maverick Heart

The Further Adventures of Zane Grey

Stephen J. May

OHIO UNIVERSITY PRESS

ATHENS

Ohio University Press, Athens, Ohio 45701
© 2000 by Stephen J. May
Printed in the United States of America
All rights reserved

Ohio University Press books are printed on acid-free paper ⊗ ™

09 08 07 06 05 04 03 02 01 00   5 4 3 2 1

Frontispiece: Zane Grey in Australia, ca. 1936. Grey made
two important trips to Australia in the 1930s, both of
which increased his stature as a world-class angler.

All photographs courtesy of the Ohio Historical Society

Library of Congress Cataloging-in-Publication Data

May, Stephen.
     Maverick heart: the further adventures of Zane Grey /
Stephen J. May.
        p.   cm.
     Includes bibliographical references (p.) and index.
     ISBN 0-8214-1316-3 (cloth : alk. paper) —
     ISBN 0-8214-1317-1 (paper : alk. paper)
     1. Grey, Zane, 1872–1939. 2. Novelists, American—20th
century—Biography. 3. Adventure and adventurers—United
States—Biography. 4. Western stories—Authorship.
I. Title.

PS3513.R6545 Z78 2000
813'.52—dc21
     [B]   00-021235

FOR TREVOR,

FELLOW ADVENTURER

Sea Gypsy

I am fevered of the sunset,
I am fretful with the bay,
For the wander-thirst is on me
And my soul is in Cathay.

There's a schooner in the offing
With her topsails shot with fire,
And my heart has gone aboard her
For the islands of desire.

I must forth again tomorrow!
With the sunset I must be
Hull down on the trail of rapture
In the wonder of the sea.

—RICHARD HOVEY

CONTENTS

ILLUSTRATIONS

In *Zane Grey: Romancing the West* (Ohio, 1997) I attempted to demonstrate the special relationship between Zane Grey and the American West and how that relationship influenced his great novels. The focus of that book was on the crucial period of 1903–25, when Grey first developed as a writer.

In *Maverick Heart: The Further Adventures of Zane Grey* I've sought to complete the survey of Grey's life by focusing on the other aspects of his multifaceted career, in particular his life as a sportsman, outdoorsman, angler, explorer, baseball player, essayist, and desert sage. *Maverick Heart* is intended as a companion volume to *Zane Grey: Romancing the West*.

Born Pearl Zane Gray on January 31, 1872, in Zanesville, Ohio, Zane Grey (he changed the spelling of his surname after graduating from college in 1896) died October 23, 1939, in Altadena, California. Between 1920 and 1939 he lived comfortably in a Spanish-style house in Altadena, surrounded by gardens, lawns, tennis courts, and fan palms. He and his wife Dolly also owned residences on Santa Catalina Island and in Lackawaxen, Pennsylvania. Additionally, they owned cabins in Winkle Bar, Oregon, and in the Tonto Basin, Arizona. However, Grey invariably headed to Altadena when his wanderings were over.

In 1928 Grey asked Dolly to have a huge study added to the big house. While Grey was in New Zealand, Dolly and the contractors created for Zane a forty-eight by seventy-five-foot office, which was soon filled with mementos, boxes of letters, Navajo rugs, bearskins, bookshelves, and the famous Morris chair in which Grey did his writing. Nearby was a fireplace bearing an Indian petroglyph design. On Grey's desk were photos of Dolly and the three children.

If there was a place that best reflected the many lives of Zane

Grey, it was this rambling study in Altadena. On one end of the bookshelves were the authors who deeply influenced Grey: Wordsworth (*Lyrical Ballads*); Defoe (*Robinson Crusoe*); Shakespeare (the tragedies); Hugo (*Les Misérables*); Hawthorne (the Romances); Stevenson (*Treasure Island*); and the various works of Tennyson, Conrad, Matthew Arnold, and John Ruskin.

On another shelf were books authored by Grey. The variety of their subjects reveals the breadth of his interests and talents. To one side were his baseball books for boys: *The Short Stop, The Young Pitcher,* and *The Redheaded Outfield.* Next came the classic angling books: *Tales of Fishes, Tales of Fresh-Water Fishing, Tales of Tahitian Waters, Tales of Swordfish and Tuna,* and *An American Angler in Australia.* Beside them were his outdoor books: *Tales of Lonely Trails* and *Zane Grey's Book of Camps and Trails.* On the next shelf were some of his great western novels: *Riders of the Purple Sage, The Rainbow Trail, The Border Legion, The Desert of Wheat, Nevada, Wanderer of the Wasteland,* and *The Vanishing American.*

No telephone or radio intruded on the silence and seclusion in Grey's office. Grey hated distractions; if a phone call came for him, he took it in the main wing of the house. Amid his solitude and personal mementos, Grey could plunge into the business of writing.

Because Grey was so prolific and his interests so diverse, his biographers have had difficulty in selecting the essential features of his life. Too often there is the temptation to see the forest instead of the trees. In *Maverick Heart: The Further Adventures of Zane Grey* I have concentrated on what I feel are the key ingredients of Zane Grey's other lives. In some chapters I have focused on individual essays and stories, instead of trying to discuss his entire production, which by a conservative estimate would exceed five million words.

For some reason, observers of Grey have either merely alluded to his life as an adventurer or entirely avoided mentioning it. I assume the reason is that their foremost concern is with Grey as writer of western fiction, and that discussions of his other roles would only distract from that focus. I agree. Not often does one find in a writer or artist such a wealth of avocations, which, quite naturally, makes it difficult to write of the totality of their lives. That is why I decided to treat Zane Grey's western fiction and his sporting life in separate volumes. In this book I've tried to give the reader an assessment of Grey as an adventurer, explorer, and outdoor writer.

In *Maverick Heart: The Further Adventures of Zane Grey* I advance the argument that further consideration of Grey's nonfiction work reveals a well-rounded writer with diverse interests and unsuspected strengths. Those readers who enjoy Grey's western novels will probably be further impressed by his abilities in nonfiction. Those critics who dismiss his western novels might reconsider their opinion of Grey as a writer upon the review of his outdoor essays. In my mind, most of Grey's work discussed in this book contains splendid description, insightful narration, frequent humor, surprising vitality, pungent wit, and provocative philosophy.

In this book I also draw upon Grey's private letters, which I found to be a rich source of material. I additionally discuss his important short stories and novelettes, as well as his "other" novels, *The Reef Girl* and *Wilderness Trek*. These fresh perspectives, in combination with his western novels, afford the reader what I hope is a more comprehensive portrait of the man—and the phenomenon—who was Zane Grey.

Also new in this book is a more thorough view of the relationship of Zane and Dolly Grey. Without a doubt, Zane Grey could not have led the adventurous life he did without the assistance and devotion of Dolly. Dolly has long been acknowledged as the force behind Zane; she was also a unique personality in her own right. In *Maverick Heart* I again assert her significant role in Grey's writing career, but I add to it a survey of her many talents, loves, and idiosyncrasies.

Zane's and Dolly's marriage was riddled with secrecy, melodrama, and hypocrisy. It was also filled with tenderness, dedication, and great love. The story of their life together is as compelling as any story Zane Grey ever wrote. Frequently it was turbulent; other times it contained long separations followed by happy reunions.

Both Zane and Dolly blossomed during the era of Theodore Roosevelt. Roosevelt, the cowboy commander of the Rough Riders, exerted much more influence on Grey than has previously been acknowledged. To my mind, the popularity of the western novel was enhanced by the public's perception of T.R. as a western hero. Roosevelt's experiences in the Dakotas in the 1880s and his exploits in Cuba in 1898 had made him an honorary westerner. He expressed this vigorous cowboy image to his countrymen during his presidency. Along with Owen Wister, Frederic Remington, Buffalo Bill's Wild West Show, and the proliferation of the dime novel, Roosevelt probably influenced the sales of Zane Grey's books more than any other factor.

Partly at Dolly's insistence, Grey headed to the Colorado River Basin in 1907. It was a journey that began in curiosity and ended in pilgrimage. Grey came to love this landscape. And if there is one feature that sets him apart from other western writers it his devotion to the varied countryside of the Southwest. Where other observers might treat the land as a scenic backdrop, Grey worshipped the beautiful and grotesque rock monuments like holy shrines.

While Grey became famous for authoring western novels, he also developed a significant reputation as an outdoorsman. When *Outdoor Life* celebrated its one hundredth year of publication in 1998, the editors decided to include some of the luminaries of its pages over the years. Among those featured in the centennial issue were Ernest Hemingway, Theodore Roosevelt, and Zane Grey. In outdoor essays such as "Colorado Trails" (*Outdoor Life*, March 1918), Grey became one of the gurus of hunting and fishing in the western United States. Despite Grey's outdoor expertise he was remarkably humble in his writing, frequently playing the role of a supporting character or trusting the forest knowledge of his guides over his own. While Roosevelt and Hemingway projected aloof egotism on the hunting trail, Grey was often self-deprecating and ambivalent. "Hunting is magnificent," he wrote, "up to the moment the first shot is fired."

Ultimately, Grey was a loner. In the roles of adventurer, essayist, explorer, and western novelist, he inevitably sought sanctuary in himself. Because of his shyness and reluctance to remain in the limelight, he sprinted from most publicity. If he wished he could have been as popular as any movie idol of the time. With his flinty, midwestern good looks he could have been a superstar of the Jazz Age. He simply did not have the desire for such status. Rather, he sought the anonymity of the writing life. In that role, he found enough fame and attention for his own liking.

A book of this scope and nature could never have been written without the inspiration and kind assistance of many people. I would like to thank the following from Zane Grey's West Society: Todd Newport, president; Joe Wheeler, executive director; Charles Pheiffer, Carolyn Timmerman, Loren and Bonnie Grey; Terry Bolinger, Sonny Heath, Jim Vickers, and Les Smith. For permission to use information from the *Zane Grey Review,* I'd again like to thank Carolyn Timmerman, editor, whose love of Zane Grey's work is balanced by her dedication to the truth. For reading parts of the manuscript and providing her support, I thank Professor Mary Karen Solomon.

A huge debt is owed to the work of the late G. M. Farley, who amassed a significant body of Grey scholarship and was always ready to share this knowledge. I still miss his inspiration and kind spirit. I would also like to acknowledge the work of Grey scholars Carlton Jackson, Candace Kant, and George Reiger for their groundbreaking work in Grey studies. At the Ohio Historical Society I would like to thank Lisa Wood, research assistant, for helping me to select the appropriate photographs, and appreciation also to Mr. Duryea Kemp for tracking down some information. Thanks also must go to Alan King and Kit Gibson of the National Road/Zane Grey Museum in Norwich, Ohio, for extending numerous courtesies. My thanks also to Bradford R. Cole, curator of manuscripts at the Cline Library, University of Northern Arizona, for granting permission to quote from the letters of Zane and Dolly Grey in the G. M. Farley Papers and to the staff at the Ohio Historical Society for allowing me to cite letters from their collection.

Sections of chapter 3 on the Colorado River were originally delivered in different form as a presentation to the Zane Grey's West Society on June 17, 1998, at the group's annual convention in Grand Junction, Colorado.

An incurable romantic and maverick of the first order, Zane Grey rebelled against society's norms and chose the lifestyle that pleased him. In our own time, when the pressures to conform are great and the demands on our time are endless, it seems an enviable decision.

AUTHOR'S NOTE

When he was in his twenties, Zane Grey changed the spelling of his last name by replacing the *a* with an *e*. His brother, R. C. Grey, made the same change. I have taken the liberty of spelling their last name Grey throughout.

1872   Zane Grey (birth name: Pearl Zane Gray) born January 31 in Zanesville, Ohio.

1875   R. C. Grey born in Zanesville.

John Wesley Powell: *The Exploration of the Colorado River.*

1876   Battle of the Little Big Horn, Montana.

1878   Publishing firm Beadle and Adams introduces the dime novel.

1883   Lina Elise Roth—later known as Dolly Grey—born February 6 in New York.

1884   Theodore Roosevelt in the Badlands, North Dakota.

Helen Hunt Jackson: *Ramona.*

1885   Owen Wister in Medicine Bow, Wyoming.

Theodore Roosevelt: *Hunting Trips of a Ranchman.*

1886   Capture of Geronimo.

Z.G. enters Zanesville High School.

1888   Theodore Roosevelt: *Ranch Life and the Hunting Trail.*

1889   Theodore Roosevelt: *The Winning of the West* (vol. 1).

1890   Z.G. moves with his family to Columbus, Ohio.

1892   Z.G. enrolls at University of Pennsylvania with baseball scholarship.

Sierra Club founded.

Owen Wister: "Hank's Woman."

1893   Z.G. plays summer baseball in Delphos, Ohio.

William Jackson Turner delivers speech: "The Significance of the Frontier in American History" in Chicago.

1895   Z.G. plays summer baseball in Findlay, Ohio, and Jackson, Michigan. Hits .295 at Findlay and .398 at Jackson.

1896   Z.G. leaves Philadelphia for New York City, where he opens a dental office.

William McKinley elected president of the U.S.

1897	Z.G. joins Campfire Club in New York.
	Gold Rush in Klondike territory.
	Owen Wister: *Lin McClean*.
1898	Theodore Roosevelt leads the Rough Riders in Cuba.
	Z.G. plays baseball in Newark, New Jersey.
1900	Z.G. meets Lina (Dolly) Roth on the Delaware River.
1901	President McKinley assassinated in Buffalo, New York.
	Theodore Roosevelt becomes twenty-sixth president of the U.S.
1902	Zane Grey: "A Day on the Delaware" (*Recreation*), his first published article.
	Owen Wister: *The Virginian*.
1903	Zane Grey: *Betty Zane*, his first novel.
	Mary Austin: *The Land of Little Rain*.
	Andy Adams: *The Log of a Cowboy*.
1904	Theodore Roosevelt elected to a second term.
	John C. Van Dyke: *The Desert*.
1905	Z.G. marries Dolly in New York City.
1906	Z.G. and Dolly honeymoon in the West.
	George Wharton James: *The Wonders of the Colorado Desert*.
1907	Zane Grey: "Byme-by-Tarpon" (*Field and Stream*).
	Z.G. travels with Buffalo Jones and Jim Emmett in Arizona and Utah.
	Beginning of the California Aqueduct.
1908	Z.G. (with Buffalo Jones and Jim Emmett) explores Grand Canyon area.
	Zane Grey: "Tige's Lion" (*Field and Stream*).
1909	Zane Grey: *The Short Stop*, his first baseball book; "Roping Lions in the Grand Canyon" (*Field and Stream*).
	Z.G. in Nassau, Cuba, and Mexico.
1910	Zane Grey: *The Heritage of the Desert*, his breakthrough novel; "The Rube" (*Popular*); "A Trout Fisherman's Inferno" (*Field and Stream*).

1911   Zane Grey: "The Rubber Hunter" (*Popular*); "Down an Unknown Jungle River" (*Field and Stream*).

Z.G. travels with Al Doyle on Navajo reservation.

1912   Zane Grey: *Riders of the Purple Sage* (*Field and Stream*); "Tigre" (*Munsey's*); "The Fighting Qualities of Black Bass" (*Field and Stream*).

Titanic sinks.

1913   Z.G. travels with John Wetherill to Rainbow Bridge.

Willa Cather: *O Pioneers!*

California Aqueduct completed.

1914   Zane Grey: *The Light of Western Stars.*

Panama Canal completed.

World War I begins.

1915   Zane Grey: *The Rainbow Trail;* "Nonnezoshe" (*Recreation*); "Monty Price's Nightingale" (*Popular*).

1917   Zane Grey: "Two Fights with a Swordfish" (*Recreation*).

Z.G. travels in northwest Colorado ("Colorado Trails").

U.S. enters World War I.

1918   Zane Grey: *The U.P. Trail;* "Gladiator of the Sea" (*Field and Stream*).

Z.G. and family move to southern California.

Z.G. hunts in Tonto Basin, Arizona ("Tonto Basin").

Spanish influenza spreads across the world.

World War I ends in Europe.

1919   Zane Grey: *Tales of Fishes;* "Swordfish of the Sea" (*Field and Stream*); "Big Tuna" (*Field and Stream*).

Z.G. travels in Death Valley, California ("Death Valley"), the Pacific Northwest, and Tonto Basin, Arizona.

Theodore Roosevelt dies.

1920   Zane Grey: "Yaqui" (*Country Gentleman*); "Crater Lake Trout" (*Country Gentleman*); *The Redheaded Outfield and Other Stories.*

Z.G. moves to his final residence on Mariposa Street, Altadena, California.

1921   Z.G. visits Zanesville, Ohio, his boyhood home.

1922   Zane Grey: *Tales of Lonely Trails.*

1923   Zane Grey: *Tappan's Burro and Other Stories; Wanderer of the Wasteland;* "Steelhead" (*Country Gentleman*); "Fishing the Rogue" (*Country Gentleman*).

Emerson Hough: *North of '36.*

Dolly Grey vacations in Europe.

1924   Zane Grey: *Tales of Southern Rivers; The Wolf Tracker* (*Ladies' Home Journal*); "What the Desert Means to Me" (*American*); "Help Us Save Vanishing America" (*Success*).

Z.G. buys *Fisherman* in Nova Scotia; travels in Oregon.

1925   Zane Grey: *The Vanishing American; Tales of Fishing Virgin Seas; Don: The Story of a Lion Dog* (*Harper's*).

Z.G. travels to Galapagos, Cocos Island, and Mexican coast.

Z.G. sails to New Zealand.

1926   Zane Grey: "Shooting the Rogue" (*Country Gentleman*); *Tales of the Angler's El Dorado, New Zealand;* "From Missouri" (*McCall's*).

Z.G. in Tahiti and New Zealand.

Dolly Grey in Europe.

1927   Zane Grey: *Tales of Swordfish and Tuna.*

Z.G. in New Zealand.

1928   Zane Grey: *Tales of Fresh-Water Fishing; Nevada;* "Avalanche" (*Country Gentleman*).

Z.G. in Tahiti.

Herbert Hoover elected president of the U.S.

Boulder Canyon project authorized by Congress.

1929   Zane Grey: "Amber's Mirage" (*Ladies' Home Journal*); *The Ranger* (*Ladies' Home Journal*).

Z.G. in Tahiti, Arizona, and Utah.

Stock market collapses.

1930   Zane Grey: "Canyon Walls" (*Ladies' Home Journal*); "Giant of the South Seas" (*Outdoor Life*).

Z.G. buys *Fisherman II*; sails in Tahiti.

Max Brand: *Destry Rides Again.*

1931 Zane Grey: *Tales of Tahitian Waters; Zane Grey's Book of Camps and Trails.*

Z.G. sails to Tahiti, relinquishes idea of sailing around the world.

Boulder Dam Project begins.

1932 Z.G. and Dolly establish Zane Grey Corporation.

Franklin Roosevelt elected president of the U.S.

1933 Z.G. in New Zealand and Tahiti.

1934 Zane Grey: "Outlaws of Palouse" (*Country Gentleman*).

Z.G. travels in Oregon.

R. C. Grey dies.

1935 Zane Grey: "North Umpqua Steelhead" (*Sports Afield*).

Boulder Dam completed.

1936 Zane Grey: *The Trail Driver.*

Z.G. visits Australia, films *White Death.*

Franklin Roosevelt elected to a second term.

1937 Zane Grey: *An American Angler in Australia;* "Australian Angling" (*Field and Stream*).

Z.G. suffers heart attack in Oregon.

1938 Z.G. returns to Australia.

1939 Zane Grey: *Western Union*, his last book signing.

Zane Grey dies October 23 in Altadena.

Maverick Heart

CHAPTER ONE

❧ ❧ ❧

The Boy of Summer

I see the boys of summer in their ruin
Lay the gold tithings barren,
Setting no store by harvest, freeze the soils;
There in their heat the winter floods
Of frozen loves they fetch their girls,
And drown the cargoed apples in their tides.

— DYLAN THOMAS

Two clear and forceful images emerge from Zane Grey's childhood and early adult years. The first is of a young boy, his pants knotted below the knee, his hair hand-combed or catlicked, as he heads with fishing pole to the river. The second is also of a youngster, his left hand cradling a baseball glove while his right hand holds a bat.

Fishing—and writing about it—would dominate Grey's life to the degree that he would probably consider himself an angler first and human being second. This inverted order of perceptions never seemed to bother him very much. Between 1924 and 1936 he set fourteen world fishing records in such varied locales as Nova Scotia, Mexico, and Australia. He became an articulate spokesman for the sport, developing and endorsing key pieces of fishing tackle.

As for baseball, he followed it devoutly, both in its amateur and professional varieties. When his playing days were over in his late twenties, he became an avid spectator and baseball journalist, following the growth of the sport from a modest diversion before 1910 to its virtual monopoly of American culture in the 1920s.

When Zane Grey was in his teens in Zanesville, Ohio, baseball fields sprouted everywhere, from empty sandlots to front lawns to remote patches of turf tucked away by the Muskingum River. Boys, and sometimes girls if they were lucky, descended on these rough diamonds, playing games of "choose-up" and emulating the exploits of the minor-league players in places such as Pittsburgh and Columbus.

At one time Grey played for a team called Madden's Hill, named for a local landmark. Frequently he used a hard rubber ball stitched with yarn to simulate a real baseball. When Madden's Hill played a team from Seventh Ward, the rubber ball was so "lively that you could hardly hold it."[1] When Grey pitched he threw a regular baseball. However, when Seventh Ward was on the field, Grey substituted the lively ball for the baseball. The Seventh Ward pitcher had no idea of the switch. At the plate, Grey and his teammates crushed the rubber ball, resulting in a twenty-seven-run inning. Perplexed, disheartened, and "hopelessly rattled," the Seventh Ward team left the field badly beaten—and unaware of Grey's trickery.

In 1890, the Gray family moved from Zanesville to Columbus, Ohio. Zane was eighteen and built like a solid bull terrier. His dreamy eyes and slumberous strength fooled people. Few could imagine that such a mild-mannered pup could become such a competitor on the diamond. But when Grey walked onto the playing field, he unleashed restless energy on virtually anyone in his path.

This combination of physical strength, abandon, and mental toughness would show up in other Grey roles: as writer, adventurer, explorer, and family man. Once he committed to any venture, Grey attacked it with a singular vengeance.

Above all Grey wanted to be a star pitcher. Seemingly, it was young rural hurlers who became the stuff of legends—and Grey wanted to be just like them. These podunk phenoms and sandlot pitchers came from virtually every remote spot in America: places like Blue Ash, Ohio; Salt Lick, Kentucky; Birdsboro, Pennsylvania; and Peach Orchard, Arkansas. If they were good and maintained their velocity they ended up in the majors alongside the likes of Walter Johnson and Christy Mathewson. Generally they were rangy and thin as saplings, with straw hair sprouting from under their baseball caps. While other boys played marbles or the piano, these young pitchers often hurled three hundred hardballs a day into a tipped apple basket. Frequently they could not spell their team name, but they could smoke a fastball from sixty feet or finesse a curve past an unwary batter. They knew next to nothing about nervous tension. In front of a roaring crowd in Buffalo or Philadelphia they were as cool as a pasture cow.

These hurlers appealed deeply to Grey, who could easily see himself in their shoes. He would probably have gone on to pitch in the majors if the distance from the rubber to home plate had remained the same. Later, in college, he tried for several seasons to get accustomed to the new distance of sixty feet six inches, but he never did succeed.

In Columbus in 1892, he quickly started pitching for the Capitols, the city league team. He had a strong arm, due in part to pulling teeth on the side. His dentist father usually assigned him this task as a way of keeping him out of trouble and letting him make some extra money. Zane traveled to the outlying areas of Columbus, creating something of a reputation as a tooth-puller. Before dentistry was regulated, a large segment of the population was serviced this way.

On these rural missions, Grey frequently mixed business with sport. One outing took him to Baltimore, Ohio, a farm town about thirty miles southeast of Columbus. Baltimore fielded a respectable team, but its pitching staff was weak. They were scheduled to play a team from nearby Jacktown. Sensing he could help, Grey boasted of his pitching prowess to the Baltimore manager, telling him that he played for the pennant-winning Columbus Capitols. The manager had indeed heard of Pearl Gray, and was sufficiently impressed to hire Zane as a "ringer"—an impromptu substitution. Grey's assignment was to start the game against rival Jacktown.

Jacktown's team was an assortment of bullies and conscripted farmhands, who arrived in gaudy baseball outfits. "Raw-boned and rangy," they played without shoes.[2] Moreover, they brought their own umpire, named Starleet, to the game. Starleet dressed more like a dandy than a baseball official. According to Grey, he wore "black velvet knickers, a white ruffled shirt, a flowing tie, and a little cap with a tassel."[3] Despite his looks, Grey considered him a "a tough hombre" behind the plate. Zane's teammates confirmed that Starleet was a Jacktown man, and that they would have to hit the ball hard to have a chance to win.

Jacktown's pitcher was a bumptious oaf of three hundred pounds named Ben Orth, whose post-game brawling was legendary. Orth first intimidated players with his scowl and size. He then punished them in the game. And if they needed more, he saved his remaining aggression for the barroom and the back alley.

Ben Orth's only pitch was a fastball, and he hurled it "like a bullet." He retired the Baltimore lineup in the first inning on nine pitches. The visiting Jacktown crowd roared its approval. Grey thought it might be quick game.

Pearl Zane Gray went to the mound for Baltimore. Using his curveball, change-up, and fastball he mowed down the Jacktown lineup. The innings fled briskly. By the fifth, it was apparent to Grey that Starleet was favoring Jacktown. The umpire was calling clear strikes as balls, and Zane was getting frustrated.

The game remained scoreless through six innings, but in the bottom of the seventh a Baltimore player beat out a grounder past the cumbersome Orth. The next man singled the runner to third. The catcher walked, loading the bases. On an 0–2 pitch, Grey homered into the hay wagons lined up in the outfield. Baltimore scored two more runs and led 6–0 after seven innings.

When Grey took the mound, the Jacktown rooters booed him endlessly. After striking out the first batter, he got the second on a slow curveball. The man was so doubled-up by the pitch that he crumpled to the dirt. Grey swelled with pleasure. By then the Jacktown team and fans were chanting at Grey: "Ringer! Ringer! Ringer!"[4]

Starleet called a time-out, walked to the mound, and accused Grey of doctoring his pitches. "Game called!" snapped the umpire. "Nine to nothing! Favor Jacktown! Baltimore's ringer pitcher throws a crooked ball!"[5]

Grey was stunned. More significantly, however, the Jacktown crowd and players were storming the field and heading after him. Grey darted from the mound, ducked into the dugout, and headed out of the ballpark. In hot pursuit, the Jacktown players and fans were right behind him. Big Ben Orth grabbed a fence rail and swung it as easily as a baseball bat. Grey ran to the nearby barn, where he had left his street clothes, and began madly undressing. After he pulled his shirt on, the Jacktown mob burst into the barn. Trouserless, Grey bolted for the rear door, dashed from the yard, and kept running into an adjacent cornfield. Finding a good furrow amid the six-foot-high corn, he waited and slept.

The following morning a farmer stumbled on Grey sleeping in his cornfield. Grey explained the events of the previous day. The farmer told him that he had seen the game, the ensuing melee, and Zane's sprinting abilities. They shared a good laugh. Before they parted, the farmer gave Grey a pair of overalls to wear on the train back to Columbus.

After Grey (still known as Pearl Zane Gray) secured a baseball scholarship to the University of Pennsylvania in 1892, he began the tradition of playing summer ball for various midwestern teams. One of his first stops was Delphos, Ohio, where he played alongside his brother, R.C.

In 1893, R.C. Grey was eighteen and a versatile outfielder. At 5

Zane Grey ca. 1895, just prior to his graduation from the dentistry program of the University of Pennsylvania.

foot 10 inches and weighing 170 pounds, he batted left and threw left. After playing for Delphos he joined clubs in Findlay, Ohio, and Jackson, Michigan (1895); Ft. Wayne, Indiana (1896); Buffalo, New York (1897); and Toronto, Ontario (1898–1900). R.C. was a better pure hitter than Zane, who worked more on his rotation of pitches. In 1895, R.C. hit a sizzling .454 while playing for Jackson, and went on to a lifetime .370 batting average in the minor leagues. Nick-named "Reddy," R.C. had a fiery head of hair that matched his temper. It was Reddy or R.C. who would inspire the events in Zane Grey's *The Red-Headed Outfield* (1920).

Both Zane and R.C. played for Delphos during the successful summer of 1893. The following year, they reprised their roles on the team. The Delphos manager called Pearl "not only a great ball player but a gentlemanly one." The manager added that "he would rather have nine good, gentlemanly, brainy players than nine heavy-batting lushers."[6]

During the time he played baseball in Delphos, Grey experienced events that brought him face to face with the world's evil and that ultimately threatened his life. It was common in Delphos—although it was illegal—to play baseball on Sunday. Grey and other players frequently broke the law. Zane soon learned that the mayor planned to enforce the law, and was sending the police to arrest Grey. Zane reckoned that such an arrest would not look good back at Penn, so he decided to leave immediately for Columbus, telling R.C. to mail his clothes home.

Grey steered for the railroad yards and hopped a freight train that would take him home via Lima, Ohio. At Lima the train slowed to a halt, and a passing brakeman shined his light into Grey's darkened box-car. The brakeman asked if Grey had any money. Zane admitted that he had a little. "Give it to me," said the man, "and get back in there." Grey retreated to the dark end of the box car and listened as the train lurched through Lima. Presently the door rattled open and three burly tramps heaved themselves onto the floor. Grey remained silent and motionless in the shadows. As Grey watched the men began arguing about how to divide some stolen goods. One of the men was African American. The argument became heated. The two other tramps hit the black man over the head with a heavy instrument. The man crumpled over, and Grey thought he was dead. Too panic-stricken to move or cry out, Zane remained frozen in the shadows.

The two men moved away from their victim and soon fell asleep. Grey lay prone until dawn. He felt the train slow to a crawl. Gingerly he crept to the door, opened it, leaped from the box-car, and did not quit running until he was under a canopy of trees. Later he learned he was in Upper Sandusky, about seventy miles north of Columbus. Returning to the railyards, he caught another freight train—this one an open car loaded with soft coal—and headed for Columbus.

During the journey it poured. The rain, combined with the wind and coal dust, turned Zane's skin jet-black. Convinced it was a good disguise, he hunkered down in the soft bed of coal and felt the wind swirl around him. When he finally arrived in Columbus, he could hardly wait to tell his parents and the police of one of the most harrowing experiences in his young life.[7]

By 1895, the year before Grey graduated from Penn, Zane and R.C. were playing for clubs in Findlay, Ohio, and Jackson, Michigan. Zane was in the outfield, having pretty much abandoned the idea of becoming a pitcher. At Jackson he played in twenty-seven games, hit .398 for the season, and stole nineteen bases. Playing under the name of Pearl Zane helped protect his college eligibility at the University of Pennsylvania.[8]

When Pearl Zane Gray came to New York in 1896, he entered a Babylon garden festooned with the promises of wealth, fame, and romance. It was at this point that he adopted the name Zane Grey.

He arrived to set up a dental practice, to further his literary ambitions, and to make money. For Grey, who had known nothing but lean times in college, the prospect of making money was particularly attractive. New York seemed a likely place to accomplish that end. In 1861 there were only three millionaires in America; by 1896 there were over 3,500, most inhabiting Manhattan Island and environs. Not only could one make a fortune in New York, but, according to one financier, it would take a damned fool not to.

Urban growth in New York was staggering. In 1870, the city boasted a population of one and a half million people. By 1890, swelled by a stream of immigrants, the figure rose to two and half million.

The president of the New York City Board of Police Commissioners in early 1896 was Theodore Roosevelt. At thirty-eight years of age, Roosevelt had rolled up his sleeves, pounded his fist into his hand, and declared war on the evils of New York City. One of his first goals was to clean up police corruption. True to his word, T.R. began a tradition of prowling the streets at midnight, partly to monitor criminal activities but primarily to check on his own police officers. On one occasion, Roosevelt came upon one of his officers talking to a prostitute. It appeared that an arrest was not imminent, so Roosevelt intervened.

> "Officer, is this the way you attend to your duty, talking to women?"
>
> "What are you looking for—trouble?" the cop retorted, not recognizing Roosevelt. "You see that street? . . . Now run along there or I'll fan you, and I'll fan you hard." He turned to his friend. "Will I fan him, Mame?"
>
> Mame thought he would, but Roosevelt didn't. "Oh, no, officer. You will neither fan me hard nor easy. . . . I am Police Commissioner Roosevelt. Instead of fanning anybody, you report at Headquarters at 9:30 o'clock."[9]

Under Roosevelt's administration, New York's crime rate plummeted, as he earned respect from his officers on the beat.

Into Roosevelt's Gotham came Zane Grey, age twenty-four and as yet unpublished. He opened his dental office; in the rear of the office were his cramped living quarters. "The shapes arise," wrote Walt Whitman. By the end of the century, the shapes had risen in New York into an eruption of skyscrapers and a labyrinth of ethnic neighborhoods. Grey came to loathe the bigness, congestion, and din of the city. On weekends he crossed the bridge and took the twelve-mile trip to East Orange, New Jersey, where he played for a baseball team sponsored by the Orange Athletic Club. He played outfield for the team through the 1901 season. He played briefly on the Newark team until it went bankrupt in 1898. Baseball, like fishing, helped save Grey's sanity in the huge metropolis.

By the turn of the century baseball was out of its infancy and entering its prime, competing with football for spectator support. While football was as rough as a medieval siege, baseball, at least in appearance, was gentlemanly, placid, and leisurely. The players were nicely spaced in baseball, as in any utopia. They sported handlebar mustaches, pointed sideburns, and long stockings. In football twenty-two ruffians banged away at each other; in baseball the players worked at making things pleasant and genteel.

However, this was baseball as seen from the stands. On the field there were more maneuverings and plottings than in a Shakespearean tragedy. The manager wished to murder the opposing pitcher, who was knocking down his batters like bowling pins; the first baseman barked incessantly at the batter at the plate; the runner on second sought to test his cleats on the third baseman's leg. And so on and so on. Whereas football was outwardly barbaric, baseball was subtle, underhanded, and mischievous.

Grey loved these distinct features of the game as well as the others: the nail-biting moments of the late inning rallies, the individual dramas of the players on the field, the manager's anxiety at inserting a greenhorn in the lineup, and the crowds' pointed appraisal of the umpires. In works such as *The Short Stop* (1909), *The*

Grey (far right) as an outfielder for the Orange Athletic Club, in Orange, New Jersey.

Young Pitcher (1911), and *The Red-Headed Outfield and Other Stories* (1920), Zane Grey would reveal these singular aspects of the sport to a generation of young and adult readers.

Perhaps the best of his baseball books is *The Red-Headed Outfield and Other Stories* of 1920. Published the same year as his *Man of the Forest,* this collection of stories discloses Grey's bubbling energy and fierce dedication to the game. Most of the stories were first published in *National Post, Popular,* and *Success* between 1910 and 1911. Out of the tradition of Horatio Alger, they are among the best baseball stories for young adults ever written.

Like the book *The Short Stop, The Red-Headed Outfield* was inspired by Grey's experiences in the minor leagues in Ohio and

Michigan when he was in his twenties. The title work "The Red-Headed Outfield" describes the fictional Rochester Stars team and its trio of red-headed outfielders: Red Gilbat, Reddy Clammer, and Reddie Ray.

Red Gilbat, the nuttiest member of the three, is "a weird, long-legged, long-armed phantom." He is also unpredictable. Sometimes he shows up for a game, and sometimes he does not. He often watches the game from the stands or through a hole in the fence. When Red Gilbat does play, he swats a home run every third trip to the plate. Such behavior drives manager Delaney crazy.

The second member of the outfield is Reddy Clammer, who makes "circus catches, circus stops, circus throws, and circus steals—but particularly circus catches. That is to say he makes easy plays appear difficult." Clammer craves the limelight, and is always "strutting, posing, talking, arguing, and quarreling."[10]

The third member of this unique trio is Reddie Ray, a sprinting champion and marvelous hitter. A cheetah on the basepaths, he is always surprising Delaney with his clutch hitting and acrobatic fielding.

Alternately tormenting, confounding, and surprising Delaney, the three tow-headed wonders lead Rochester to a pennant show-down with the Providence Grays. On a beautiful September day the teams grapple into the late innings. With two out, the bases full, and Rochester needing three runs for a tie and four for the win, Delaney munches his fingernails and watches his star runner warm up in the on-deck circle:

> Bases full, Reddie Ray up, three runs to tie!
> Delaney looked at Reddie. And Reddie looked at Delaney. The manager's face was pale, intent, with a little smile. The player had eyes for fire, a lean, bulging jaw and the hands he reached for his bat clutched like talons.
> "Reddie, I knew it was waitin' for you," said Delaney, his voice ringing. "Break up the game. . . !"
> . . . Clean and swift, Reddie leaped at the first pitched ball. Ping! For a second no one saw the hit. Then it gleamed, a

terrific drive, low along the ground, like a bounding bullet, straight at Babcock in right field. It struck his hands and glanced away to roll toward the fence.

Thunder broke loose from the stands. Reddie Ray was turning first base. Beyond first base he got into his wonderful stride. Some runners run with a consistent speed, the best they can make for a given distance. But this trained sprinter gathered speed as he ran. . . . His strides were long. . . . He had the speed of a race horse, but the trimness, the raciness, the delicate legs were not characteristic of him. Like the wind he turned second, so powerful that his turn was short. All at once there came a difference in his running. It was now fierce, violent. His momentum was running him off his legs. He whirled around third base and came hurtling down the homestretch.

His face was convulsed, his eyes were wild. His arms and legs worked in a marvelous muscular velocity. He seemed a demon —a flying streak.

He overtook and ran down the laboring Scott, who had almost reached the plate.

The park seemed full of shrill, piercing strife. It swelled, reached a highest pitch, sustained that for a long moment, and then declined.

"My Gawd!" exclaimed Delaney, as he fell back. "Wasn't that a finish! Didn't I tell you to watch them redheads?"[11]

In the second story, "The Rube," Grey adopts the first-person point of view, which is unusual in his work, and becomes the manager of a pitching phenom named Whitaker Hurtle. The manager's Worcester club is in the dumps, his players are banged up, and his record is plunging. Moreover, the Worcester fans are enraged and the reporters are raking the team over in the papers. Everything looks dismal indeed. Enter Whitaker Hurtle. "He was as lean as a fence rail, raw-boned as a horse and powerful," observes Grey. At first, however, the manager thinks Hurtle is a "rube"—a bumpkin with no sense. Hurtle gradually proves himself on the mound, as Grey had done years before on the diamonds around Columbus and Zanesville.

During a big game, though, Hurtle begins to lose confidence.

He can't find the plate with his pitches and his manager starts worrying. He calls aside Spears, Worcester's captain. "Go after the rube. Wake him up. Tell him he can't pitch. Call him 'Pogie!' That's a name that stirs him up." Spears goes to the mound and growls at Hurtle: "Come now, you cross between a hayrack and a wagon tongue, get sore and do something. . . . Show us, you tow-headed Pogie."

Angered and flushed, Hurtle gets his rhythm going. He mows down the Bison nine with a barrage of pitches. His manager gloats:

So, with the wonderful pitching of an angry rube, the Worcester team came into its own again. I sat through it all without another word; without giving a signal. In a way I realized the awakening of the bleachers, and heard the pound of feet and the crash, but it was the spirit of my team that thrilled me. Next to that the work of my new find absorbed me. I gloated over his easy, deceiving swing. I rose out of my seat when he threw that straight fast ball, swift as a bullet, true as a plumb line. And when those hard-hitting, sure-bunting Bisons chopped in vain at the wonderful drop, I choked back a wild yell. For Rube meant the world to me that day. . . .

We scored no more. But the Bisons were beaten. Their spirit was broken. This did not make the Rube let up in their last half inning. Grim and pale he faced them. At every long step and swing he tossed his shock of light hair. At the end he was even stronger than at the beginning. He still had the glancing, floating airy quality that baseball players call speed. And he struck out the last three batters.

In the tumult that burst over my ears I sat staring at the dots on my scorecard. Fourteen strikeouts! One scratch hit! No base on balls since the first inning! That told the story which deadened senses doubted. There was a roar in my ears. Someone was pounding me. As I struggled to to get into the dressing room the crowd mobbed me. But I did not hear what they yelled. I had a kind of misty veil before my eyes, in which I saw that lanky Rube magnified into a glorious figure. I saw the pennant waving and the gleam of a white cottage through the trees. . . . Then I rolled into the dressing room.

Somehow it seemed strange to me. Most of the players were

stretched out in peculiar convulsions. Old Spears sat with drooping head. Then a wild flaming-eyed giant swooped upon me. With a voice of thunder he announced:

"I'm a-goin' to lick you, too!"

After that we never called him any name except Rube.[12]

In the next few stories, Grey continues the Rube's exploits in "The Rube's Pennant," "The Rube's Honeymoon," and "The Rube's Waterloo," all with the same gusto and acute knowledge of the sport that characterizes the initial narrative. *The Red-Headed Outfield and Other Stories* was Grey's last baseball book, revealing just how deeply the game penetrated his and the American character. By its publication in 1920, the men with the big lumber—Babe Ruth, Hack Wilson, and Rogers Hornsby—were turning Grey's youthful stories into reality, and making baseball the huge money game of the roaring twenties.

Zane Grey's other passion was fishing, and growing up in Zanesville he became, by his own admission, prince of Muskingum River and Dillon's Falls. He knew the fishing holes by their special names: Big Rock, Pot Shop, Head of Falls, Big Channel, Long Hole, Shady Rift, and Sycamore Hole. Young Zane was surprised by the fecundity of the waters, which yielded rock bass, calico-bass, mud-cats, goggle-eyes, and chub.

On one summer day he met the resident hermit of Dillon's Falls, Old Muddy Miser. Old Muddy became Grey's fishing and outdoor mentor, counseling the boy about the importance of proper tackle and reminding him of the necessity of being a good citizen. Grey never forgot him. For Zane, whose parents held contempt for fishing, it was an ideal relationship. During the hot summer days on the shady banks of Dillon's Falls, Grey played and laughed with Old Muddy Miser, while he developed a fishing knowledge that would go with him from Eastern Ohio to the shores of Tahiti and New Zealand.

Old Muddy Miser inspired in Grey not only a love for freshwater fishing, but also an interest in one day searching out the great fish of the open sea. Muddy Miser tutored his student about the beauty of the striped marlin and the ferocity of the broadbill swordfish. Moreover, he taught Grey that fishing was a noble enterprise, something that Grey remembered all his life.

One August, when Grey was in his early teens, he and Old Muddy sampled the angling at Poverty Run, a notable fishing hole six miles from Dillon's Falls. Muddy Miser told Zane that Indians often sojourned in the nearby woods, a fact that, for Grey, always made a place more haunting and special. For several days, Zane and Old Muddy camped by the river, discussing everything from Zane's future in dentistry to the remote possibility of his becoming a writer.

In his late seventies, Muddy encouraged Zane to read, to experience the world, and to remain a fisherman regardless of his primary occupation.

For the young Zane Grey it was a perfect setting: the campfire and smell of woodsmoke; the bass and chub fishing; the important conversations in the forest's hallowed sunlight. Muddy Miser stressed the rituals of freshwater fishing. Together they caught minnows for bait, watched ducks and geese wing overhead, and cooked their meals over an open fire. The time was spoiled only by the notion that Grey would soon have to return to civilization and the certainty of his father's stern parenting.

Young Zane possessed an uncanny knowledge of the territory around Zanesville. Most children are aware of the limits of their neighborhoods. Zane, however, charted the landscape within a five-to-ten-mile radius of Zanesville. He knew hideouts and havens, byways and secluded lanes. His love for fishing and a persistent need to escape his father's wrath led him far from home, to remote creeks such as Bartlett's Run and Timber Run, both feeding Licking Creek. Often such excursions involved fishing, although Zane also met young girls from time to time.

Zane's father blamed him for introducing fishing to brother Romer. It seemed to Lewis Gray that Zane and Romer spent more time down by the fishing hole than at home doing their chores. One time Romer failed to come home. Zane was so beside himself that he feared telling his father. Instead, he sought out his mother's advice. "Find him before your father comes home," she told Zane. The young Grey immediately began covering the countryside, seeking out the hidden places he knew so well. Failing to find Romer, Zane trudged home, telling his mother, "I didn't find him, but I will." His father quickly declared, "You better had and be quick about it too, you young Muddy Miser. I'll go out and cut me a nice apple switch."

Zane admitted that "the threat of a switching had no particular effect" on him. In fact he would have welcomed "a dozen switchings if it only would have brought Romer back." Once again, Zane scoured the territory. He thought of searching the area around Joe's Run, a forbidden fishing hole "made dreadful by two drownings," but chose instead Sunderland's Lake. The latter was "full of big golden sunfish." However, farmer Sunderland refused to let the neighborhood boys fish in his pond. Zane tramped barefoot for hours in the waning summer light. As darkness fell on the lane leading to the lake, he spied "a dim little figure—a boy in white cotton blouse and short pants." Romer! They clung together for a moment, then Zane took his brother's hand and headed home into the night. "I was scared turrible," R.C. admitted. Pearl Zane explained that their father was so angry he would probably whip them both with an apple switch. "Pa," said Zane "thinks it's my fault you run off fishin'—and I guess that's so." Romer suggested that Zane take him fishing more, thereby alleviating his need to run away with other boys. Zane agreed to the idea, and for the next fifty years or so the two were inseparable.[13]

Zane and his father were always at odds regarding Zane's fishing. Even into his teens, Pearl Zane derived perverse joy from defying his father's authority. Not finding enough time through the week for angling, Zane began sneaking down to Dillon's Falls and Licking Creek on Sundays. On one summer sabbath he tiptoed home and started to wash off the mudstains from a tub in the yard. As he was bending over, his father sneaked behind him and gave Zane "a terrific whack with a good stiff willow switch." Zane bolted from the yard and climbed a neighbor's tree, his father pursuing him. For several minutes Zane hung precariously from a branch high up while his father taunted him from below. Only his mother's intervention prevented Zane from tumbling to the ground and facing his angered father. Mrs. Gray calmed her husband, allowing Zane to shinny down the tree and slouch back to the house.[14]

Such incidents were common around the Gray household. When Zane grew up and had children of his own, he made it a point to make angling an important part of the family's activities.

One humiliating experience during Zane's sophomore year in high school threatened his fishing and baseball activities and, in his own mind, his very existence in Zanesville. Grey felt depressed after being jilted by his girlfriend. Feeling that he needed to do something "terrible," he and two older friends, Charley and Harvey, decided to visit a brothel located between the river and railroad tracks.

The boys knocked on the back door and entered. While they talked to Jumbo, the proprietess, the police raided the place and attempted to arrest Zane and his friends for being underage in a house of "ill-fame." Jumbo tried to persuade one of the officers to drop the charges. "These boys must not be taken to jail," she told him, "they belong to the best families in Zanesville. If you arrest them it can't be kept a secret." The officer refused her entreaties, even reminding Jumbo that "harboring minors would cost her plenty." The police locked up the place and carted a frightened and embarrassed Pearl Zane off to jail.

Eventually the charges against Zane and his friends were dismissed, and he was released to his father. "I expected a terrible upbraiding," Grey wrote, "and a promise of direful punishment, but neither was forthcoming. Manifestly my father was too deeply shocked to think of punishment." For the next several months Grey spiraled downward into shame and guilt. He stopped fishing, playing baseball, and lost interest in his schoolwork. Only later, long after he had left Zanesville for Columbus and Philadelphia, was he able to remember the incident at Jumbo's with some amusement.[15]

When Grey moved from Philadelphia to New York City in 1896, he made the rather astute move of joining the Campfire Club, an organization composed mainly of eastern bluebloods who were dedicated to life in the outdoors. With this club he could further his love of fishing and nature. Not only did it allow him to meet some of the most notable sportsmen in the country, but it also brought him in close contact with publishers and editors of outdoor periodicals. Among its members when Grey joined included: Ernest Thompson Seton, writer and naturalist; Dan Beard, organizer of the Boy Scouts of America; Gifford Pinchot, conservationist; Theodore Roosevelt, writer, naturalist, and politician; George Shields, publisher of *Recreation;* Robert Hobart Davis, editor of *Munsey's;* and Eltinge Warner, who later took over as general manager of *Field and Stream* after the death of John Burkhard. It was through association with these people that Zane Grey furthered his ambitions as a writer, naturalist, and outdoorsman.

Inclusion in the Campfire Club was not simply gained by breeding and notoriety. Often it included the ability to pass tests in woodlore and boating. Zane Grey, in particular, excelled at the annual canoe race, in which his forte was paddling standing up—rather than using the traditional manner of squatting in the canoe. He could also out-fish and out-hunt most of the other members, and, if necessary, out-boast them as well.

By the year 1900 Grey's relationships with publishers in the club deepened. Both Shields of *Recreation* and Davis of *Munsey's* encouraged him to write articles for their respective publications. His brief nature essay "A Day on the Delaware" appeared in the May 1902 issue of *Recreation;* the following year "Camping Out" was published in *Field and Stream.* Before Grey had made his mark as a serious novelist, he was very much the observer of nature in nonfiction.

Perhaps Grey's strongest relationship with a magazine publisher was with *Field and Stream's* Eltinge Warner, a cigar-puffing dynamo who took the periodical from a respectable journal in 1907 to one of the premier sporting magazines in America. For forty-four years, Warner fostered the magazine's emphasis on conservation, encouraging new writers such as William Hornaday and Aldo Leopold to write for his magazine. From 1910 to 1917 *Field and Stream* was the official publication of the Campfire Club, so Zane Grey became familiar with its editorial staff. Gradually, Warner added departments on camping, conservation, boating, and on what became the magazine's signature—the true-life wilderness adventure. Over the years Grey wrote essays for *Field and Stream* on fresh- and saltwater fishing, camping, wilderness ecology, and western travel. With a few other writers such as Florence Tasker and his friend Bob Davis, he became one of the magazine's most frequent contributors.

His first published article, "A Day on the Delaware," is rich in fishing lore. Since it is Grey's initial offering as an outdoor essay, its opening paragraph bears repeating:

> Our summer outing slipped by swiftly as only such days can, and the last one arrived. As we started out in the early morning the fog was rising from the river, and hung like a great grey curtain along the mountaintops; while here and there, through rifts, the bright sun shone making the dew sparkle on the leaves. . . . The air was keen with a suspicion of frost in it, and fragrant with pine and hemlock. This was to be our last day. We were going to improve every moment of it, and, perhaps, add more achievements to memory's store. I looked at Reddy and

marveled at the change a month could bring. He was the color of bronze and the spring of the deerstalker was in his rapid step.[16]

This outdoor kingdom eventually became Grey's sanctuary, nurturing him to health when the city and his job had very nearly destroyed his spirit. As he distanced himself from his dental practice in New York, he retreated to the Delaware wilderness, purchasing land at the convergence of the Delaware and Lackawaxen Rivers. Amid the "gray cliffs and hills black with ragged pines" he bloomed as a nature writer. In August 1900 he met his future wife Lina Elise Roth on the Delaware River, and from then on he considered its bends and shallows sacred.

The Lackawaxen and Delaware River country dominate Grey's early nonfiction writing. He was proud of his knowledge of these rivers and their secrets, once proclaiming that he knew "every rapid, every eddy, almost . . . every stone from Callicoon to Port Jervis."[17] If New York City was too large, too congested, too civilized, this corner of the Pennsylvania was all he truly needed. It was a place he could chart, observe, digest, and reflect on while easing his burgeoning talent safely into its quiet spaces.

Grey always had a particular affection for the diminutive Lackawaxen River, but he was apparently unable to determine if it was a spring, a creek, or truly a river. The Lackawaxen bubbles out of the Pennsylvania Appalachians, swings into the hamlet of Lackawaxen, and flows into the Delaware River. In an early article he describes this terrain vividly: "Winding among the Blue Hills of Pennsylvania there is a swift amber stream that the Indians named Lackawaxen. The literal translation nobody seems to know, but it must mean, in mystical and imaginative Delaware, 'the brown water that turns and whispers and tumbles.' . . . All its tributaries, dashing white-sheeted over ferny cliffs, wine-brown where the whirling pools suck the stain from the hemlock root, harbor the speckled trout. Wise in their generation, the black and red-spotted little beauties keep to their brooks; for, farther down, below the rush and fall, a newcomer is lord of the stream. He is an archenemy, a scorner of beauty and blood, the wolf-jawed, red-eyed, bronze-backed black bass."[18]

Grey loved the qualities of bass, their gaminess and their color, but he loved the isolation of the river even more. Often in summer, tourists descended on his river paradise and the results were predictable:

> Often as I reached the pool I saw fishermen wading down the stream, and on these occasions I sat on the bank and lazily waited for the intruders to pass on. Once, the first time I saw them, I had an angonizing fear that one of the yellow-helmeted, khaki-coated anglers would hook my bass. The fear, of course, was groundless. The idea of that great fish rising to feathery imitation of a bug or lank dead bait had nothing in my experience to warrant its consideration. Small, lively bass, full of play, fond of chasing their golden shadows, and belligerent and hungry, were ready to fight and eat whatever swam into their ken. But a six-pound bass, slow to reach such weight in swift running water, was old and wise and full of years. He did not feed often, and when he did he wanted a live fish big enough for a good mouthful. So, with these facts to soothe me I rested my fears, and got to look humorously at the invasions of the summer-hotel fishers.
>
> They came wading, slipping, splashing downstream, blowing like porpoises, slapping at the water with all kinds of artificial and dead bait. And they called to me with a humor inspired by my fishing garb and the rustic environment:
>
> "Hey, Rube! Ketchin' any?" I said the suckers were bitin' right pert.
>
> "What d'you call this stream?" I replied, giving the Indian name.
>
> "Lack-a-what? Can't you whistle it? Lack-awhacken? You mean Lackafishin'."
>
> "Lackarotten," joined in another. "Do you live here?" questioned a third.
>
> I said yes. "Why don't you move?" Whereupon they all laughed and pursued the noisy tenor of their way downstream, pitching their baits around.

"Say, fellows," I shouted after them, "are you training for the casting tournament in Madison Square Garden or do you think you're playing lacrosse?"

The laugh that came back proved the joke on them, and that it would be remembered as part of the glorious time they were having.[19]

By 1910, after having lived at Lackawaxen for more than five years, Grey could claim some expertise as both a fresh- and saltwater fisherman. Important articles such as "Byme-by-Tarpon" (*Field and Stream*, December 1907) and "Cruising in Mexican Waters" (*Field and Stream*, January 1908), began to establish him as a new voice in saltwater fishing; in freshwater fishing, the Lackawaxen and Delaware Rivers continued to be his focus. By 1910 he had completed his first and second trips west with Buffalo Jones and Jim Emmett, and had written "Roping Lions in the Grand Canyon" (serialized in *Field and Stream* beginning January 1909) and *The Last of the Plainsmen*. The summer of 1910 saw the publication of *The Heritage of the Desert*, the novel that would secure his reputation and allow him the rest of his life for fishing, writing, and adventuring.

In January 1912, *Field and Stream* serialized *Riders of the Purple Sage* before it was published in book form by Harper and Brothers. While Grey's western novel was running, the magazine also published one of his significant fishing essays, "The Fighting Qualities of Black Bass" (May 1912).

The two emotions that Grey knew intimately were melancholy and anger, and nothing could rouse his ire more than someone who pretended to know more about the upper Delaware River than he did. In "Black Bass" he tried to defend his knowledge of the river and advance his own ideas about the great qualities of bass fishing. On this occasion he responded to an article in *Field and Stream* written by an angler named W. P. Corbet, who claimed that the smallmouth bass was superior as a game fish to the largemouth bass. Grey, like another writer he supported, Will H. Dilg, believed that the fighting qualities of bass had nothing to do with size but depended solely on temperature and conditions of the river. When Corbett in his article mentioned casually that he had fly-fished the Delaware as part of his experiment, Grey had enough ammunition to respond. In "The Fighting Qualities of Black Bass," Grey declared:

If I know any fishing water at all it is the Delaware River. I live on it. I own nearly a thousand acres along it. I have fished it for ten years. . . . Mr. C. remarked that "thousands of bass are taken every summer with the fly from the Delaware." If it was meant seriously, I think it should have been made clear. I fancy that in his enthusiasm Mr. C. just "talked." He was not clear, deliberate, and absolutely sure of his facts. . . .

Every fishing water has its secrets. A river or lake is not a dead thing. It has beauty, wisdom and content. And to yield these mysteries it must be fished with more than hooks and for more than fish. Strange things happen to the inquiring fisherman. Nature meets him halfway on his adventure. He must have eyes that see. One fisherman may have keener eyes than another, but no one fisherman's observation is enough. . . . In July, when the water gets low and clear, I go up river. I build a raft and lie flat upon it and drift down. I see the bottom everywhere, except in rough water. I see the rocks, the shelves, the caverns. I see where the big bass live. . . . I never caught one on the day I first saw him. I never caught one on any day he saw me or the boat. I never caught a very large bass, say over five pounds, until after the beginning of the harvest moon. Furthermore, I know that these big bass do not feed often.

One day at a certain place I caught a smallmouth bass, next day a largemouth then a salt-water striped bass, all out of the same hole. They were about the same size, upward to two pounds; none of the fish jumped and they all fought well and equally. I could not have told the difference. This was in the Delaware, not a mile from my home. I have seen striped bass with the shad, and once I think I saw a sturgeon. While fishing for bass I have caught big trout. I have had a small bass bite my bare toes in the water. I have seen bass engaged in pitched battle with what appeared to be some kind of order. I have seen a bass tear a water snake to pieces. These last two instances I heard of from other fisherman before I saw them myself.

I repeat, no one fisherman's observation is enough. We must get together or forever be at dagger's point.[20]

"Lord of Lackawaxen Creek" and "The Fighting Qualities of Black Bass" were collected in book form in *Tales of Fresh-Water Fishing*, published in 1928 by Harper and Brothers. Among the other later angling essays in that book are "Crater Lake Trout," "Fishing the Rogue," and "At the Mouth of the Klamath."

Grey, however, was not always the obsessive, dedicated fisherman. In any given situation he could always view himself with a whimsical eye, as he did in the hilarious essay titled "A Trout Fisherman's Inferno" (*Field and Stream*, April 1910). In this essay, Grey recalls Dante's classic work, imagining himself dying and descending into a shadowy world by the banks of a river:

> . . . I saw that I stood in a great dim amphitheatre veiled in golden shadows and vapors. The dome was as black as night; the sides were obscured in distance. Subdued voices and whispers and low cries rose about me, and shapeless forms moved to and fro. I was led along the sand for many leagues of an opaque river where there was great confusion.
>
> "Where am I?" I asked.
>
> "This is the Fisherman's Inferno," replied my captor.
>
> "What are you going to do with me?"
>
> "I don't know. I'm leading you to the judges. We must consult your record."
>
> Then I could see quite plainly, though my sight seemed obscured by a haze. The place was immense, and fearful, yet it was quite beautiful. Everywhere were scurrying, noiseless brooks, and huge mossy stones and giant hemlocks, all dim under the strange veil. . . .
>
> "Have you looked up his record?" inquired my captor.
>
> "Yes, it is bad," replied an old gray trout, slapping a huge book with his fin. In abject fright I recognized this trout. He had several long straggling whiskers and each one was an old leader of mine. Evidently the hooks were still fast in his gullet. He looked sour-complexioned, and as if his character had been set during a painful experience. . . . There I stood, facing my captor,

judge, and jury, old trout that I had wronged. What mercy could I expect ? I tried not to hear the reading of the record, but my guard held down my hands. . . .

The wise old trout bent their gray heads close together round the learned judge, and they nodded and held council.

I awaited my fate in a feverish fear that was more dreadful than any I had ever felt in my life on earth. My future looked desperate, indeed.

"Fisherman," began the old gray judge, with his head cocked wisely to one side, and a gleam of revenge in his dark eye, "it has been your wont to haunt the trout streams. . . . You write that you love the mossy stones, the gnarled old roots, the dripping ferns and violets; and you wade serenely downstream, building your philosophy of life—while you yank murderous hooks into the throats of hungry trout. I shall give you the severest sentence I can under the law of this court."

He paused to lend dignity and weight to his final stroke.

"You are sentenced to spend eternity here reading your own stories!"

I fell blindly on my knees.

"Mercy! Mercy! judge. I never deserved that! Mercy!"

"Immutable decree of the Trout Fisherman's Inferno! Lead him away!"

The sonorous command rang in my ears like a bell of doom. My guard dragged me away over the sand; the bronze shafts of light darkened; the murmuring voices died away, and—Then I awoke.[21]

Between 1900 and 1912 Grey developed from a casual weekend angler into an informed expert on tackle and technique. His Lackawaxen home provided him a spot to fish virtually from his front porch, and this locale yielded a score of fishing articles, baseball essays, and all of his early western novels.

For most of his life Grey refused to take himself too seriously as a fisherman. A revealing example of this occurred in the same year—1910—that he published "The Trout Fisherman's Inferno." It was customary for the three Gray brothers—Ellsworth, R.C., and

Zane—to meet once in a while and catch up on their busy lives. They frequently chose Lackawaxen or a nearby fishing hot spot on the Delaware River for these get-togethers. Ellsworth, nicknamed Cedar, was eleven years older than Zane. Cedar never had the passion for angling shared by Zane and R.C. After injuring his back as a youngster in Zanesville, he settled for more sedentary activities. He eventually became an illustrator in New York, spending an occasional weekend with Zane and Dolly at Lackawaxen.

For the rendezvous in summer 1910 the brothers chose Mast Hope Brook, a pastoral retreat on the Delaware River not far from Lackawaxen. Wearing their khaki suits and waders, they clambered down to the river through thickets of maple, hemlock, and clumps of rhododendron. By the time they reached the roar of the falls, they were already sharpening their tongues for the ensuing combat. "I know where my big fellow I lost last year is," said Cedar. "Mind you stay clear of me when we get to that hole." R.C. scoffed at this and said: "Have either of you guys any money you can afford to lose?" Zane added finally: "Boys, I'll be sorry to take this money. It'll be as easy as picking blossoms from these laurels."

The brothers split up, Zane hoping to return with the biggest, and certainly the most, fish. Despite a morning full of promise, "rich in the amber of light of June," Grey encountered dismal fishing. Tramping back to camp for lunch, he met Cedar and R.C. who related similar woeful stories. "They're not rising to flies," moaned R.C. "Maybe they will this afternoon."

Shortly thereafter they dispersed again, each brother heading to his secret bonanza. This time, however, Zane had some trickery in mind. He reached into his pocket and pulled out a tin of ordinary worms—the respectable fly fisherman's last resort. "These were the backbone of my campaign," he wrote. "These were the strength of my boast to my brothers. These were the secret source of my assurance. All was fair in love, in war—why not in fishing?"

Zane proceeded to use his hook and worms, but without great

results. He did land several medium-sized trout, which he took with pride back to camp. R.C. and Cedar asked if he had any luck, whereupon he produced his silver bounty. "Not so bad," said R.C. "Did you catch those on the fly?" Zane tried to dodge the question. R.C. reached into his basket, producing ten beautiful trout, "not one under ten inches." Zane stammered: "What—did you get them—on?" "Worms," said R.C. While R.C. smirked, Cedar revealed his catch—an eighteen-inch trout that they all recognized as "the massive many-hued monarch of Mast Hope Brook." "Lord, you got him!" Zane exclaimed. "Say! What did you catch him on?" Cedar dryly replied: "My boy, he broke his back reaching for a nice big fat fishing worm."[22]

While freshwater fishing was a staple in Grey's life, he began, as early as 1905, to integrate saltwater fishing into his regimen. He was attracted to tarpon fishing in the Gulf of Mexico, particularly the area in and around Tampico, Mexico. As the nineteenth century closed, tarpon fishing increased in prominence, as evidenced by this note in the *London Observer* of August 1886: "Here at last there is a rival to the black bass of North America, to the Siluria glanis of the Danube, to our own European salmon, and possibly even the sturgeon. . . . Sportsmen may go to Florida for tarpon, as they now go to the Arctic Zone for reindeer, walrus, and musk ox."

"Byme-by-Tarpon"—Grey's sixth outdoor article and his fourth for Eltinge Warner at *Field and Stream*—set the tone for most of his subsequent deep-sea fishing essays. It contains, among other standard features, a resourceful companion figure, in this case, Attalano, whom Grey describes as being "in harmony with the day and the scene. He had a cheering figure, lithe and erect, with a springing stride, bespeaking the Montezuma blood said to flow in his veins. Clad in a colored cotton shirt, blue jeans, and Spanish girdle, and treading the path with brown feet never deformed by shoes, he would have stopped an artist."[23] In some essays this companion is replaced by a mentor figure who pilots Grey through some dangerous shoals or guides him over unblazed trails.

"Byme-by-Tarpon" also features Grey's acute descriptive abilities, as in this instance he related the actions of his tarpon prey:

> When the first long, low swell of the changing tide rolled in, a stronger breeze raised little dimpling waves, and chased along the water in dark, quick-moving frowns. All at once the tarpon began to show, to splash, to play, to roll. It was as though they had been awakened by the stir and murmur of the miniature breakers. Broad bars of silver flashed in the sunlight, green backs cleft the little billows, wide tails slapped lazily on the water. Every yard of water seemed to hold a rolling fish. This sport increased until the long stretch of water, which had been as calm as a lake at twilight, resembled the quick current of a Canadian stream. It was a fascinating, wonderful sight.
>
> But it was also peculiarly exasperating, because when the fish roll in this sportive, lazy way they will not bite. For an hour I trolled this whirlpool of flying spray and twisting tarpon, with many a salty drop on my face, hearing all around me the whipping crash of breaking water.[24]

The third feature of Zane's early fishing essays is usually some complication that concerns, frustrates, sometime amuses him, but ultimately provides philosophical insight. In "Byme-by-Tarpon" these stages unfold in the following way:

> I began to recover the long line. I pumped and reeled him closer. Reluctantly he came, not yet broken in spirit, though his strength had sped. He rolled at times with a shade of the old vigor, with a pathetic manifestation of the temper that became a hero. I could see the long, slender tip of his dorsal fin, then his broad tail, and then the gleam of his silver side. Closer he came and slowly circled the boat, eyeing me with great accusing eyes. I measured him with a fisherman's glance. What a great fish! Seven feet, I calculated, at the very least.
>
> At this triumphant moment I made a horrible discovery. About six feet from the leader the strands of the line had frayed, leaving

only one thread intact. My blood ran cold and the clammy sweat broke out on my brow. My empire was not won; my first tarpon was as if he had never been. But true to my fishing instincts I held on morosely; my eye on the frail place in my line, and gently, ever so gently, I began to lead the silver king shoreward.

Grey realized, with some horror, that his frayed line would not hold the tarpon long enough to bring him to shore. He then encountered a vivid sense of his own helplessness:

> . . . One moment he lay there, glowing like mother-of-pearl, a rare fish, fresh from the sea.
> Then, as Attalano warily reached for the leader, he gave a gasp, a flop that deluged us with water, and a lunge that spelled freedom.
> I watched him slowly swim away with my bright leader dragging beside him. Is it not the loss of things which makes life bitter? What we have gained is ours; what is lost is gone, whether fish, or love, or fame.[25]

Attalano, with a "smile, warm and living" on his dark face, merely said: "Byme-by-Tarpon."

For the next three decades, Grey would increasingly seek adventure beyond American shores. Often this involved searching for greater exploits, more attractive ports, and larger, more exotic fish. As with most things in his life, he proceeded from little to big to biggest, and seldom knew what to do with himself once he had achieved his loftiest goals.

CHAPTER TWO

❧ ❧ ❧

Those Damned Cowboys

Yesterday I was eighteen hours in the saddle—
from 4 A.M. to 10 P.M.—having a half hour each
for dinner and tea. I can now do cowboy work
pretty well.

— THEODORE ROOSEVELT

ON September 6, 1901, in Buffalo, New York—just over four
months before Zane Grey's thirtieth birthday—Leon Czolgosz, an
anarchist, stepped in front of President William McKinley and
fired two shots into him. The first wound in the chest was minor;
the second in the stomach proved fatal. At first it appeared that the
president might make a full recovery. But on September 13, Vice
President Theodore Roosevelt, vacationing in the Adirondacks, received a telegram informing him that McKinley's condition had
worsened. Roosevelt threw on his clothes and began the journey to
Buffalo to be near the dying president. Roosevelt did not arrive in
time to see McKinley alive. On September 14, the former police
commissioner, governor of New York, colonel of cavalry, and a man
once curtly referred to as "that damned cowboy," Theodore Roosevelt, became the twenty-sixth president of the United States.

After Roosevelt settled into the Oval Office, neither Washington nor Zane Grey's life were ever quite the same. T.R.'s face and manner soon became as recognizible as the Statue of Liberty: the close-cropped hair, the easy, vigorous smile, the pompous strut, the spectacles that looked as if they were screwed into his forehead and flashed in the sunlight like round, opaque windowpanes. Aptly described by a contemporary as a "steam engine in pants," Roosevelt came to embody America's boundless optimism and restless energy.

The New York–born Roosevelt also possessed most of the qualities that Zane Grey admired: intelligence, savvy, physical power, literary talent, and fame. Grey was never totally aware of the debt he owed to Roosevelt and his circle of acquaintances. Between 1885 and 1902, while the American frontier era was coming to a close, Roosevelt, along with Owen Wister and Frederic Remington, was promoting the idea of a romantic West—an idea that, following the lead of dime-novel publishers Beadle and Adams, Zane Grey would soon adopt. Largely, it was this trio of chroniclers—Roosevelt, Wister, and Remington—who kept the Old West alive during the waning years of the nineteenth century.

Although Roosevelt was not born in the West, or even raised there, he became a rather shrewd impostor. "I always told you," he once told a friend, "that I was more of a Westerner than an Easterner."[1] His influence on Grey is evident in six key areas: hunting, fishing, the outdoors, conservation, writing, and of course, a devotion to the West. Frequently, too, T.R.'s mere persona—aggressive, confident, even bullying—had a magnetic hold on Zane Grey.

Roosevelt's western experiences began in summer 1883 and unfolded like a Zane Grey novel. He was asthmatic from birth. Often he wheezed and coughed the day away, or lay prone for hours gasping for air. As a child, he was slight of frame and physically weak. Unlike Zane Grey, "Teedie" idolized his father, who represented everything the young Roosevelt wished to be: powerful of body, healthy, handsome, robust, and influential. To a young Theodore, he was "a sort of benevolent Norse god."[2] Theodore Sr., realizing that his son was not developing any physical stamina, took Teedie aside and said: "You have the mind but you do not have the body, and without help of the body the mind cannot go as far as it should. You must make your body. It is hard drudgery to make one's body but I know you will do it."[3]

Through clenched teeth, young Theodore muttered: "I will make my body."[4] And so he did. For the next several years, Theodore walked, exercised, rode, hiked, and mountain-climbed. Gradually his reedy chest and spindly legs developed mass and muscle. By the time he reached Harvard University in 1876 he was a first-class boxer, wrestler, and body-builder; he even had time for a few dancing lessons across Harvard Yard. He met the great love of his life, Alice Lee Hathaway, and had a whirlwind courtship. After being initiated at the Porcellian Club, Theodore got drunk on wine. "Wine makes me awfully fighty," he complained later. It also gave him such a hangover that he resolved to use alcohol sparingly.[5] Although Roosevelt was not the teetotaler Grey was, he remained a spartan drinker.

Throughout 1879, Theodore chummed around with Owen Wister, a nineteen-year-old Philadelphian interested in the theater, opera, and music. Wister soon sensed the super-charged aura of the maturing Roosevelt. "He was his own limelight, and could not help it," observed Wister. "A creature with such voltage as his became the central presence at once."[6]

After graduating from Harvard in 1880, Roosevelt entered an extremely happy period: he married his sweetheart Alice, wrote his first book, had a baby girl, and became an assemblyman for the state of New York. All the days were full of promise, love and success—and then in one brief twenty-four-hour period his whole world collapsed.

On a fog-shrouded St. Valentine's Day, February 14, 1884, Theodore journeyed from Albany to his home in New York, where he found his wife Alice and his mother Mittie both struggling with death. Alice, bedridden with Bright's disease, was upstairs; Mittie, with acute typhoid fever, lay in a downstairs room. At three in the morning, Mittie expired, causing Theodore to mutter: "There is a curse on this house." He had barely enough time to grieve her death, when his dear wife Alice died fourteen hours later. Later, he scrawled a large X in his diary for that day and jotted a note beneath it: "The light has gone out of my life."[7]

On and off for the next two years, Theodore Roosevelt tried to bury his anguish in the hard granite soil of the Badlands of Dakota Territory, enduring the spiritual makeover of a Zane Grey character. He had visited the Little Missouri River country in the autumn of 1883 and liked it so much that he decided on a more extended sojourn. Additionally, the family tragedy kept him away from New York; he thought the West might also help restore his mind and body.

On the family-owned Dakota ranch in the summer of 1884, Theodore worked diligently on becoming a westerner. He spent many days driving cattle, mending fences, and making friends with the local stockmen. He got his cowboy garb tailor-made from a widowed seamstress who lived nearby. "You should see me," he wrote a friend, "in my broad sombrero hat, fringed and beaded buckskin shirt, horse hide chaparojos . . . with braided bridle and silver spurs."[8] He wrote his sister that he now looked like "a regular cowboy dandy." With the same ardor that he attacked virtually everything, Theodore made himself a range rider, even though most of his time was spent taking care of mundane matters.

As time went on the bleak Dakota landscape became more pleasant for Roosevelt. "I grow very fond of this place," he noted, "and it certainly has a desolate, grim beauty of its own, that has a curious fascination for me."[9] Away from politicians and his circle of thoroughbred friends in New York City, Roosevelt came to love the isolation and rugged hills beyond his verandah. "I love to sit and watch their hard, gray outlines gradually growing soft and purple . . . while my days I spend generally alone, riding through the lonely, rolling prairie and broken lands."[10]

Sometimes his outlandish dress and bespectacled appearance got him into trouble. Once, on a cold winter night, he ran into a drunk bully in Nolan's Hotel in Mingusville, a town just west of the Dakota ranch. With "a cocked gun in each hand," the stranger approached Roosevelt, calling him "four eyes" and telling him to set up drinks for everybody in the saloon. Roosevelt briefly complied. "As I rose," he recalled, "I struck quick hard with my right just to one side of the point of his jaw, hitting with my left as I straightened out, and then again with my right. . . . When he went down he struck the corner of the bar with his head. . . . I took away his guns and the other people in the room . . . hustled him out and put him in the shed."[11]

These Dakota showdowns were somehow far sweeter than any he experienced on the floor of the state assembly in Albany or in the Harvard debate classes. Roosevelt reflected on them all his life. On another occasion in Dakota Territory, he learned that a neighbor rancher named Paddock was claiming one of Roosevelt's cabins as his own. Paddock and his drunken henchmen began raiding the cabin for food and supplies, declaring that if "four eyes" wanted to purchase it, he could do so with money or blood. Rarely troubled by diffidence, T.R. mounted his pony and galloped up to Paddock's ranch. Paddock answered the door. Roosevelt said smoothly, "I understand that you have threatened to kill me on sight. I have come over to see when you want to begin the killing." Taken off guard, Paddock mumbled something about being "misquoted."[12] Roosevelt returned home, assured that his lands and cabins would be left alone.

After Roosevelt finished hunting, punching cattle, or loping leisurely over the prairie, he retreated to his desk at the ranch, where he prepared to become an evangelist for Dakota in particular and the West in general. He made copious notes of his daily wanderings and musings. Back in New York, between January and March of 1885, he worked on the account of his experiences in Dakota Territory, which he called *Hunting Trips of a Ranchman*. In the frontispiece photograph he is wearing his fur cap, silver dagger, and garish buckskins, looking very much the dude hunter. Draped in cartridges, surrounded by cardboard rocks and artificial grass, Roosevelt assumes the pose of a brave hunter. For unknown reasons, his spectacles have slipped to the end of his nose. Despite the efforts to dramatize the photograph, the whole effect seems contrived—even humorous. Indeed, his biographer, Edmund Morris, observes that "one doubts that he could hit the photographer, let alone a distant grizzly."[13]

Hunting Trips of a Ranchman was published in a lavish edition by G. P. Putnam's Sons. Filled with Roosevelt's hunting and ranching exploits in Dakota Territory, it reads much like another "education of the greenhorn" book—Zane Grey's *Last of the Plainsmen*. Roosevelt, like Grey, was a hunter of considerable skill. He also thought nothing of studying the habits of a meadowlark for hours or observing the warm freshness of a deer's bed—and then head out for an afternoon of bloodletting on the hunting trail. Naturalist and hunter, preserver and destroyer, lived together in Roosevelt in some weird symbiosis. It also did with Zane Grey, but Grey was never the scientist that Roosevelt was.

In 1885, T.R. mentioned to Harvard friend Owen Wister that a western trip might help cure Wister's poor health. "For a good healthy experience," Roosevelt had declared to friends, "I would strongly recommend that some of our gilded youth go West and try a short course in riding bucking ponies."[14]

Wister certainly fit the "gilded youth" image. At twenty-five years of age, two years younger than Roosevelt, he was wealthy, footloose, and bored. After graduating from Harvard in 1882, he traveled around Europe, playing his musical compositions for the likes of Franz Liszt. He eventually ended up as a bank clerk in Boston, when Roosevelt, fresh from Dakota Territory, tempted him to change his life. The advice for a rest cure for Wister was seconded by his doctor.

That summer Owen headed to a friend's ranch—the Deer Creek Ranch—near Medicine Bow, Wyoming. It was seductive countryside: mountains, rolling green prairies punctuated with gambel oak and pine clumps. He worked on the ranch, bathed each morning in Deer Creek, and pronounced the air "delicious . . . as if it had never been in anyone's lungs before." Like Roosevelt, Wister adopted the cowboy life quickly and passionately. "This existence," he wrote, "is heavenly in its monotony and sweetness. I'm beginning to feel I'm something of an animal and not a stinking brain alone."

Meanwhile, Theodore Roosevelt returned to Dakota Territory in spring of 1886, and became a local folk hero by rounding up some notorious horse thieves. In late March, while the Little Missouri River was still clogged with ice floes, Theodore pursued three bandits as they fled northward. Characteristically, he had packed a copy of Matthew Arnold's poems, as well as *Anna Karenina*. "My surroundings were quite grey enough to harmonize with Tolstoy," he admitted.[15] He finally overtook the thieves on April 1, delighting in surprising them from some bushes. Roosevelt could have shot them on the spot, but he decided that justice should prevail. With his three desperadoes in tow, he trudged forty-five miles south through mud, snow, and a cold wind to Dickinson, North Dakota. "It was a gloomy walk," he remarked. "Hour after hour went by always the same, while I plodded along the dreary landscape—hunger, cold, and fatigue struggling with a sense of dogged, weary resolution."[16] Arriving in Dickinson on April 11, Roosevelt was able to surrender his "unwilling companions into the hands of the sheriff."[17]

The only doctor in Dickinson noticed Roosevelt leaving the sheriff's office. "He was teeth and eyes," observed the doctor. "His clothes were in rags. . . . He was scratched, bruised, and hungry, but gritty and determined as a bulldog. . . . I told my wife that I had met the most peculiar and at the same time the most wonderful man I ever came to know."[18]

Word spread quickly of Roosevelt's derring-do on the Little Missouri River. He reported to his sister that "these Westerners have now pretty well accepted me as one of themselves." Gone quickly were the labels of "four eyes" and "that dude Rosenfelder." Instead, the cowboys, much to his delight, called him "a hell of a good rider" and "a fearless bugger."[19] In just a little over two years, the tentative dude Roosevelt had become the robust, self-assured drover of the Dakota Badlands—a distinction that he came to revere more than that of being governor of New York, and even president of the United States. He wrote his sister Bamie: "I should say this free open air life, without any worry, was perfection. I write steadily for three or four days, then hunt, or ride on the roundup for many more."[20]

Roosevelt's second book of cowboy culture, *Ranch Life and The Hunting Trail* (1888), soon followed. Only this time, he had an illustrator by the name of Frederic Remington to give his words pictorial depth and richness.

Of all the prominent writers and artists of the 1880s and 1890s, perhaps the one to have the earliest and most profound impact on Zane Grey's generation was Frederic Sackrider Remington. His covers and illustrations for *Harper's Weekly, Youth's Companion, Outing,* and *Century* featured hard-riding cowboys, thundering horses, fearless scouts, marauding Indians, vacant wastelands, and brave soldiers—all the images of the romantic, disappearing West. It was these images that would stay in the minds of a generation and make Remington, in the words of Theodore Roosevelt, "a national treasure."

Zane Grey turned fourteen in January 1886. That month Rem-

Grey in 1903, at the time of the writing of his first novel *Betty Zane*.

ington's first cover illustration for *Harper's Weekly* appeared. The illustration, "Indian Scouts on Geronimo's Trail," depicted a scene from the army's desperate search for the rebel Apache leader. Remington himself came very close to seeing Geronimo in his Southwest travels.

Only weeks before his January cover illustration was published, Remington's life was quite different. After looking for a lost gold mine in Arizona and searching for Geronimo—and finding neither —Remington traveled to New York. He had three dollars in his pocket and a bundle of sketches and line drawings under his arm. He quickly sold some of the illustrations to *Harper's Weekly.* He then took an unsold portfolio of drawings into the editorial offices of *Outing* magazine. The art editor was Poultney Bigelow, his old friend from Yale. Years later, Bigelow remembered his encounter with Remington: "I was interrupted by a vast portfolio in the hands of some intruding one. I did not look up at the huge visitor but held out a hand for the drawings. He pushed one at me. . . . here was the real thing, the unspoiled native genius dealing with Mexican ponies, cowboys, lariats, and sombreros. These were the men of the real rodeo, parched in alkali dust, blinking out from barely opened eyes under the furious rays of the Arizona sun. I looked at the signature —Remington. . . . I bought all he had in his portfolio, and I loaded him with orders."[21]

From then on, the burly Remington waited on no one. The sobriquet often applied to him—that "he knew the horse"—may also include the rider as well. For Remington was one of the first illustrators to popularize the cowboy as an American frontier image. In sometimes sparse compositions he focused on the routines, dangers, and hardships of the lone drover. Sometimes he depicted him in silent vigils, or trying to direct cattle stampeded by thunder and lightning. Always Remington's distinctive style emerged as he portrayed lean ponies, rollicking vaqueros, or mustachioed riders. His subjects reflected his keen eye for authenticity.

By 1890 Remington had achieved the market domination that Zane Grey would enjoy thirty years later. Like Grey, Remington was an active researcher. He lived in cattle camps and army forts throughout the West, gathering sketches and first-hand observations. In December 1890, on assignment from *Harper's Weekly*, he narrowly missed the Wounded Knee debacle in South Dakota, which was the symbolic end of the Indian's struggle in North America. His absence may account for the melodramatic painting he did of the battle.

If Remington flirted with melodrama in other works, he never really crossed the line. Like Grey, he usually relied on direct observation, personal experience, and visual accuracy. The result was an extensive body of work that for all its romanticism was extremely reliable in its visual truth.

The year of the Wounded Knee Massacre, Owen Wister graduated from the Harvard Law School and was admitted to the Philadelphia bar. Since his 1885 trip to Medicine Bow, Wyoming, he had periodically refreshed his spirit in the West. Sensing the law might be his ultimate calling, he pursued it diligently. Upon being admitted to the bar, however, he became disillusioned once again.

One night in Philadelphia in 1891, Wister and a friend were ruminating about life

> One evening . . . fresh from Wyoming and its wild glories, I sat in the club dining with a man enamored of the West as I was. From oysters to coffee we compared experiences. Why wasn't some Kipling saving the sagebrush for American literature, before the sagebrush and all that it signified went the way of the California forty-niner? What was fiction doing, fiction, the only thing that has outlived fact? Must it be perpetual teacups? Was Alkali Ike in the comic papers the one figure which the jejune American imagination could discern in that epic which was being lived at a gallop out in the sagebrush? "To hell with teacups

and the great American laugh," we two said. . . . The claret had been excellent. "I'm going to try it myself!" I exclaimed. "I'm going to start this minute."[22]

Wister grabbed his claret, walked down the hall to the library of the Philadelphia Club, and began his first story of the West. Titled "Hank's Woman" (*Harper's Monthly*, August 1892), the short story was a sordid tale of seduction and murder, which contained most of the features of Wister's romantic West. It also introduced a character known simply as "the Virginian."

Writing and trying to sell the story also brought him in contact with the House of Harper, one of the major forces in New York publishing. One arm of the publishing firm produced *Harper's Weekly*, known as "a journal of civilization" and a leading voice in modern cultural commentary. By the 1890s the West had become a popular item in its pages, first with Remington and then with Wister and others. On the other end of the publishing arm was Harper and Brothers, who published such notable authors as Mark Twain and Willliam Dean Howells. More than a decade after Wister, an aspiring Zane Grey would also knock on the door of the House of Harper, hoping to follow in the footsteps of his western contemporaries. Harper rejected Grey's work repeatedly. In 1910 Grey finally found success with *The Heritage of the Desert,* and he remained with Harper and Brothers for the rest of his life.

The modest success of "Hank's Woman" lured Wister from his practice of law back to the circuitous trails of the West. He wrote and published more in the early 1890s than ever before. In a normal year he would spend six months in the West, and then return to his office on Chestnut Street in Philadelphia to write of his experiences. Ironically, the unpublished and unsung Zane Grey was an undergraduate at the University of Pennsylvania at this time, and would have been a stone's throw from Wister's office.

In 1893 Wister had a chance encounter with Frederic Remington at Yellowstone Park. They became friends and often corresponded with each other. Later Remington invited Wister to write an article that Remington could illustrate. "Make me article on the evolution of the puncher," he told Wister. "I want to make some pictures of the ponies going over the hell-roaring malpais after a steer on the jump."[23] The result was Wister's article in the September 1895 issue of *Harper's Monthly,* "The Evolution of the Cowpuncher."

Even before Zane Grey popularized the idea that the West held the moral cure for the American malaise, Owen Wister was declaring it in such articles as "Evolution." Moreover, Wister asserted that the cowboy's virtues stemmed from his pure Saxon bloodline and a landscape free from the "hordes of encroaching alien vermin, that turn our cities into Babels and our citizenship into a hybrid farce."[24] In his colorful and often turgid prose, Wister championed the cowboy as a free-spirited holdout from the corruption of civilization. In Wister's hands, the knight of the open range was no whimsical fairy tale hero, but a serious racial stereotype.

Nevertheless, Owen Wister would develop his ideas of the cowboy into two significant works of fiction: *Lin McLean* (1897) and *The Virginian* (1902). The latter was, more than any other work, the book that Zane Grey would have liked to have authored. It became the pacesetter for the genre, and inspired movie cowboys to walk with a swagger and talk with a drawl. Dedicated to Theodore Roosevelt, *The Virginian* grabbed the American consciousness and never really let go. Published in the first years of the twentieth century, it anticipated the work of Zane Grey and the movies of William S. Hart, Gary Cooper, John Wayne, and Clint Eastwood.

While Wister and Remington were enjoying immense popularity, the dime novel—that much-maligned offering of the firm of Beadle and Adams—was also soaring in sales. Ridiculed by teachers, parents, and critics alike, the dimes nevertheless found their way into many boys' and girls' darkened closets. As a youth Grey fed on them, placing dime novels alongside Defoe and Cooper as some of his earliest literary influences. His particular favorites among authors were Prentiss Ingraham and Edward L. Wheeler. The former, for instance, wrote the nationally famous paperback, *Wild Bill, The Pistol Prince,* which related both the historical and fictional exploits of James Butler "Wild Bill" Hickok. The young Grey identified with the superhuman qualities of these western folk heroes. In Hickok's case, Ingraham transformed him from a respectable lawman into a six-shooting, bear-fighting adventurer. Wild Bill cleans up Kansas and even fights the notorious McCandless gang, eventually gaining his nickname from "this desperate affray, in which one man whipped ten desperadoes." Both lawman and outlaw gained notoriety from their appearance in the dime novel. Zane Grey's understanding of the mythmaking capabilities of dime-novel fiction would figure prominently in his works.

During the 1890s Theodore Roosevelt had packed away his chaps and spurs for a career in politics. After leaving his post as the police commissioner of New York City, Roosevelt headed to Washington to become assistant secretary of the navy.

By 1898, war with Spain was imminent. Congress quickly authorized the mounting of a cavalry unit, and Roosevelt, chafing to return to the saddle, reminded key people of his experience as a cowboy, rancher, and hunter. He even brandished a copy of *Ranch Life and the Hunting Trail* in the halls of the War Department.[25]

The First Volunteer Cavalry soon emerged, composed mainly of westerners. "They shot straight, lived straight, and rode like the wind."[26] And according to the marketing of the regiment, "they broke broncos before breakfast, roped and branded longhorns until dinner, and shot wild Indians after supper."[27] Tabbed the "Rough Riders" by a journalist, the unit quickly attracted volunteers from all over America. The original limit of 780 men swelled to 1,000 after the war department generated more funds. The men's demeanor was exactly what Roosevelt had witnessed in the Dakota badlands: "They were a splendid set of men," he exclaimed, "tall and sinewy, with resolute, weather-beaten faces, and eyes that looked a man straight in the face without flinching."[28]

Roosevelt received a lieutenant colonelcy to command the Rough Riders against the Spanish. His chest was never larger or his heart stouter. The regiment trained in the heat and dust of San Antonio, Texas. "We are working like beavers," wrote Roosevelt, "and we are getting the regiment in shape."[29] For official photographs, Roosevelt donned his elegant khaki cavalry hat with its crossed swords insignia; for drilling his men, however, he wore a rumpled Stetson that looked as if it had already seen battle.

At last, on June 14, 1898, the ships bearing Roosevelt and the Rough Riders steamed out of Tampa harbor, heading for Cuba and their encounter with the Spanish forces.

The Rough Rider battles in Cuba were viewed by many as full-fledged western cavalry skirmishes, even though they occurred more than a thousand miles east of Kansas and were accomplished without horses. Of course, they *were* a western regiment in spirit and dress, and they could have charged up Madison Avenue and still have ridden into western history. In their slouch hats, loose neckerchiefs, leggings, and boots, the Riders looked "exactly," said Roosevelt fondly, "as a body of cowboy cavalry should look."[30]

Journalists from competing newspapers descended in a swarm on Cuba, prepared to cover all aspects of the war. Among them were Richard Harding Davis of the *New York Tribune* and Edward Marshall of the *New York Journal*. Also in Havana was Frederic Remington in the employ of newspaper magnate William Randolph Hearst. Remington at first was disgruntled by the lack of hostilities, cabling Hearst that he wished to come home. Hearst supposedly telegrammed back: "Please remain. You furnish pictures. I'll furnish war."[31]

When military action did come, journalists along with the Rough Riders were thrown into the conflict. After a brief but bloody skirmish with the Spanish at Las Guasimas on June 24, Roosevelt and his men moved into position below the Spanish entrenchments on San Juan Heights.

In the battle that followed on July 1, Roosevelt was transformed from an admired, bespectacled lieutenant colonel into "the most famous man in America." Largely it was journalists such as Richard Davis, Stephen Crane, and Edward Marshall who made Roosevelt an overnight hero.

They, as well as Roosevelt himself much later, described how the colonel of the Rough Riders filled his legendary "crowded hour"; how he rallied his men wearing a blue polka-dot scarf dangling backward from his hat; how on horseback he urged his men up San Juan Hill, while Spanish bullets perforated the leaves and sounded "like the ripping of a silk dress"; how he reached a wire fence near the top of the hill, turned his horse loose, and fought the remaining way on foot; how, despite numerous Rough Rider casualties, his men yelled and cheered as they drove the Spanish soldiers from their positions on the summit; and how Roosevelt, with "the wolf rising in his heart," stormed and secured the top of the hill for the advancing American forces.[32] "San Juan was the great day of my life," he wrote later.[33] Richard Harding Davis, observing the battle, declared in a dispatch that Roosevelt was "the most conspicuous figure in the charge."[34] Along with the war, Theodore Roosevelt's brief military career soon ended. His name, however, would soon be on everyone's lips.

In early August 1898, the Rough Riders sailed home. Crowds cheered, "Hurrah for Teddy and the Rough Riders!" "Oh," barked T.R. on his return, "but we have had a bully fight!"[35]

Three years and a month later, after stops as governor of New York and vice president of the United States, Theodore Roosevelt, that "damned cowboy" and Rough Rider, sat in the White House as a somewhat reluctant but thoroughly prepared American president.

❧ ❧ ❧

In early 1907 Zane Grey met the redoubtable Charles Jesse "Buffalo" Jones at a Campfire Club dinner in New York. Still just an aspiring writer who had briefly been west, Grey was smitten with Jones's tales of mountain lions, canyons, deserts, and the wild Southwest. Jones invited Grey to northern Arizona and the Colorado River country on the trip that would launch Grey's career.

Also that year Theodore Roosevelt was well into his second term as president. Still as vigorous as ever, he visited and hunted in the West as often as his cramped schedule would allow. With the windfall success of *The Virginian,* Owen Wister became something of bon vivant and lifelong friend of Roosevelt's, often showing up at the White House for special occasions. Here Wister and Roosevelt would talk over the presidency and the state of the country, their conversations often punctuated with western memories and old-fashioned yarns. Wister never repeated the success of his 1902 masterpiece, nor did he make much of an attempt to try.

Frederic Remington was by then a contemporary legend, turning out canvases and illustrations at a prodigious rate from his New York studio. He died prematurely at forty-eight years of age in 1909, probably without ever hearing the name of Zane Grey.

The year of Remington's death, Roosevelt, who had recently vacated the White House, was on a hunting expedition in Africa. He compared his experiences there, somewhat incongruously, to his exploits in the badlands of Dakota. A few years later, as president of the American Historical Society, he proclaimed with some delight that the romantic West was still lingering in the hearts of most Americans. In a speech delivered in 1913, Roosevelt wistfully recalled "the hesitating early ventures into the Indian-haunted forest" and "the endless march of white-topped wagon trains across plain and mountain to the coast of the greatest of the five great oceans." The words were vintage Roosevelt, who tended to regard the West as sanctified territory.

In the last two decades of the nineteenth century, Remington, Wister, and Roosevelt used their own unique styles to turn the lowly, illiterate cowboy into a national symbol. Now, in the new century, it was Zane Grey's turn.

CHAPTER THREE

✠ ✠ ✠

The Strong Brown God

> To look at the river was to court terror, but I had
> to look. It was an infernal thing. It roared in a
> hollow, sullen voice, as a monster growling. It
> had a voice, this river, and one strangely change-
> ful. It moaned as if in pain—it whined, it cried.
> The current was as complex and mutable as
> human life.
>
> —ZANE GREY

"I DO not know much about gods," wrote T. S. Eliot. "But I think that
the river is a strong brown god—sullen, untamed, intractable." The
Colorado River—the strong brown god of the American Southwest
—influenced the works and excited the imagination of Zane Grey.
Several Grey novels are set here: *Riders of the Purple Sage, The
Heritage of the Desert, The Rainbow Trail,* and *Wildfire,* among
others. The river and the surrounding countryside would deeply
influence his philosophy of life. Grey had known other rivers—the
Muskingum and the Licking, the Delaware and the Lackawaxen;
later in life, he would fish the Rogue and Umpqua in Oregon and
the Tongariro in New Zealand. But perhaps no other artery carved
such an intricate path through his nervous system as the muddy,
magnificent Colorado.

For all of its greatness, the Colorado has humble origins. It
trickles out of the west face of Long's Peak, Colorado, at an elevation

of nearly 13,000 feet. Fed by streams and creeks, it gathers momentum as it travels westward across the state of Colorado. By the time it reaches the serene pastures and orchards of the Grand Valley near Grand Junction, it has dropped almost 8,000 feet in elevation.

It is this quick drop, combined with the amount of snowmelt gorging the river, that accounts for the river's volume downstream. In March the volume is relatively modest, with most of the river in Colorado still in the grips of winter. But in April and May, the water volume begins to increase, and by June, when the snow pours into the river as if into a funnel, it starts to brim above its banks.

At Grand Junction the Colorado is fed by the Gunnison and Dolores Rivers. In Utah it is joined by the Green, a major tributary snaking southward from Wyoming. Through countryside marked by red sandstone canyons, wind-sculpted rocks, and striated cliffs, the Colorado begins to thrash and boil. It is quite muddy, looking like chocolate, when it takes in the San Juan River just above the Arizona border. At this juncture, it has doubled in volume since beginning its journey.

This part of the river, from the entry of the San Juan to the Colorado's passage at the far end of the Grand Canyon, is the one most admired by Zane Grey. Before the Colorado River was dammed so much (it is the most dammed river in the world), the water flowed unimpeded from Colorado to the Gulf of California. Before the erection of Glen Canyon and Hoover Dams, the river's annual flooding destroyed ranches, crippled livelihoods, and eroded rich farmlands. It was also a wild, untamed river—something that appealed to Easterner and novitiate Zane Grey.

Before the dam, Glen Canyon was pristine, enchanting, and labyrinthine. Maidenhead ferns dangled from the sculpted rocks; canyons twisted into darkened eternities; underground springs trickled down the shoulders of salmon- and vanilla-colored stone. Today, with Lake Powell extending well into Glen Canyon, its unearthly beauty is but a memory.

In the canyon the Colorado passes west of the Rainbow Bridge, one of Grey's sacred sites, and enters northern Arizona near Lee's Ferry. It plummets southward through Marble Canyon and, gaining momentum, prepares to roar through the east entrance of the Grand Canyon. Like water shot through a straw, the current, tumbling and writhing, is jettisoned down the narrow canyon. This violent stretch of river in June would crack a wooden boat like a peanut shell, and before 1970, boats were the only mode of travel.

Ahead are Soap Creek Falls, Badger Creek Rapids, Crystal Creek Rapids, and the notorious Lava Falls, which has horrified virtually everyone who has stared into its hellish waters. Sounding like a hurricane or volcano in progress, the falls are treacherous even today. The beauty of the surrounding canyon is lost in the panic of surviving the furious river. The bottom drops out of the river at Lava Falls, plunging thirty feet instantaneously and creating wave crests as high as three-story buildings. Boiling over the basalt rocks, the Colorado surges past the rock faces.

In the Grand Canyon the river changes course at a point below Walhalla Overlook. Losing none of its force, the river begins to twist, turning southwest, west, northwest, southwest, northwest again, and then northeast. Its coiling path has no predictability until it reaches a spot below Great Thumb Peak, where it flows southwest again through the canyon.

After leaving the Grand Canyon, the Colorado loses most of its hysteria, evening out like a well-behaved watercourse. Running mainly westward, it takes a huge comma turn in Nevada, and makes its final spiritless journey south to the Gulf of California. Its water used totally, the river dies in the sand before reaching the Gulf.

In spring 1907, at the age of thirty-five, Zane Grey witnessed the flooding of the Colorado River for the first time. Traveling up from Flagstaff in a party that included Buffalo Jones and Jim Emmett, he saw how a river could act like a raging monster. He looked at this part of the West with wide, absorbing eyes. With two books published (*Betty Zane* and *Spirit of the Border*) as well as a handful of magazine articles, he thought of himself as a writer searching for new material. When he got to the Colorado, he realized he had found it:

> The first sight of most famous and much-heralded wonders of nature is often disappointing; but never can this be said of the blood-hued Rio Colorado. If it had beauty, it was beauty that appalled. So riveted was my gaze that I could hardly turn it across the river, where Emmett proudly pointed out his lonely home—an oasis set down amidst the beetling red cliffs. How grateful to the eye was the green of alfalfa and cottonwood! Going round the bluff trail, the wheels had only a foot of room to spare; and the sheer descent into the red, turbid, congested river was terrifying.
>
> I saw the constricted rapids, where the Colorado took its plunge into the box-like head of the Grand Canyon of Arizona; and the deep, reverberating boom of the river, at flood height, was a fearful thing to hear. I could not repress a shudder at the thought of crossing above that rapid.
>
> The bronze walls widened as we proceeded, and we got down presently to a level, where a long wire cable stretched across the river. Under the cable ran a rope. On the other side was an old scow moored to a bank.
>
> "Are we going across in that?" I asked Emmett, pointing to the boat.
>
> "We'll all be on the other side before dark," he replied cheerily.
>
> I felt that I would rather start back alone over the desert than trust myself in such a craft, on such a river. And it was all because I had had experience with bad rivers, and thought I was a judge of dangerous currents. The Colorado slid with a menacing roar out of a giant split in the red wall, and whirled, eddied, bulged on toward its confinement in the iron-ribbed canyon below.[1]

In April of 1908 Grey returned to Lee's Ferry in Northern Arizona with Buffalo Jones and Jim Emmett. Jones, the buffalo hunter-turned-conservationist, was tracking mountain lions on the North Rim of the Grand Canyon. Once captured, the lions were transported to newly opened zoos in Philadelphia, New York, and St. Louis. This particular journey produced two important works: "Roping Lions in the Grand Canyon" and *Don, The Story of a Lion Dog* (discussed in chapter 9).

This 1908 expedition was the last extensive journey of Grey with Jones and Emmett. The irascible Jones and the taciturn Emmett were Grey's first frontier mentors, and together they personified the two approaches Zane would take to nature writing. Through Jones and his bold experiences, Grey developed the action narrative that would characterize some of his best nonfiction essays and carry over into his western fiction. Emmett, on the other hand, inspired in Grey a philosophical and stoical approach to the study of nature. Grey, like Emmett, could look at the desert for hours, watching the sun pass over the eroded cliffs or a hawk soaring on the high currents of air. Grey paid Emmett the supreme compliment by calling him a white Navajo. Emmett's gift of silent observation would give Grey's descriptions their pronounced spirit of place.

Although Grey's introduction to the western frontier involved the stalking and capturing of cougars, he never really had the stomach for it. Grey was a hunter, but he was not one to simply arrest the spirit of a wild animal. During one of the chases, he thought the practice would be less cruel if they killed the lions "outright."[2] On one hand, Grey admired Jones's wilderness acumen; on the other, he disliked Jones's casual indifference to cruelty and suffering. Although Grey profited greatly from Buffalo Jones's instruction, he began to distance himself from the aging hunter after the 1908 journey.

After Jones's death seven years later, Grey, however, would eulogize him this way: "Buffalo Jones was great in all the remarkable qualities common to the men who opened the West. . . . No doubt something of Buffalo Jones crept unconsciously into all the great fiction characters I have created."[3]

Essential to Grey's sense of adventure and his personal code of ethics was the idea that the sweat and exertion in attaining a goal must be equal to, or greater than, the prize itself. Hence, in "Roping Lions in the Grand Canyon" (serialized in *Field and Stream* beginning January 1909) Grey reveled in the days and weeks leading up the capture of mountain lions. He at first acknowledged the challenge of the Colorado River terrain and described his imposing companions:

> The Grand Canyon of Arizona is over two hundred miles long, thirteen wide and a mile and half deep; a titanic gorge is which mountains, tablelands, chasms and cliffs lie half veiled in purple haze. It is wild and sublime, a thing of wonder, of mystery —beyond all else a place to grip the heart of a man, to unleash his daring spirit.
>
> On April 20th, 1908, after days on the hot desert, my weary party and pack train reached the summit of Powell's Plateau, the most isolated, inaccessible, and remarkable mesa in all the canyon country. Cut off from the mainland it appeared insurmountable; standing aloof from the towers and escarpments, rugged and bold in outline, its forest covering like a strip of black velvet, its giant granite walls gold in the sun, it seemed apart from the world, haunting with its beauty, isolation and wild promise.
>
> The members of my party harmoniously fitted the scene. Buffalo Jones, burly-shouldered, bronze-faced, and grim, proved in his appearance what a lifetime on the plains could make of a man. Emmett was a Mormon, a massively-built gray-bearded son the desert; he had lived his life on it; he had conquered it and in his falcon eyes shone all its fire and freedom. Ranger Jim Owens had a wiry, supple body and careless, tidy garb of the cowboy, and the watchful gaze, quiet face and locked lips of the frontiersman.[4]

Jones's and Emmett's camp contained saddle and pack horses and numerous dogs, among them Sounder, Jude, Moze, and Don. Don, of course, would figure prominently in Grey's later novelette. The dogs, rambunctious and slobbering, worked constantly at searching out and treeing mountain lions. Grey viewed the dogs with sympathy and concern.

Perhaps the most artful action—and certainly the most dangerous one—consisted of the actual roping of the lion so that it could be restrained for transport. In one instance, as Jones and Emmett closed in on a treed lion, Grey reported:

> . . . Emmett ran directly under the lion with a spread noose in his hands. Jones pulled and pulled, but the lion held on firmly. Throwing the end of the lasso down to Jim, Jones yelled again, and then they both pulled. The lion was too strong. Suddenly, however, the branch broke, letting the lion fall, kicking frantically with all four paws. Emmett grasped one of the four whipping paws, and even as the powerful animal sent him staggering, he dexterously left the noose fast on the paw. Jim and Jones in unison let go of their lasso, which streaked up through the branches as the lion fell, and it dropped to the ground, where Jim made a flying grab for it. Jones, plunging out of the tree, fell upon the rope at the same instant.[5]

Once restrained by ropes, the lion was prepared for the trek out of the forest. But, as Grey observed, this stage was not without its peril:

> Transporting our captives to camp bade fair to make us work. Jones had brought a pack saddle and two panniers. When Emmett essayed to lead the horse which carried these, the animal stood straight up and began to show signs of his primal desert instincts. It certainly was good luck that we unbuckled the pack saddle straps before he left the vicinity. In about three jumps he had separated himself from the panniers, which were then placed upon the back of another horse.[6]

Jones and Emmett tried to coerce several horses to accept the load of a bagged mountain lion, but most bucked and refused. A sorrel even "broke his halter and kicked like a plantation mule." Finally, Jones tried a big stallion who showed "no hesitation" in accepting his dangerous role. After they returned to camp, they tethered and restrained the lions. Before one of the lions was eased down from the back of a horse, Grey approached the big cat:

> I . . . put my face within six inches of the lion's. He promptly spat on me. I had to steel my nerve to keep so close. But I wanted to see a wild lion's eyes at close range. They were exquisitely beautiful, their physical properties as wonderful as their expression. Great half globes of tawny amber, streaked with delicate wavy lines of black, surrounding pupils of intense purple fire. Pictures shone and faded in the amber light. . . . Deep in those live pupils, changing, quickening with a thousand vibrations, quivered the soul of this savage beast, the wildest of all wild Nature, unquenchable love of life and freedom, flame of defiance and hate.[7]

As the captured lions snarled in camp and the wind whistled through the pines, Grey felt singularly alive amid the wild beauty. He noted that he felt that "all was mine . . . the stupendous unnamable thing beneath me, this chasm that hid mountains in the shades of its cliffs . . . and all that was deep and far off, unapproachable, unattainable, of beauty exceeding, dressed in ever-changing hues."

Ultimately "Roping Lions in the Grand Canyon" ends in tragedy, as a hunted lion is senselessly killed. The dogs emerge as heroes, while the human engage in self-pity and remorse. "I'll never rope another lion," Buffalo Jones avers. For Grey, however, a lion's death is an insignificant part of a larger universe, reinforcing for him "eloquently a lesson of life—that men are still savage, still driven by a spirit to roam, to hunt, to slay."[8]

The years 1909 and 1910 were particularly good writing years for Zane Grey. He wrote his breakthrough novel, *The Heritage of the Desert,* as well several angling articles and baseball stories at Lackawaxen. Enjoying a sudden burst of success, Grey returned to the Colorado River Basin in 1911.

By then the river had become less of a physical part of nature and more a symbol of the West he wished to capture on the printed page. While Delaware and Lackawaxen Rivers could be seduced by hook, line, and sinker, the Colorado refused. Like the wild mustangs and cougars who roamed the surrounding mesas and mountains, the river was untamed and free. And this wildness appealed deeply to Zane Grey. In all its frenzied and peaceful moods, the river god spoke its oracles clearly and distinctly—and mankind listened.

On this 1911 journey Grey had the additional benefit of traveling with two great western scouts: Al Doyle and John Wetherill. Doyle knew the countryside in and around Flagstaff, the Mogollon Rim and the Tonto Basin; Wetherill traveled extensively in the rugged terrain of Monument Valley, the Colorado River, Glen Canyon, and east to Hovenweep and Mesa Verde. Doyle would guide Zane for the next several years throughout Arizona. Wetherill, along with his wife Louisa, managed the trading post at Kayenta, where Grey often stayed on his rambles to Monument Valley, the Navajo reservation, and the Rainbow Bridge. Also in Kayenta was Nas ta Bega, the Paiute guide who accompanied Wetherill on so many trips. Nas ta Bega figured prominently in Grey's western tutelage. He taught Grey how to look "with slow contracted eyes from near to far." He also showed Grey how to gesture, without speaking, when recognizing a landmark in the distance. Grey observed that there "was something significant and impressive about an Indian when he points anywhere."[9] With Buffalo Jones and Jim Emmett, Doyle, Wetherill, and Nas ta Bega completed Zane's schooling in Western lore; and Grey was humble enough to listen—and watch—attentively.

Doyle and Grey stayed with the Wetherills in 1911. Deep in the heart of Navajo country, Kayenta was Grey's northern base for exploring the land east of the Grand Canyon. Wetherill, with his slouch hat and lanky frame, was perhaps the most influential white man living in northeast Arizona. He guided Grey and Doyle to some of the most famous places in Zane's fiction and nonfiction:

Surprise Valley, the Rainbow Bridge, the Keet Seel ruins, Laguna Creek, the canyon country above the Colorado River, Bubbling Spring, Canyon Segi, Navajo Mountain, and Monument Valley. Later, Wetherill guided Theodore Roosevelt's party into Monument Valley. Grey was thrilled by the idea that he had gotten there ahead of his hero.

Of all his guides, Grey was most in awe of Wetherill. The latter had come from one of the most famous families in the Southwest. In the late 1880s the Wetherills lived on a cattle ranch in southwestern Colorado. John and his four brothers—Richard, Clayton, Benjamin, and Winslow—loved exploring the hidden canyons and secluded arroyos around their property. In the winter of 1888, Richard Wetherill and his cousin Charles Mason were searching for stray cattle in a remote canyon. Looking down into the dense foliage, they saw what appeared to be mammoth stone houses lodged underneath the rock overhangs. They had discovered Mesa Verde, the now-famous national landmark abandoned by the Anasazi in the thirteenth century.

For the next several months, Richard, John, and their brothers combed the ruins atop Mesa Verde. It was here, while sifting through the artifacts of the ancient cliff dwellers, that John Wetherill developed a passion for amateur archeology and exploration that would inspire him the rest of his life. The Wetherill brothers excavated numerous sites on and under the mesa, giving names to the stone houses such as Cliff Palace, Spruce Tree House, Square Tower House, and Spring House. For three years the Wetherills virtually owned one of the great archeological sites in the world. John unearthed pottery, arrows, and baskets, as well as discovering numerous mummies in the kivas. Eventually, John's father approached the Smithsonian Institution about supporting their excavation efforts, an offer the musuem declined for lack of money. Later, the Wetherills sold many of the artifacts to the Colorado Historical Society in Denver.

Grey, ca. 1913, in Monument Valley, scene of many of his most famous novels and one of his favorite areas of the West to explore.

John married Louisa Wade in 1900 and left Colorado for the Navajo reservation. As a self-trained doctor, mentor, and friend, Louisa established a strong rapport with the Navajo people. After sojourning with the Wetherills, Theodore Roosevelt claimed that Louisa had "the keenest sympathy not only of their bodily needs, but with their mental and spirtitual processes. . . .They trust her so fully that they will speak to her without reserve about those intimate things of the soul which they will never even hint at if they suspect want of sympathy or fear ridicule."[10]

From his trading post at Kayenta, John continued his exploration of northern Arizona and southern Utah. In 1909 he and Byron Cummings discovered Betatakin ruins, now part of Navajo National Monument. Later that year he journeyed across the Arizona border and became the first white man to gaze upon the Rainbow Bridge. By 1910, when the bridge became a national monument, John

Wetherill was something of celebrity in the Southwest. Soon, tourists like Zane Grey and Theodore Roosevelt were seeking out his services, particularly when they wished to enter the rugged, unknown interior regions of the Colorado Plateau and Monument Valley.

Unfortunately, the word spread quickly about the wonders of Monument Valley, despite Grey's claim that "the leisure traveler" would have a difficult trek to reach it. By 1924 the Gouldings erected their trading post in the valley. By the 1930s, movie companies discovered its prime location and began shooting around Goulding's. Director John Ford soon made Monument Valley famous, filming several notable western movies there, including *Stagecoach, She Wore a Yellow Ribbon,* and *The Searchers.* By the 1960s, Glen Canyon Dam had sent fingers of Lake Powell so close to the Rainbow Bridge that tourists could moor their houseboats and trudge up to the monument in shorts and flip-flops. Grey's remote cathedral became a victim of the age of technology.

In April 1911 Zane made the landscape sketches for *Riders of the Purple Sage.* Apparently, he left his entourage and headed up into the Four Corners area, holing up in a remote cabin in Dove Creek, Colorado, just east of the Utah state line. Surrounded by cottonwoods, juniper, and great patches of sagebrush, he began the preliminary work on his most famous novel. The color of sand is particulary striking. Blood-hued, it declares itself against the rich green of the foliage and bright grandeur of the sky. After leaving Dove Creek, he seems to have returned to Kayenta before making the trip east to Lackawaxen.

Grey's treatment of Mormons in the novel hung over the book from the outset, initially deterring Harper's from publishing it and sending Grey to see his fishing buddy Bob Davis, editor of *Munsey's* magazine. Davis wanted to serialize it, but his boss Frank Munsey refused to publish the novel. While at a Campfire Club meeting, Grey approached Eltinge Warner, his friend and editor of *Field and*

Stream magazine, and told Warner of his dilemma. At first Grey was surprised that Warner expressed interest in *Riders*, since the magazine's outdoor emphasis was beyond the range of his novel. Warner reviewed the novel, accepted it, and in January 1912 *Riders of the Purple Sage* began running in serial form. Only after its introduction in *Field and Stream* did Grey get an audience with Harper and Brothers. The novel appeared that spring in book form, and quickly became one of the blockbuster novels of that year.

To some people in the early twentieth century, the Colorado River was a scenic annoyance. To others it was a useable resource. To Zane Grey, it was the river of action and adventure. In 1913 he returned to the Wetherill's trading post at Kayenta and began the journey northward that would yield his beautiful essay "Nonezoshe" and his novel *The Rainbow Trail*. During the writing of the novel, Grey read the journal of another of his Western heroes, John Wesley Powell. Powell's adventures presumably gave Zane the idea of sending a fictional boatload of fugitives on a dynamic, dangerous escape route down the rapids of the Colorado River.

In May of 1869, Powell and a band of explorers sailed in four wooden dories from Green River, Wyoming, down the Green and Colorado Rivers. Although Powell did not resemble a frontiersman, he certainly embraced the lifestyle of one. In photographs from the time of the expedition, he appears grizzled and distracted, even half-awake. He had lost his left arm at Shiloh and did not attempt to hide the fact. He had short dark hair, restless eyes, and a crinkly beard that could have doubled as a wren's nest.

Powell's single-minded purpose was to explore the Colorado River and record as many of his observations and impressions as he could. The rapids of the Green River were scary enough for Powell and his men, but they proved to be simply an overture to the main event on the Colorado. By the first part of August they had entered

Glen Canyon, an Edenic place where the river glided smoothly. From Glen Canyon down through Marble Canyon, however, the river, as Powell quickly discovered, got angry. Powell negotiated a series of rapids in a fifteen-foot pilot boat made of pine. His men were in twenty-one-foot oak dories. As Powell's boat hit the rapids, he strapped himself in. Powell's arm was waving crazily over his head as the boat bobbed and lunged. Several days they spent running the rapids, days of exhaustion, hopelessness, and alarm. "A few more days like this," wrote Powell, "and we are out of prison."[11]

In late August they emerged from the belly of the whale. The river straightened and grew less wild. In their wooden dories, they had barely made it through the rapids. It had taken them three months and six days to run the river from Wyoming to the Grand Wash Cliffs, Arizona. Most of it had been routine. The last stretch of the river had been harrowing.

More than forty years later, Zane Grey found Powell's wild ride irresistible. At the climax of *The Rainbow Trail,* the central characters —Joe Lake, Nas ta Bega, John Shefford, Lassiter, Jane Withersteen, and Fay Larkin—huddle together in their wooden craft as they prepare to descend the Colorado River:

> The rugged overhanging walls grew sinister in Shefford's sight. They were jaws. And the river—that made him shudder to look down into it. The little whirling pits were eyes peering into his, and they raced on with the boat, disappeared, and came again, always with the little, hollow gurgles.
>
> The craft drifted swiftly and the roar increased. Another rapid seemed to move up into view. It came at a bend in the canyon. When the breeze struck Shefford's cheeks he did not this time experience exhilaration. The current accelerated its sliding motion and bore the flatboat straight for the middle of the curve. Shefford saw the bend, a long, dark, narrow, gloomy canyon, and a stretch of contending waters, then, crouching low, he waited for the dip, the race, the shock. They came—the last stopping the boat—throwing it aloft—letting it drop—and crests of angry waves curled over the side. Shefford, kneeling, felt the

water slap around him, and in his ears, was a deafening roar. There were endless moments of strife, and hell and flying darkness of spray all about him, and under him the rocking boat.

When they lessened—ceased in violence—he stood ankle-deep in water, and then madly he began to bail. . . .

After the fury of the rapids, the Colorado finally becomes serene:

> Mile after mile they drifted through the silent gloom between those vast and magnificent walls. After the speed, the turmoil, the whirling, shrieking, thundering, the never-ceasing sound and change and motion of the rapids above, this slow, quiet drifting, this utter, absolute silence, these eddying stretches of still water below, worked strangely upon Shefford's mind and he feared he was going mad. . . .
>
> And then the fugitives turned through a V-shaped vent in the canyon. The ponderous walls sheered away from the river. There was space and sunshine, and far beyond this league-wide open[ing] rose vermilion-colored cliffs. A mile below the river disappeared in a dark, boxlike passage from which came a rumble that made Shefford's flesh creep.
>
> "Shore, if I ain't losin' my eyes, I seen an Injun with a red blanket," said Lassiter.
>
> "Yes, Lassiter," cried Shefford. "Look, Fay! Look, Jane! See! Indians—hogans—mustangs—there above the green bank!"
>
> The boat glided slowly shoreward. And the deep, hungry, terrible rumble of the remorseless river became something no more to dread.[12]

In 1918 Zane, Dolly, and their three children moved from Lackawaxen to Los Angeles. He was riding the crest of popularity, and commercial successes such as *Riders of the Purple Sage, Desert Gold, The Light of Western Stars,* and *The Border Legion* had made his name synonymous with the western novel. He was also becoming quite wealthy through numerous serializations of his works and his association with Hollywood.[13] And even though the Colorado

River was two hundred and fifty miles from Los Angeles, it would still figure prominently in his future.

The California phase of his writing career, which lasted from 1918 to 1939, would produce, among other works, *Boulder Dam*, Grey's final and poignant farewell to the Colorado River. Although the great Colorado River projects were conceived in the 1920s, the story of how Los Angeles got water from the Colorado—and its effect on Zane Grey—really began in the early part of the century.

The idea of bringing water to a thirsty Los Angeles began in the crafty mind of the city's chief engineer, Irishman William Mulholland. In 1900, when the population of Los Angeles was peaking at a hundred thousand, Mulholland first put in motion the plans to secure water from somewhere else. No one in Los Angeles at that point had any intention of siphoning off Colorado River water. Instead, Mulholland and city officials chose the Owens River in central California as the most readily available and renewable source of water for the City of the Angels. Given Mulholland's temperament, however, he would have selected Lake Superior if he could have erected an aqueduct long and durable enough.

The scrappy Mulholland worked his way to the top by digging ditches and working in lumber camps. Arriving in Los Angeles, he was asked what education and background he possessed to manage L.A.'s vast water system. With a cigar characteristically lodged in his lips, he replied: "Well, I went to school in Ireland as a boy, learned the three R's and the Ten Commandments—most of them—made a pilgrimage to the Blarney Stone, received my father's blessing, and here I am."[14] What Mulholland lacked in formal education, he made up for in guts and guile. The city, for reasons of its own, hired him.

Begun in 1907 and completed in 1913, the California aqueduct stretched 223 miles and brought water from the Owens Valley, through the Mojave Desert, and down into the Los Angeles Basin. Within three to five years, the region that was once an arid, sleepy pueblo was transformed into a palm-fringed and orchard-filled paradise.

By 1920, however, when Zane Grey moved into his permanent home in Altadena near Los Angeles, the California Aqueduct was simply unable to keep up with the demand. Los Angeles's population was soaring past five million and growing daily. The city was swank, fashionable, and booming economically. What it needed was more water.

The next logical move was to use the Colorado River, and that meant building an enormous dam to control and harness its energy. In 1922, negotiations to establish the Colorado River Compact took place near Santa Fe, New Mexico; but it wasn't until six years later, in 1928, after extensive, sometimes brutal debate and litigation, that Congress authorized the construction of Boulder Dam, a decision that would forever alter the course of the Colorado River and the livelihoods of people in six states.

By the end of the 1920s the number of people, automobiles, highways, and bridges had drastically changed the face of the Golden State. Grey was particularly concerned about the proliferation of the "stinking automobile" and the crowding out of the remaining open spaces. He wrote several cautionary articles for magazines and newspapers that indicated his displeasure with the destruction of California and its coastline. He supported conservation groups who sought greater control over California's forests and fishing grounds. In the tradition of Theodore Roosevelt, Grey, in his fifties, began to treasure—and fight for—the West's dwindling resources. He thought that bringing water from the Colorado River to Los Angeles was a bit far-fetched, but as the project progressed, he became interested and later infatuated by the idea.

Shortly after Congress authorized Boulder Dam in 1928, Grey took his daughter Betty Zane and his son Romer on a motor trip to his old haunts in Monument Valley and the Colorado River country near Lee's Ferry. They visited Argon Rock, the San Juan River,

Grey leading the horse "White Stockings" over Glass Mountain in southern Utah, ca. 1922.

southern Utah, Surprise Valley, the Rainbow Bridge, and Navajo Monument. This journey, his swan song for this particular itinerary, left him with sore loins and a troubled heart. Riding on horseback through the Monument Valley, he remarked that the vistas were "simply epic." He added that "it damned near killed me. It was too much without rest." After seeing the growth around Flagstaff, he told Dolly bluntly: "I shall never come back to Arizona. The main reason is that the country has been ruined by motorists. The Navajos are doomed. The beauty and romance of their lives is dead."[15] Nearing sixty years of age and feeling the divorce from the romantic West, Grey felt his interest in seeking out the byways and backroads diminishing and in some cases, evaporating. However, he did use the trip to pen several romances set in a bygone age: *Robbers' Roost, The Drift Fence, The Hash Knife Outfit,* and *West of the Pecos.*

Grey with a canine companion in the Grand Canyon ca. 1906, just prior to discovering the West as an important venue in fiction.

✦ ✦ ✦

Back in California, Grey was as excited as most Americans by the Boulder Dam Project at a site near Las Vegas, Nevada. The actual digging was not in Boulder Canyon, but in Black Canyon, ten miles south. The name "Boulder" stuck, however. Grey liked big things: cars, boats, novels, yarns, and natural landmarks. This project was going to be enormous indeed—in some people's minds the next wonder of the world. Grey envisioned that his *Boulder Dam* novel would equal the "epical turmoil" of his *U.P. Trail,* with intense human drama set against a large-scale backdrop. Like the Union Pacific story, it would employ legions of work groups, ramshackle cities, fierce conflicts, and moments of physical ardor and personal danger—all the features that in Grey's mind molded people and inspired epic novels.

If Boulder Dam's engineering dimensions were impressive, the human factors were even more compelling. Begun in 1931, the building of the dam occurred just as America was sinking into the Depression. With the unemployment rate at 30 percent, thousands of work-hungry men hitchhiked, rode boxcars and buses, or drove the family car out to the searing Nevada desert to compete for the jobs. A makeshift town emerged near the Black Canyon dam site. Known as "Ragtown," the village was composed of cardboard or sheet metal hovels stitched together with chicken wire and twine. Whole families occupied these shacks while the men waited for the jobs that in many cases never came. With temperatures in the summer approaching 120 degrees and rattlesnakes prevalent, many women and children did not survive. In terms of human misery and futility, not even the nineteenth-century mining camps and railroad towns could hold a candle to Ragtown on the Colorado River.

The few men who secured jobs got to live in Boulder City, a model town near the site with schools, hospitals, and fire and police departments. Workers made four dollars a day in often perilous conditions—scaling rock, pouring concrete, digging with pneumatic drills, and mucking soil. Cheap labor and willing workers were abundant. If a man refused a dangerous job, there were always twenty or more men lined up behind him ready to take his place. Work proceeded on the dam with few interruptions or complications. If the project was an example of vastness, it was also a model of speed and efficiency.

And then there was the river. For millions of years it had determined its own course, as it carved a bed from the Rockies to the Gulf. In November 1932 four massive explosions changed all that. These opened the four diversion tunnels that lured the Colorado from its centuries-old channel and forced the water through rock tunnels on each side of the dam site. Once the river was temporarily diverted, work could begin on digging into the dry bedrock and beginning the actual dam.

The men with the most dangerous jobs were the high scalers, who hung five hundred feet over the sheer canyon walls cleaning the rock faces and inserting dynamite. Four hundred of these men dangled over the naked bed of the Colorado River in summer temperatures that could fry eggs on sun-heated stone.

Zane Grey followed the progress of the dam in the Los Angeles newspapers. He later wrote to officials in Six Companies, the organization that managed construction of the dam. After some correspondence back and forth, an official invited Grey to Boulder City to witness some of the operations. Grey motored up through the Mojave Desert and arrived in Las Vegas. Looking much like Cheyenne, Wyoming, during the roaring days of the Union Pacific Railroad, Las Vegas was a boomtown brimming with bootleggers, gamblers, white slavers, prostitutes, and drifters. Grey met the chief of police, a rugged and unarmed Texas Ranger, who preferred to settle arguments with his fists rather than with a gun.[16]

Grey loved the tarnished glitter of the place. A guide from Six Companies showed him Boulder City, Ragtown, and the huge cavity of the dam, filled with milling workers. Six miles from Boulder City, the dam site was endless din from morning through the night. Huge banks of floodlights illuminated the floor of the canyon, allowing men to work in four continuous shifts. From a high observation point, Grey could see several aspects of the project: the high scalers, the concrete workers, the truck drivers, and the steam shovel operators. Grey was impressed by the vastness and complexity of the project and the indifference to personal danger of the men. From his intense observations, Grey began to formulate the plot and characters of *Boulder Dam*.

The actual novel, however, was not completed until much later. Written hastily on a December 1933 cruise to Tahiti with daughter Betty and son Loren, *Boulder Dam* recounts the harnessing of the Colorado River. It was not published until 1963, making it one of Grey's final novels to reach print. *Boulder Dam* is not one of Grey's best efforts, but it does reveal his attitude about the damming of this once unbridled river.

Although Grey continued to endure an emotional separation from the interior West—especially Arizona—he still clung determinedly to a belief in American idealism. To Grey the American values were the traditional frontier ideals of courage, integrity, grit, and ingenuity. All these seemed manifest in the building of Boulder Dam. In his novel he hoped to remind his readers of these values and to lift their spirits amid a worsening economic depression.

The central character of *Boulder Dam* is Lynn Weston, an ex-football hero who migrates to Nevada to land a job building the dam. In the process he gets mixed up with white slavers, racketeers, and shady women. Lynn progresses through eleven different jobs, from mixing concrete to dangling over the canyon as a high scaler. Grey writes: "Always behind Lynn's passion for the construction of Boulder Dam were two forces that vied with each other for supremacy.

One was elemental, sensorial, and the other intellectual and constructive. The latter grew as the months of contact and thought passed by, but always the stronger was the sheer physical joy of sweat and blood, the thunder and boom, the conquest of muscle over granite."[17] Lynn is fiercely proud to be part of the ambitious project, but secretly he believes "that only the elemental forces that had given birth to this strange river could ever change its course or dam it permanently."[18] This ambivalence runs through the novel.

The erection of Boulder Dam proved to be a major challenge to Grey's philosophical belief in the supremacy of nature. He, like his character Lynn Weston, wished to believe that human ingenuity was limitless: "Right there Lynn received his first mystic conception of the colossal and vain obligations of man pitting himself against the elements of time. He would succeed, too, temporarily, this bull-headed, ingenuous, and extraordinary man."[19] Lynn further muses: "Was not Lindbergh a classic example of the unlimited possibilities of mind, of the heroic spirituality of man, of the endless growth toward perfection, or whatever the inscrutable thing life meant for its highest creation?"[20]

Lynn Weston struggles with the notion that human monuments can survive the ravages of time and nature. Specifically, can this monument—Boulder Dam—outlast the inevitability of natural destruction and survive the fury of the Colorado River? The question is answered, somewhat ambiguously, at the end of the novel.

When the labors on the dam are completed, Lynn returns to witness the towering monument he helped create:

> Lynn's heart was full to bursting. Boulder Dam was beautiful in the extreme. It had sublimity, grace, translucent changing color, and perpetual melody and movement. But all this, and Lynn's elation, could not restrain his mind from envisioning the grand scene five hundred thousand years hence.
>
> The canyon yawned there black and dark under a pale and failing sun. The wide V-shaped gap was open as it had been in the beginnings of time, after the great inland water had cut its

tortured way to the sea. On the canyon walls colossal scars showed the action of a recent glacial period. Far up the canyon gleamed the pale green teeth of the retreating ice, sinister and deadly, yielding only to another age.

Below foamed and thundered the rapacious river, augmented to its old volume, no longer red but dirty white, remorseless and eternal.

Life had failed on earth. Inscrutable nature had gone on with its work, patient, terrible, and endless. . . . But the earth, with its long past age of creation, its dreamers and builders who had passed on, was only a tiny globe in the universe. Other planets were evolving. And the divine Thing felt by Lynn in his vision had no beginning and no end. The spirit moved ever toward perfection and immortality.[21]

In Grey's romantic visionary way, the Colorado River—the river of John Wesley Powell, Buffalo Jones, John Wetherill, Jim Emmett, Fay Larkin, John Shefford, and Nas ta Bega—returns ultimately to reclaim the desert earth.

For more than thirty years, Zane Grey saw both the tamed and untamed aspects of the Colorado River. In books such as *The Last of the Plainsmen, The Rainbow Trail, Wildfire,* and *Boulder Dam,* Grey worshipped and capitalized on the Colorado and its spirited plunge through the Southwest. For Grey, fording the Colorado River was something like a rite of passage, with strange and wonderful things on the other side.

For beyond the river was the "immutable desert, the leagues and leagues of slope and sage and rolling ridge, the great canyons and the giant cliffs . . . the pine-fringed plateaus, the endless stretch of horizon, with its lofty, isolated, noble monuments, and the bold ramparts with their beckoning beyond!"[22]

In short, beyond the Colorado lay Zane Grey country.

✠ ✠ ✠

My Dear Dolly

There was never any more inception than there is now,
Nor any more youth or age than there is now,
And will never be any more perfection than there is now,
Nor any more heaven and hell than there is now.

— WALT WHITMAN

WHEN Lina Elise Roth, known as "Dolly," married Zane Grey in November 1905, she knew that she had a gem of a writer on her hands. She also knew that he could be distracted, naive, moody, idealistic, and frequently undisciplined at the writing table. Realizing that editors often bloodied novice writers, she was always there to buoy his spirits, especially during the lean writing years of 1904–8. It helped that they were both romantics, although Dolly favored the German writers—particularly Goethe and Heine. It took a while for Grey's American West to seep into her pores.

Dolly had an instinctual knowledge of Grey's talent, but as they exchanged vows, neither she nor Grey had any idea of his future success. The Zanesville newspaper carried their joyful news:

Happily Married
Dr. P. Zane Grey, Author of
Betty Zane, weds Miss Roth in New York City.

Mrs. Lina Roth

Announces the marriage of her daughter, Lina Elise

to

Dr. Zane Grey

on Tuesday, November the twenty-first,

Nineteen hundred and five,

New York City.

The announcement continued: "Dr. Grey is the author of *Betty Zane,* one of the most popular stories ever read in this section of Ohio. It will be gratifying to his many friends to know that the doctor is now engaged on a companion book to *Betty Zane* and the manuscript will be delivered to the publisher probably before the close of the holidays."[1] The manuscript referred to in the news story was *Spirit of the Border,* and Dolly helped Zane prepare it for publication.

After returning from honeymooning in the West, the Greys settled into the house at Lackawaxen. From the outset, Zane set the tone for the marriage. He wished to pursue writing full time, even though it meant that the couple had to scrape by financially for a while. He wanted to travel, fish, and write magazine articles based on his experiences. His worst fear was that he would fail as a writer and be forced to return to his dental practice. At one point early in his marriage, when rejections mounted, he even seriously contemplated the idea. However, with Dolly's support and an overwhelming belief in himself, he managed to struggle along as an author.

Their first year of marriage was a happy one. They read aloud their favorite authors, played cards, strolled by the Delaware River, and hiked the surrounding hills. Zane loved the attention of his adoring bride. Dolly was the dutiful wife, enjoying their private moments together, tidying the house, and providing her husband the time to write in the nearby cottage. *The Spirit of the Border* was published in 1906, and Grey pushed ahead on the third volume of the Ohio River trilogy, *The Last Trail.*

Dolly Grey in the fields at Lackawaxen, ca. 1906. During the early years of her marriage to Zane Grey, Dolly enjoyed gathering fresh flowers.

Dolly did her best to ensure her husband's happiness. Frequently she was as star-struck as he was by the prospect of his future success as a writer. In her heart she worried about being equal to the task. "Sometimes I fear," she told Zane in a letter, "I'm not worthy to hold so high a place in your life, for after all I'm only a woman and dependent for love, life even, on you. But your faith in me gives me strength and courage to be what you wish me to be. . . . I'm glad I have you and that you love me, and I'm going to try hard to do and be everything you want."[2]

By 1908 Zane was traveling so often that Dolly became concerned for his career. He had once told her: "I need this wild life, this freedom. . . . The spirit of my ancestors is dominant in me. . . . I want the broad open free wilderness, to be alive, to look into nature, and so into my soul."[3] Dolly soon realized that worldly temptations could easily sidetrack her otherwise dedicated husband. In an important letter of 1909, she reminded him to place his writing at the forefront and to recognize threats to his time and craft: "Try to get into the attitude of making everything subservient to your work, for you have a great work to do, and a great destiny to fulfill, if you will but do it. You've always made your work secondary to your desire. The time has come when you must reverse that if you want to be as great as it is in you to be. And I think you have come to the time in your life when that is what will mean most to you."[4] Evidently Dolly's words struck home. Grey folded the letter and tucked it into his billfold, where it remained the rest of his life.

Later on in their marriage, Dolly became even more emphatic concerning her husband's responsibility to his career and her role in supporting it. She once remarked to Zane:

> It is froth of your enthusiasms that is always planning these new trips. That is all right, but get down to the solid matter between. Your one *aim* and *object* in life should be your *work*. . . . All your life you have pandered to your own desire. Pander now, for a little to your work. It will repay you so infinitely more. . . . And when you get a new enthusiasm ask yourself a few ques-

tions. Is this trip going to further my work, either in inspiration or solid material it brings me? Will the financial outlay equal the income?

My dearest, don't ever think I fail to appreciate what your enthusiasm and emotion and anticipation mean to your work. They are you, and you'd never have been great without them. But also you need the balance that I provide. Is it not so? Have I ever steered you wrong? It's my job to keep your feet on the earth while your head was in the clouds. Contact! You may not have thanked me for it at times, but you're living on this earth and writing for the people in it, and it provides the necessary wherewithal for you to carry out your cherished plans.[5]

One of the couple's happiest outings occurred in early 1909, when Zane and Dolly cruised to Nassau, Cuba, and Mexico. While soaking in the Caribbean sunshine, they visited the tourist haunts and strolled the beaches. In Mexico, Grey took part in adventures on the Alacranes Reef on the Yucatan Peninsula and on the Santa Rosa River near Tampico. According to Dolly, it was during the couple's stay on the Alacranes Reef that their first child, Romer, was conceived.

Although a happy event, the arrival of Romer Grey on October 1, 1909, upset routines around the house. Zane was accustomed to a set schedule of writing, fishing, and wandering along the Delaware. A crying baby often annoyed and distracted him from his work. While on one hand he craved a family life, on the other his need for solitude created tension in the Grey household.

By 1912, after six years of marriage, the Grey's relationship began to unravel. Dolly cited two reasons for their relationship's decline: the first was Zane's frequent and prolonged absences from home; the second was his inclusion of young women on his western "research" journeys. For Dolly, the former was maddening; the latter was heartbreaking.

Zane could justify his trips as essential to his writing career. They also alleviated some of his major depressions. His philandering, on the other hand, proved a thornier issue to explain. When Dolly accused him of spending too much time with "the girls"—as they both referred to his female acquaintances—he could become angry, defensive, and verbally abusive. In defending his behavior, Zane could blame Dolly for virtually anything—her "German" heritage that made her "too intellectual," or her "scornful" nature as a woman.[6]

As early as 1911, the year before the publication of *Riders of the Purple Sage,* Grey was taking women on his western research journeys. Perhaps he needed the excitement that these "girls" could give him. Certainly they provided the kind of approval he required from Dolly or from virtually every woman who walked into his life.

The reason for and the source of Grey's behavior are more difficult to determine. Was Zane Grey's philandering influenced early in his career by a prurient interest in Mormon polygamy?

Between 1907 and 1911, Grey's work was steeped in Mormon culture and history. In these years he traveled throughout Utah and Arizona, gathering information and visiting numerous Mormon settlements. Although the Mormon church officially restricted polygamous marriages in the early 1890s, and a restriction on polygamy was one of the conditions of Utah's statehood (1896), the practice continued, most notably in isolated regions of northern Arizona and southern Utah. Grey's important trips to Arizona occurred in 1907 and 1908, when significant percentages of the Mormon population were still practicing plural marriages.

Two popular misconceptions dominated the anti-Mormon sentiment of the late nineteenth and early twentieth centuries. The first was that Mormon men were over-sexed religious madmen who kept "harems" of young women. The popular press, from Bulwer-Lytton to Mark Twain to Arthur Conan Doyle, often focused on this highly sensationalized viewpoint. The second—and perhaps more volatile to the public—was that Mormon wives lived dehumanized, repressed existences under the domination of their husbands.[7] This second misconception probably produced more lascivious tales of "masters" enslaving and sexually dominating innocent young women than any other myth in Mormonism. In truth, Mormon women lived highly domestic and ordered lives, regarding the practice of polygamy as an honorable way of being married and bearing children.[8] Mormon leaders often stressed that plural marriage was commanded by God as a way of raising a morally pure generation.

Also adding to the public's misperception was that Mormon wives tended to be much younger than their husbands. A Mormon male in his early twenties generally married a women in her late teens. When the man married for a second time he was generally in his thirties and his second wife was between seventeen and nineteen.[9] Moreover, Mormon men in polygamous marriages were thought by some to remain younger longer. One Mormon leader explained it this way: "I have noticed that a man who has one wife, and is inclined to that doctrine, soon begins to wither and dry up, while a man who goes into plurality looks fresh, young, and sprightly."[10]

Before Zane Grey made his journeys with Buffalo Jones and Jim Emmett, he was already aware of the sensational aspects of Mormonism. His visits to drowsy hamlets in Arizona and Utah, however, showed him additional features. Mormon polygamy both attracted and repelled him. On one hand it shocked his Protestant sensibilities; on the other it excited a libidinous need in him. Afterward, Grey began to feel some justification for traveling with women friends. After all, his Mormon friends engaged in plural marriages and yet led highly moral lives; why shouldn't he?

Polygamy in Mormon culture, more than any other issue, provoked conflicting feelings in Zane Grey. He, like the protagonist John Shefford in *The Rainbow Trail,* might admit with some moral ambiguity: "His judgment of Mormons had been established by what he had heard and read, rather than what he knew. . . . One wife for one man—that was the law. Mormons broke it openly; Gentiles broke it secretly. Mormons acknowledged all their wives and protected their children; Gentiles acknowledged one wife only. Unquestionably, the Mormons were wrong, but were not the Gentiles more wrong?"[11]

Perhaps because he had exhausted the melodramatic features of Mormonism, or perhaps because his ambivalent feelings troubled him too much, Grey virtually abandoned the theme of Mormon culture in his novels after *The Rainbow Trail* in 1915. However, one aspect remained in Grey's life and that was having several women friends accompany him on his research journeys.

For many years, Zane Grey showed to the world a highly conservative, upright persona. In fact he had numerous affairs, spent lavishly, and was something of a libertine. In the back of Grey's mind, did the justification for the sexual aspects of such behavior begin somewhere in the Arizona and Utah desert villages?

In February 1913, Zane headed to Long Key, Florida, where he fished and wrote parts of his novel, *The Light of Western Stars*. Dolly Grey celebrated her thirtieth birthday at home. Having to raise two young children, edit Zane's manuscripts, and run the household at Lackawaxen, her life had become increasingly stressful. She had put on weight. However, she still bore the radiant expression and sparkling eyes of her teens.

While Grey was in Florida, Dolly took the train to New York and visited the editorial offices of Zane's publisher, Harper and Brothers. There she met the wily editor Ripley Hitchcock and an aspiring dramatist named Van Brunt. Van Brunt, it seemed, wished to write a stage play based on Grey's blockbuster novel *Riders of the Purple Sage,* and the three were meeting to work out copyright and financial arrangements.

Dolly clearly enjoyed her role as a business wizard. In a letter to Zane, Dolly related how she maneuvered Hitchcock and the novice playwright.[12] She asked for a third of the royalties for the play, should it be staged. Hitchcock agreed to her terms; Van Brunt meekly consented. After the deal, Dolly felt suddenly confident because of her face-to-face business acumen. She underlined to Grey in her letter that Hitchcock "didn't get the best" of her.

Hitchcock had rejected Grey's early novels. Even by 1913, his name continued to resonate in the Grey household. "He [Hitchcock] was as sweet as molasses to me," declared Dolly, with some venom.[13] After this meeting, Hitchcock's respect for both Dolly and Zane increased significantly.

On one hand, acting as Zane Grey's business manager appealed deeply to Dolly. On the other it meant that she would have to endure a prolonged absence from her husband. During these separations she was not above using some subtle means to provoke a reaction in Zane. She might in a letter enumerate the cost of household repairs, or mention an expensive purchase she was contemplating. In April 1913, while Zane was still in Long Key, she took the children over to Uncle R.C.'s farm, which was near the Grey home at Lackawaxen. Dolly noticed R.C.'s growing influence on her son Romer, and she used the occasion to tell Zane that Romer "wants to be Uncle Rome's boy now and live with him." Dolly also chided Zane about his next destination—northern Arizona. "What's your idea in going to Flagstaff," she wrote. "Just to drag those girls over the same country you've been over twice before?"[14]

In 1916, just shortly after their tenth wedding anniversary, the Greys' marriage was in trouble. Zane's absences, coupled with his numerous diversions, left Dolly alone much of the time. With three small children to raise and with little time for herself, Dolly's self-esteem began to erode. She mentioned to Grey that she wished to write a novel, but she realized that she lacked any leisure time to complete it. The plot, however, as well as the characters of her novel, continued to spin in her head for a long time. Her writing was relegated to correspondence and journal notations. Ten- to twelve-page letters were common. In them she usually developed scenes and supplied abundant feeling. She was a natural storyteller and a sensitive observer.

At various times Zane Grey's output was so prodigious that people thought Dolly or one his secretaries was responsible for writing parts of his novels. However, there has never been any clear evidence that anyone but Zane wrote material under his byline. Later, in the early 1920s, Dolly got formal training in novel and short story writing. While she edited and proofread her husband's work, she also studied other major writers of the time and assiduously worked on her own style.

Meanwhile, Grey's journeys and dalliances continued to unsettle her. The list of "girls" who seemed to come and go in his life included Lillian and Claire Wilhelm (who were sisters and also cousins of Dolly Grey), Elma Swartz, Dorothy Ackerman, Louise Anderson, and later Mildred Smith. These women were frequently mentioned as secretaries and traveling companions. Smith, for instance, remained personally involved with Grey until the early 1930s. The role of these women was unclear, but apparently some of their duties included accompanying Zane on his travels, typing portions of his manuscripts, and checking with Dolly on items of content and narrative.

The Wilhelm sisters frequently accompanied Grey to the Southwest. To avoid scandal that might arise from their traveling with him, Grey simply referred to them as his "nieces." This was particularly evident when the local newspaper in Flagstaff announced the arrival of Grey for one of his hunting or research journeys. For instance, in 1918 when Grey arrived for his Tonto Basin, Arizona, excursion, he was accompanied by Lillian and Claire Wilhelm, Elma Swartz, and Dorothy Ackerman, as well as by R.C. Grey and his wife. The women gave their names to the *Arizona Daily Sun* as "Mrs. Westbrook Robertson" (Lillian) and "Miss C. Williams" (Claire). Dated September 29, 1918, the brief newspaper article continued: "Mrs. Robertson is a niece of the distinguished author, Zane Grey,

and joined her uncle here to make a trip into the Indian country."
While Zane and R.C. hunted near the Mogollon Rim in October
1918, the women slipped away and toured the Colorado River near
the Grand Canyon. It was common for Grey's traveling guests to
engage in a variety of pursuits once they got to their destination.

By late summer of 1916 the Grey marriage was at a turning point.
Zane was traveling in the West. Dolly was at Lackawaxen—or
"Lacky"—as Grey sometimes affectionately called it. In September,
obviously distressed, she wrote to him: "Yesterday, I was reviewing
all the married couples I knew. You are the only man of them all
whose wife doesn't subjugate you, literally, figuratively or both. Well,
perhaps I would if I could. I could, but I wouldn't. . . . I wonder
how many men a *good* woman can love. A good man can love only
one; but a good woman has a larger capacity."[15] She also drove
home her loneliness: "I'm the 'alonest' person I've ever met, regardless of how many people are around me." In the same letter she reminded him that she would stand beside him when all of his more
frivolous friends had slipped away. "I'm the only one who has never
gone back on you and who never will."[16]

Grey felt cornered. It was customary for him to store up guilt
and resentment and then release them in a torrent. He fired back
to her in a note: "As for me I'd rather go to hell than stand your
scorn and bitterness and discontent any longer. If I must continue
to be made to feel as you have made me feel lately, I do not want
your love, or you as a wife, or as anything. For a long time I have
seen the futility of my life."[17] Several times Zane implied that he
might be contemplating suicide, as if to arouse sympathy in Dolly.
He then engaged in a defense of his women friends: "I know that
you consider me a whore-master. My friends are not what you think
them. They all have weaknesses, as indeed the whole race have.
But they are worth, to me, all and more than I have given them. If
as you say they must fail me, one by one, then I say that when that
day comes I am done for good and all. . . . These girls have kept

something alive in me. And now it is dying."[18] Zane's response is important because he sensed that his showdown with Dolly was imminent. He finished his letter curtly: "I will be home in October. Then we can settle the matter. I shall not stay long but go to New York in November, and south for the winter." Finally, in a postscript, he admitted painfully that his "great Babylon [was] tottering."[19]

To make matters worse for them, Dolly was quite fearful that a nationwide outbreak of infantile paralysis (polio) might spread to their corner of Pennsylvania. Hearing that the disease could be borne by envelopes and postcards, she burned each one as it arrived by mail. "I'm not taking any more chances than necessary," she told Zane in a letter. "I was never so terrified in my life." In adjacent New York, health officials prevented children from leaving the state without a certificate. School openings were delayed to control the epidemic. A relative of Dolly's, a young boy of two, succumbed to the disease. "The children are so wonderful,"she told Zane, "and in such fine condition. But oh, it strikes the rich and the sanitary and the careful people, just as it does the poor unhealthy ones; and they can't account for it."[20] Fortunately, the Grey family was not affected by the disease, but the summer of 1916 provided some anxious moments.

A year later Zane mounted a camping and hunting expedition to the Colorado Rockies, taking with him R.C. and two "nieces"— presumably Lillian Wilhelm and Elma Swartz. In Colorado, he conscripted two guides, named Teague and Virgil, who led Grey and his group into the wilds of the northern Rockies. From their base in Yampa, Colorado, near Steamboat Springs, they first headed west to Trapper's Lake in the Flattop Mountains, where they fished and hunted. The lake was nationally famous for its placid setting, abundant wildlife, and superb fishing. In 1901 Theodore Roosevelt put the region on the map with a highly publicized hunting trip (*Outdoor Life,* April and May 1901), and now Grey, long a Roosevelt fan, was treading in the footsteps of his outdoors hero. Grey's account of

Grey with his children at Lackawaxen ca. 1916, as he was approaching the zenith of his career.

this trip was published in *Outdoor Life* the following year. Although the guides Teague and Virgil thought Grey a daring hunter and resourceful outdoorsman, they both agreed that he had a hair-trigger temper and was unaccountably moody—often sulking through dinner.

When Zane was away from home, Dolly directed the Grey literary empire from the big house at Lackawaxen. When he returned, as from the Colorado trip in autumn 1917, business activity doubled. Grey plunged into work, creating both nonfiction and fiction from his wanderings in the Rockies. Dolly sold his article "Colorado

Trails" to *Outdoor Life* (March 1918). Later, the essay appeared in book form in *Tales of Lonely Trails* (1922). Grey promptly wrote *The Mysterious Rider* (1921) and sold it to Harper and Brothers. Dolly bargained with *Country Gentleman* for serial rights to the novel (the serialization appeared beginning June 7, 1919). Any given journey could yield numerous creative works: articles, essays, serializations, novels, nonfiction books, short stories—and later, their reprints.

As time went on Dolly's editorial skills and business sense became highly developed. For one thing, she knew the essential Zane Grey. When Zane wandered in his writing or said something unusually silly, she would provide her perspective—and a heavy pencil. Generally, hers was the final word before the manuscript was mailed to Harper and Brothers or to a magazine. Zane would make some preliminary notations in the margin, but these scratches could hardly be called "editing." One of Grey's secretaries might type a second copy before it went to Dolly for final approval. When Harper's prepared the galleys and sent them to Zane, he would make minor corrections only—a word or two, or a phrase. Harper's might ask for an extensive pruning of the manuscript, or for the reworking of a scene. Zane always complied.

Dolly had an extensive knowledge of New York editors and publishers. From Ripley Hitchcock at Harper and Brothers to Bob Davis at *Munsey's* magazine, she knew their likes and dislikes, their weaknesses and strengths. If she felt she could boost the price of an article, she would; if she thought a certain article needed a particular publisher, she followed it up the editorial line.

One of Dolly's obligations while Zane was away involved taking care of the horses that figured prominently in *Riders of the Purple Sage*—Night, Black Star, and Blanco Sol. Grey had first seen them in Arizona. He admired them so much that he purchased them and brought them back to Lackawaxen. Zane stabled them in the barn, frequently taking them on rides throughout the wooded countryside. Black Star and Blanco Sol never truly adjusted to life in Pennsylvania, dying prematurely at Lackawaxen. Zane returned Night to Arizona, hoping that his native environment might foster better health. It did. On an Arizona ranch, Night proved himself the wonder horse that Grey had captured so vividly in his famous novel.

Grey's decision to move from Lackawaxen to California broke Dolly's heart. Lackawaxen had been their first home during the early years of their marriage, and Zane had written his breakthrough novels there. Also, she had raised her three children in the big house under the towering maples and bordered by the peaceful river. Although in one way she was excited by the thought of living in southern California, the idea also frightened and unsettled her. Her marriage to Zane was still precarious, and the bustle of urban Los Angeles left her alienated and alone. Moreover, she was an Easterner to the core. She loved the shopping and culture of the East, as well as its nearness to Europe and her German heritage. In her own mind, however, moving with Zane to Los Angeles meant being closer to him and his travels, and that such a change might improve their marriage.

Gradually, between 1918 and 1922, she adapted to Western ways. While Zane was reaching the zenith of his career and spearheading his own movie production company, Dolly tried to make a home in a strange city. That house—an innocuous bungalow on Western Avenue in L.A.—would serve their needs until they bought a permanent home in Altadena in 1920. And characteristically, Dolly rallied to fix it up and make it liveable for their sojourn there.

After moving to California, Zane began taking son Romer with him on various excursions, which pleased Dolly, who viewed her husband as something of a stranger to their children. Romer, age nine in 1918, was as adventuresome and curious as Zane. "I love him passionately," remarked Dolly, "but Daddy will always have first place."[21]

Although the move did not soothe the prickly tension between Zane and Dolly, it allowed them more time together. Zane frequently accused Dolly of being too cultured, too civilized, and therefore unable to understand the elemental passions that drove him both as a person and a writer. "I understand life better than any book-educated or human-educated intellectual person," Zane told her. "For life to them is only one-millionth of life in the universe. . . . It would be funny to hear you and your women crowd talk about men, love, passion and life. Not one of you would tell the truth. Not one of you would reveal herself."[22]

While their differences often separated them, they shared a great deal of love and respect. Each could be brutally honest with the other. After bitter arguments, they could be casually humorous or playfully sarcastic. Grey could admit that Dolly was "a million times too good" for him; Dolly ended an emotional letter with "I love you best on earth." Even when they were mauling each other or questioning the other's allegiance, they usually maintained an enormous reserve of compassion.

Over time, Dolly and Zane came to a separate peace. Dolly even developed a love for Zane that recalled the deep devotion of their honeymoon years. She grew more accepting of Zane's absences and his women friends. Often she reminded him of her undying love for him, but she also stressed that the welfare of the children was uppermost in her mind: "I brought them into this world, and I must stick by them." About their relationship, she remarked that "the wildness is gone . . . as is the qualities that caused me bitterness and agony. . . . But I feel a deep well of feeling in me that makes life worthwhile."[23]

Zane's philandering, which was only exacerbated by his association with Hollywood, continued unabated. Dolly accepted it, and even acted as advisor periodically on how Grey should handle female attention: "But I won't go into the matter of the girls again, it's useless. . . . Only this I say to you, no woman is ethical, can possibly be, in the relationship in which these girls are placed to you. . . . I find that the fighting spirit in the human species requires a blow for a blow, a hurt for a hurt. The Christlike spirit of turning the other cheek never manifests in a battle of woman against woman for a man! That's where nature gets in her deadly work."

It seems that Dolly could not resist further commenting on Grey's behavior with other women:

> Your friends have always been nice, more or less normal girls in the ordinary walks of life. But in their relations to you they have become just the biological "female of the species" and in that manner have reacted to each other and used their claws. It's perfectly natural—and always has been—only because to you they are different, you haven't grasped the fact that it's history repeating itself. . . . Aren't they all perfectly sweet and nice and lovely when they have you all to themselves. . . . And Mildred Smith has reacted in exactly the same way as all the rest with the modifications of her particular makeup. What is so unforgivable in Mildred to other women is the assurance of righteousness and superiority. It sticks out all over her and enrages her adversaries.[24]

Meanwhile, Zane was overdrawing his bank account. Dolly became so alarmed that she sent him a cautionary note. "If you didn't have me to look after your affairs," she admonished him, "you'd be pretty badly off." She never did understand the extravagant nature of Zane's character. "I'll never be a spender," Dolly confessed. "I can't pay $25 for a hat to save me. I start out desperately—and then I think it's a waste."

Although she scrimped on spending for herself, she doled out money for the children's education and expenses. When they moved into their Spanish-style home in Altadena in 1920, Dolly went on a shopping spree, filling her new hacienda with Southwestern furnishings and antiques.

❧ ❧ ❧

Even though she deeply missed the peaceful routines at Lackawaxen, Dolly came to love the Egyptian sun of California. After

they settled into their Altadena home, Dolly and Zane looked westward toward Santa Catalina Island as a place to have a summer
home and writing retreat. Zane, of course, had loved the fishing
coves of Catalina for over a decade, but Dolly had recently discovered its treasures. Returning from a vacation to the island, she admitted that "Avalon was heavenly. I never saw it so warm and mild,
yet so cool, hills emerald, starred with millions of beautiful flowers
—mariposa lilies, yellow violets, wild hyacinth . . . the two days I
spent there were like a little trip to paradise."[25]

They soon bought a house near Avalon harbor. Unfortunately, it
happened to be directly behind Tom Mix's house. Mix was flam-
boyant, loud, and king of the movie western. Grey was taciturn,
understated, and lord of the western novel. The two did not get
along. When Mix showed up at the Catalina Tuna Club, Grey's holy
temple on the Pacific, the author shunned him.

The Grey's home looked directly into Mix's rear windows. Mix
threw raucous parties, angering Grey. Moreover, Mix had flashing
electric lights on the front of his house, and a flashing "M" on the
roof, meant to be seen from the air. Mix's activities so incensed
Zane that he packed up and sold the house. For many years Zane
Grey refused to acknowledge that Tom Mix starred in any of the
movies made from Grey's books, although in fact he starred in
several.

Eventually the Greys built an earth-toned, pueblo-style home
high on the hill overlooking Avalon harbor. Life was peaceful, except
for an alarming number of confused tourists who mistook their
dwelling for an Indian musuem located nearby.

In the early 1920s Dolly Grey began to stretch her sense of independence even further. Zane's western novels virtually every year
had achieved best-seller status, and she longed for ways to establish her own identity. Zane was also doing his customary amount of

Dolly and the three children (Romer, lower left; Loren, lower right; Betty Zane, upper right) in 1920, the year they moved into their new house in Altadena, California.

traveling to Long Key, the Rogue River, and the Colorado River Basin.

While Zane was in Oregon in April 1921, Dolly, the three children, and Hildred, the governess, drove back east. They were accompanied by two chauffeurs, so that Dolly could enjoy the passing countryside. (Zane was often concerned for her welfare, and on one occasion the following year he reminded her about one of the drivers: "I like Ken, and he's OK, but nothing doing on the speed stuff anymore. Do you get that, beloved? Not over thirty miles on the road, at any time. Otherwise I will fire this driver and scrap the cars.")[26] Characteristically, she filled an entire notebook with her observations, which she sent to Zane: the rutted, unpaved road; the hotels, the undulating beauty of the landscape; and the unique people they happened to meet along the way. When they got to Lackawaxen, Dolly felt overwhelming nostalgia for the old place. She visited with some of Zane's family, and walked through the woods down to the Delaware River. After a brief stay, she headed back across the country to rendezvous with Zane on the Rogue River. She made notes again as they retraced the route of the pioneers across the northern United States.

Dolly never shared Zane's love of the sporting life. Her version of the outdoors was always genteel and reflective. Possessed of a Wordsworthian spirit, she loved nature as a passive but intense observer. She did, however, like to fish in the Rogue River and breathe the alpine air of Oregon. Zane often asked Dolly to accompany him on fishing trips to the Northwest, but Dolly just as often declined. The sight of a flopping fish and the grit of camping life did nothing to inspire her. Once, however, when Zane asked her to fish on the glassy surface of Pelican Bay in southern Oregon, she packed her bag and went.

Under a rainless summer sky, Dolly and a woman friend nicknamed Dal ventured out in a boat on the water. As related in Zane's *Tales of Fresh-Water Fishing,* Dolly's expressed purpose that day was to have "fun."[27] Leaving Zane and R.C. to themselves, Dolly and Dal rowed into the middle of the bay. As a matter of fact, Dolly wanted solitude to avoid the serious side of fishing that her husband seemed to crave. After a couple of hours trolling in the bay, Dolly started screaming that she had hooked a big trout. Zane and R.C. frantically rowed toward them. Dolly desperately grasped the fishing rod, the tip of which was in the water. When she saw Zane and R.C., she yelled to them to leave her alone. "It's my fish," she reminded them. "We'll catch him all by ourselves—or die." Zane yelled that he would remain at a safe distance, while Dolly reeled him in.

For several minutes Dolly grappled with the fish, finally dragging it over the gunwhale. Dal was scared to look at it, let alone touch it with a stick. When the fish flopped in Dolly's boat, they all saw that it was not a trout but a "lunker"—a three-foot-long yellow sucker. As Zane and R.C. tried to stifle their laughter, Dolly and Dal were in hysterics over what to do with it. Neither Dal nor Dolly wanted to mess with it, but both agreed that they would have to do something. Zane told them to hit it with a gaff-handle. Dolly finally grabbed the gaff and hit the sucker with an "exceedingly gentle tap that would not have hurt a mosquito." Shocked by her brutality, Dolly whispered "There, he's dead." As Dolly collected herself, the yellow sucker, sensing perhaps it had a brief moment to seek its freedom, promptly flopped over the gunwhale, into the water, and disappeared. As the sucker swam away, R.C. howled: "Oh, yes, he's dead! he's dead! Haw! Haw! Haw!"[28]

Partly to celebrate her fortieth birthday and partly to take the voyage of her dreams, Dolly sailed for Europe on her own in 1923. Arriving in Southhampton, England, on board the *Mauretania*, she visited southern parts of Britain, then France and Italy. The Great War had deeply affected her, and she roamed through areas still rebuilding from the devastation. London and Paris enthralled her, but some of her most poignant moments were spent in the war-ravaged villages outside the City of Light. In Bethune Dolly discovered a landscape still scarred by trenches, barbed wire, and shell fragments. Acres of white crosses covered the denuded hillsides. In another village she noticed statue pedestals missing; she surmised that the Germans had melted them to make ammunition. At the famous cathedral at Reims the French were in the process of restoring the facade, which was heavily damaged in the fighting. A most illuminating and disturbing visit occured in Verdun, site of one of the most crucial and hellish battles of the war. Amid a treeless landscape, she was pleased to find millions of tiny wildflowers, symbolizing new life blooming in the man-made desert of the Western Front. Driving around Verdun, she encountered the "Trench of Bayonets," which was an earth-covered bunker with rusted bayonets at various angles poking out of the ground. It was a chilling scene. Evidently, many gallant Frenchmen had been buried alive in the trench, their bayonets still poised for battle.

She wrote Zane often. To incite some jealousy in him, she remarked that a mysterious European count was chasing her across Europe. Zane, although amused, was also clearly irritated by the notion.

Back in America, Dolly motored through Lackawaxen and then headed to California. Even though the roads were often treacherous and the weather unpredictable, she loved the freedom of the roadways. On this trip she drove alone, without the aid of chauffeurs.

She frequently motored through southern California and Arizona, either heading to the Grey's cabin in the Tonto Basin or back east. Once in Holbrook, Arizona, she enjoyed bargaining for Navajo jewelry and rugs. Again she was the shrewd businesswoman, pointing out to Zane that she had bought the five-hundred-dollar rugs "for two hundred dollars before the trader found out that [she] was Mrs. Zane Grey."[29] Clearly, Dolly enjoyed the benefits of being the wife of a famous writer. She also had come to like being the footloose gypsy with money to spend, the role that Zane had reserved for himself during the first ten years of their marriage.

Much more so than her husband, Dolly loved the artistic and cultural heritage of Europe. She visited the Continent again in the summer of 1926, and probably would have gone several times more were it not for her responsibilities at Altadena. This time she took the train to Indianapolis, where Zane had arranged a gleaming Stutz for her arrival. She drove the Stutz to Zanesville, staying with friends of the family. Feeling proud of her driving skills and sudden freedom, she continued on to New York and boarded her ship on June 2. Zane spent the summer she was away at Avalon, busily writing and trying to figure what bills to pay and when to pay them. He mentioned his frustration in a letter to her. From Switzerland, Dolly calmly wrote back: "Sorry the bills, assessments, etc. worry you. I tried to dispose of as much as possible, but when I tell you that it is a never-ending business for me, perhaps you won't begrudge me my vacation. I have the faculty of forgetting those things when I get away."[30] Although Zane stormed about the house fretting about finances and calling it her "last" trip abroad, Dolly continued with her European tour.

In the mid-1920s Zane Grey began taking longer and more distant angling adventures (discussed in chapter 7). Dolly, with some difficulty, adjusted to his absences. Manuscripts, such as the one for "Stairs of Sand," often came in the mail postmarked "Wellington, New Zealand" or "Papeete, Tahiti." Since Zane was not available for textual questions, Dolly had to rely on her keen instincts and sound judgment.

As Zane's journeys became more prolonged and far-flung, Dolly's feelings for him entered a new, more intense phase. She accepted Zane's need for escape as part of his character, and at times she reveled in his accomplishments: "You are one of the world's great men, but to me you are something much nearer and more precious. You are the man I'm loving always more, in spite of and because of everything you've done and haven't done."[31] She often played the role of the long-suffering Penelope waiting for her vagabond hero to sail home. "You are still a wandering Ulysses, questing for the unknown, seeking the magic isles, dallying with romance and physical love," she wrote him in 1927. She added that he would discover the joys of family life "sooner or later."[32] Although she missed Zane on some of his four- to six-month expeditions to the South Pacific, she clearly enjoyed having her own life while he was away. In addition to editing and finding publishers for his work, she cultivated numerous relationships with women friends, monitored the children's education, saw most of the current movies, and wrote voluminous letters to her acquaintances. She was by most accounts as happy as at any time in her life.

In June 1928 the Greys' Altadena doctor advised Dolly to have a hysterectomy, which ended up being more traumatic for Zane than it was for his wife. The events surrounding Dolly's operation are best related in Zane's own words:

> She went to the Good Samaritan Hospital in L.A. on June 18. I left her there.
>
> Next day I went back with R.C. and Romer. At nine-o'clock I saw Dolly at the last moment. She was bright, cheerful, cool, game as a thoroughbred. Pride overcame my fears for a little. Then I saw her moved down the hall and into the elevator to go into the ward upstairs to take ether. She said, "I'm all right."
>
> Somehow I got over that first hour, or through it. When the second began, the minutes dragged. I paced the gloomy hall. . . . When Dr. G came down, it was about time to save me from collapse. He reported that the operation had been imperatively necessary and that it had been successful. Something caved in in me, but I could thank God.
>
> My consciousness was such that I cannot now recall the thoughts I had, the prayers, the agonies.[33]

Weeks later Dolly was recovering and gaining strength, so that Zane could note with relief that "the load is removed from my breast, and the inhibitions from my mind."

After fully restoring her stamina, Dolly Grey leaped back into her professional life. With some financial backing from Zane, she founded and later served as president of the Altadena National Bank. Not having any academic training as an accountant, she took a risk, emotionally as well as financially, even to initiate the idea. But her keen business sense and her ability to deal with people helped her through the first months in the position. Later, the bank would fail, as would most others, in the Depression. After the bank's insolvency, she felt obligated to repay all her clients from her own funds. Although the business venture ended in failure, she remained proud of the fact that she was one of the first woman bank presidents in America.

It is unfortunate that the Greys decided to enter the banking business when they did. Throughout the 1920s, the American economy was characterized by soaring optimism and frenzied spending. The Grey's annual income reached $500,000 several times during the decade. Although he was not invested heavily in the stock market, Zane acquired numerous properties, cars, and boats. The end of the dream seemed remote indeed.

By 1929, however, the economy was spiraling toward disaster. In October Zane and Dolly—as well as every family in America and the world—felt the economic earthquake that resounded from Wall Street's collapse. Dolly, the more financially astute of the two, realized its repurcussions almost immediately. It would take Zane several years and some drastic changes in his lifestyle for it to become apparent to him.

By 1930 and her forty-seventh birthday, Dolly had steeled herself to accept Zane's frequent voyages and intense writing schedule. On the eve of their twenty-fifth wedding anniversary, she acknowledged that although the sea and other women could have his time, they could not affect his "soul and its child, [his] genius." Although this might provide only feeble consolation to other spouses, to Dolly it meant that she was intimately connected to Zane and his writing.

As for the Grey children, Romer was twenty years old and had just eloped with a flapper girl, which irked Zane. Romer had dark, tousled hair spilling amply onto his forehead and possessed the ramrod bearing that Zane had at the same age. "Romer is a second edition of me," Zane mentioned to Dolly at one time. In his outdoors acumen and clownish demeanor, he tried to emulate his famous father. Betty Zane Grey was eighteen and a budding poet. Slender with bright eyes and an aquiline nose, Betty developed an intense inner knowledge that both confounded and threatened Zane. "She has a marvelous poetic imagination," observed Dolly. "They say she has a brilliant mind. But she's very much alive, nevertheless!"[34] For many years, Zane tried to understand his daughter's unusual sensitivity to the world. The youngest child, Loren, was fifteen and interested in photography and science. Like Dolly, he preferred a patient and objective reflection on nature and the world. Later, Dolly was so adamant about sending Loren to college that she told Zane in letter: "And he *is* going to college, even if my clothes fall off my back and I have to diet down to my pristine slimness."[35] Loren did attend college and went on to become a distinguished psychologist.

The big Spanish-style house at Altadena continued to be Zane's and Dolly's refuge, even though it seemed the bustle of California traffic was persistently encroaching on their world. In 1931 Dolly invited Margaret McOmie of *Better Homes and Gardens* to interview the couple in their home and write a feature article for the magazine. According to McOmie, the "vine-covered stucco house had a rambling spaciousness" that exuded "warmth and taste." Meeting Zane, she described him as "a slender wiry figure in a soft gray knicker suit. But the great strength of his tanned face! To see Zane Grey's face is like finding the key to a room that holds something promising and genuine." McOmie called Dolly "a charming woman

with soft brown curly hair, eyes that sparkle, and a fresh whole-
someness." Strolling around like a pilgrim at a shrine, McOmie
drank in the Grey estate, from the palm-lined gardens to the dark
interior rooms crowded with Navajo rugs, fishing trophies, bookshelves, and collected bric-a-brac. Zane could not resist showing
McOmie his study, which she described as "strikingly virile." The
home, remarked McOmie, seemed be a perfect statement of their
personalities. Dolly loved such exhibitions, particularly because it
meant revealing to the world her and Zane's definition of a home:
"a place for love, comfort, and sweet rest."[36]

In 1932, the Greys established the Zane Grey Corporation. Most of
the legal negotiations, however, were accomplished while Zane was
away from Altadena. Dolly told him that by incorporating they could
deal more effectively with tax issues relating to his writing income.
The actual reason was that Dolly could put her husband on a salary
and control his extravagant spending. Between 1928 and 1933, Zane
Grey's income plummeted from $385,000 to just over $33,000 per
year. Since Zane had little contact with reality, he frequently misjudged, or simply ignored, the severity of the economic collapse grip-
ping the world. He wished to spend as lavishly as he had in the early
1920s. But the funds simply were not available.

One of Dolly's proteges, Ed Bowen, was brought in to manage
the corporation. Bowen's tight-fisted style maddened Grey, causing
a major rift in the marriage. Dolly tried desperately to please her
husband and yet keep their shrinking empire healthy. Zane, often
sailing in the South Pacific, blamed the management of the corporation, or sometimes Dolly, for scuttling his sailing plans. Often she
found herself trying to educate Zane in the economic realities. "For
three years now," she noted, "we have been fighting a very terrible
situation caused, not by our own blunders, which were bad enough,
but by an economic condition that has affected the whole world.

The battlefield is strewn with the dead and dying but we are still fighting on. . . . If you think anyone else can carry it on better than the present 'lineup,' I shall be more than happy to be relieved of the responsibility. . . . And don't think I wouldn't be willing to lay down this burden and see if I still can't find a life of my own to live."[37]

Zane thought his son Romer was more fit than Bowen to run the corporation. Dolly loudly desisted. "Romer is wonderful at times, awful at others," she remarked to Grey. "He still has the complex of wanting to run everything, and resents bitterly that Ed has the balance of the control. . . . Romer gets his wild streaks and is likely to wreck us if we don't tie him down."[38] Romer Grey's interest soon drifted away from running the corporation. He founded Romer Grey Pictures in 1933 and made two animated cartoons, neither of which he was able to sell to distributors.

As Zane continued to spend more money, Dolly became frantic. "There is one thing I'm sure of," she implored him, "and that is I am almost at the end of my rope where this debt business is concerned. The only reason I have weathered it, is because of the corporation. . . . I'd rather take a job as someone's cook than keep on with this kind of burden." Realizing that Zane might dismiss her statements as mere histrionics, she underscored the family's plight: "Please believe me, Doc, when I tell you we are doing everything we can to make ends meet, that we will give you every cent we can, and that if you don't cooperate and cut things to the bone, we can't carry on."[39] In the same letter she criticized him for suggesting that the corporation was unduly picking on him. "What gets me more than anything else," she began, "is your attitude that we have oodles of money that we are witholding from you. . . . I am perfectly willing to go on as I have been serving you, helping you, fostering that which you have to give to the world . . . but I can't do it if . . . I am accused of disloyalty and cheating and going against you."[40]

Meanwhile, Zane was off the coast of Tahiti, angered by the idea that his long-planned world cruise was not financially possible. Dolly, in Altadena, stuck to her guns. In early May 1933, she penned him a letter, notable for its impatience as well as its directness. "The last month," she wrote, "has been the worst, financially, in our existence. All the money gave out and we are overdrawn when the bank examiner showed up. It's a queer sort of feeling to know that in another week or two there might not be enough money to buy food. Of course, there was still that $1250 of yours in the bank, but outside of keeping the children on just enough to prevent starvation I would not have touched that."

Toward the end of 1933 Zane finally conceded that a speedy economic recovery was not imminent and that his personal finances were in bad shape. To Dolly, it was a welcome if belated capitulation.

If Dolly Grey's time and energy were mostly exhausted by steering the corporation, she had enough remaining to edit and polish Zane's manuscripts—always the manuscripts. Even in the 1930s, as Grey entered his sixties, novels, novelettes, short stories, and fishing articles continued to pour from his pen. All had to be proofread, edited, and have parts rewritten. "He simply would not edit," Dolly said later. In contrast to the 1920s, when she could negotiate with magazines like *Collier's* and *Ladies' Home Journal* for serials fetching between $60,000 and $80,000, the 1930s were dismal indeed. For one thing, advertisers withdrew much of their financial support, causing many major periodicals to fold, cut staff, and reduce their prices for serials and articles. Consequently, by 1933 the serial market was in serious decline.

Since serials and reprints of Grey material generated a large part of his income, losing that source of revenue proved nearly disastrous to the Zane Grey empire. However, Dolly stuck faithfully to the power of the Zane Grey name and patiently waited for the economy to improve. Even during the worst times, one of her main concerns was not to do anything rash that might cheapen Zane's reputation. Temptation rose, but she did not succumb.

On several occasions Dolly advised Zane on the marketing of his stories, especially as they tried to navigate the shoals of a worsening economy. "The trouble is," she remarked to him, "we cannot shoot these stories to editors too fast. They get together and discuss things and if too many Zane Grey stories are floating around New York without a place to alight, it will create a bad impression."[41] Dolly also reminded Zane about redundancy of character and plot devices. "Get away as much as possible from your former stories and characters," she coached him. "Try to get new ideas and situations, something different in the way of plot. And have plenty of plot and action to meet the demands of the serials." She asked him to "think over all your stories. You will find that they fall into certain classes, and your heroes often repeat themselves. *Thunder Mountain* was different, so was *The Trail Driver* and *The Shepherd of Guadeloupe*."[42]

Without Dolly at the helm, Grey could easily blunder. Once, while Dolly was away from Altadena, Grey hastily mailed an unedited manuscript to Harper and Brothers. It was returned—also quickly. Apparently Zane had assumed that his reputation alone might sell a book, but he had a sobering rejection letter. He saved it for Dolly's editing, and it was accepted. In the early 1930s, unknown to Dolly, Zane entered into a contract with a young woman named Berenice Campbell. The resulting flap cost Zane dearly.

In 1929 Berenice Campbell, age twenty-one, hitchiked alone from Missouri to Wyoming, keeping a journal of her experiences on the road. She later sent the journal to Zane Grey, who was so impressed by her independence and spirit that he offered her a royalty of 10 percent on the earnings from a book he would write about her trip. For a brief time Campbell served as Grey's secretary, but she soon left his employment. The novel—*Wyoming*—was serialized in *Pictorial Review* as "The Young Runaway" (May 1932) and was modestly successful. When she was not paid her share, Campbell sued Zane.

Dolly soon found out about Zane's agreement with Berenice and was livid. "If you ever make a contract again, God help you," she admonished him. "You've done it in your sorrow and confusion several times. Look beyond the end of your nose—or your infatuation. Don't put anything in writing. . . . Human relations are unstable, my dear." And then as if to remind him about her role, she remarked: "Hereafter, my dear, let the literary end of things remain strictly in the family."[43] Thereafter, it did.

Despite their differences and often tug-of-war relationship, they achieved a harmonious marriage. The two demons that Zane struggled with throughout his thirty-four-year marriage to Dolly were finding deep intimacy with her and understanding that other people's needs, including family members', were as important as his own. During the 1930s he would often spend six to eight months away from home on a fishing expedition, while Dolly and his children were experiencing dramatic changes and upheavals in their lives. Zane never did truly understand his responsibility as a husband and father. For Dolly's part, she accepted this behavior, sometimes at great expense to herself. In general she was more enamored of being married to a famous and wealthy author than she was concerned about making crucial decisions for herself. And too often the overpowering charm of Zane Grey simply got in the way. Although she considered herself a thoroughly independent and free-thinking woman, she loved primarily Zane's genius and soul, a soul that was often sailing away from her toward a murky destination.

Right to the very end with Zane Grey's death in October 1939, she hoped that her Odysseus would wander home for the last time and they would experience together the happiness of Zane's retirement years. In fact, Zane never could relinquish his love of the sea, the trail, and the faraway sunset. At some level, Dolly always knew this simple truth.

✄ ✄ ✄

The Pathfinder

There's a land where the mountains are nameless,
  And the rivers all run God knows where;
There are lives that are erring and aimless,
  And deaths just hang by a hair;
There are hardships that nobody reckons;
  There are valleys unpeopled and still;
There's a land—oh, it beckons and beckons,
  And I want to go back—and I will.

—ROBERT SERVICE

WHILE earthbound mortals are granted a standard twenty-four-hour day, Zane Grey seems to have wooed the muses into stretching his to thirty-six. Traveling, fishing, camping, hunting, exploring, and writing left little time for such luxuries as sleeping and eating. During his rise to fame, he turned his experiences in Mexico, Arizona, and Florida into notable nonfiction essays and books. Although his western novels steal the spotlight, these often unsung nature books give balance and dimension to Grey's extensive career.

Arguably the best—and certainly the most representative—of these nonfiction outdoor books are *Tales of Southern Rivers* (1924), *Tales of Lonely Trails* (1922), and *Tales of Fishes* (1919). All three typify Grey's love of wild nature, his lark-free spirit, and his insatiable lust for life. And between them they investigate his trio of passions: the jungle, the desert, and the sea.

In *Tales of Southern Rivers*, the essay "Down an Unknown Jungle River" plays the dominant role, revealing that despite Grey's love of the desert he had an equal fascination for the dense Mexican rainforest. Moreover, he discovered this part of the world before he discovered other regions. As early as 1905, Grey was fishing for tarpon in Tampico on the Gulf of Mexico. En route to his coastal destination by train, he happened to glimpse a beautiful waterfall high in the Mexican interior. Mica Falls, as they were known, plunged down the rock face and formed a tributary of the mysterious, uncharted Santa Rosa River. The falls passed of sight but not out of Grey's mind.

The river had a reputation clouded in rumor and folklore. Grey yearned to know more, but there was scant information. A tantalizing mystery, particularly one secreted in the high, lush Mexican mountains, stimulated him like a narcotic. In early 1909 he returned to the area, experiencing the events he recorded in "Down an Unknown Jungle River" (serialized in *Field and Stream*, March 1911) and fictionalized in book form as *Ken Ward in the Jungle* (1912).

If Grey had never written a word about the American West, he still would have ranked among the century's great writers of outdoor-adventure nonfiction. In essays such as "Down an Unknown Jungle River" and later in "Tonto Basin" he achieves a superb integration of character study, narration, and strong sensory reporting. Without sentimentality or overstatement, Grey paints his vivid scenery with lucidity and precision. Moreover, his narrative essay style moves with the pace and cadence of good fiction.

In Tampico he met a young American railroad engineer named George Allen, who would serve as his companion on the expedition. Allen, reckless and ambitious, fit the profile of a youthful Zane Grey. Allen would remain a lifelong friend until his drowning death in 1932. Grey also selected a Mexican guide, Pepe, who was the best boatman in the region when sober. To Pepe the three pesos a day that Grey promised him proved irresistible. "In hiring guides," observed Grey, "or choosing companions for a wild adventure, I had learned to trust inexplicable impulse."

Zane Grey's selection of local guides and traveling companions would make good stories in themselves. Frequently his outdoor narratives hinge on humorous situations and complications provoked by an "experienced" outfitter or local guide. Whether recruiting them in Arizona, Mexico, Colorado, or Florida, Grey trusted his impulses more than his good sense. Of course he trusted implicitly his reliable guides, Al Doyle and John Wetherill, but frequently in strange locales he had to rely on someone's recommendation. The unkempt Pepe and the blustery George Allen, as it turned out, provided Grey with some hilarious moments in the midst of near disaster.

Grey's plan called for them to travel west into the Sierra Madre Mountains, then double back to Tampico by way of the river. For the next two weeks, covering over two hundred miles, the trio went down the unmapped Santa Rosa River in a rowboat. Like the Colorado River, the Santa Rosa provided its moments of panic and its bouts of bliss. Abundant wildlife surrounded the river's course: quail, pheasant, obnoxious parrots, turkey, and numerous flocks of ducks. An occasional alligator peeped above the water. Ten-foot-long black snakes sometimes dangled from the mossy cypress trees, and bitterns, herons, and kingfishers darted through the foliage. And in addition to the marauding insects, fierce ticks made the travelers' lives miserable.

There were the small ticks, called *pinilius,* and the larger variety, called *garrapata.* Both tormented the three whether in camp or out on the river. Allen became quite adept at removing them with a lighted cigarette. "Popping ticks," as Allen referred to his method, frequently took as much time as gathering firewood or hunting in the surrounding forest. Surprisingly, the ticks had favorite targets. Pepe for some reason attracted the *pinilius,* while Allen was bothered by the more vicious *garrapata.* Throughout the journey Grey referred to them as Garrapato George and Pinilius Pepe. Grey soon got the idea of burning the brush around the campsite to reduce the problem as much as possible. It worked periodically for controlling the ticks. In the middle of the night, however, an army of black jungle ants swarmed through their tent, biting Pepe and sending him howling into the night.

Once they were on the river Grey demonstrated his exceptional boating skills. Pepe was also adept in that role, but Grey was better in the shallows and rapids. Grey drew upon those skills he had developed in the Campfire Club, an organization that would later acknowledge his explorations on the Santa Rosa River. Grey loved the adrenalin rush of the boat in the rapids. Once, however, he laid too heavily on the oars, sending Pepe over the side and into the churning water. Pepe swam to shore against the current. When Grey and Allen doubled back to find him, he was shaking himself off like a doused puppy. Grey realized then and there that he would have to view the trip as a light-hearted adventure rather than as a serious expedition. Since he needed an essay that offered both human foible and courage, it was a logical decison.

After encountering numerous rapids and enduring several portages, they made their way to the lower reaches of the Santa Rosa. Along the way they hunted jaguar and were almost trampled by hundreds of wild pigs. Only a raging brush fire saved the three hunters from the marauding animals. Pepe thought that the fire might briefly help the tick problem; George Allen added that their next meal—roast pig—was a sure thing.

Allen got tropical fever, and spent the remainder of the journey so weakened that he was virtually useless as a helper. Most of the heavy work fell to Grey, who felt additional pressure to get Allen to Tampico for medical attention. Zane and Pepe spent days of hard rowing, yearning for signs of their journey's end. They reached the village of Panuco, only a short distance by cart and railroad to Tampico. All things considered, it had been an adventurous two weeks, providing Grey with the memories to write "Down an

Unknown Jungle River," and the experiences to tell several good yarns about the trip.

After Zane returned to Lackawaxen, he wrote his friend George Allen in Tampico, Mexico, that their "jungle trip caused a good deal of talk in sporting circles . . . of course, I've exaggerated other things. But I know you will uphold me in the main features, that we went down the river, shot the rapids, and had a hell of a time. And that's all I care about."[1] Grey's adventures were the talk of the Campfire Club in New York City. He sought the club's highest award for his daring exploration of the Santa Rosa River, telling Allen "if I can't get a purple I'll take a high honor red."[2] He also requested recognition for his companion George Allen: "I'll get you honors from the Campfire Club. You deserve them for taking the trip." Grey ultimately secured for Allen a high honor red badge, which he delivered to him personally.

After their Santa Rosa trip, Allen fancied himself as something of an explorer. In a letter he mentioned to Grey that he might like to reprise their expedition on the river, which prompted Zane to reply: "In regard to your coming down that river I would advise you not to, strictly not. I can see where we had more luck than sense. And if I had not known how to guide the boat, we would still be there; and your little wife would be wearing black. It was a damned fool trip, but as I look back on it I think it was great."

Over the years Zane Grey and George Allen corresponded fairly regularly. Zane and brother R.C. remained drawn to Tampico and its tarpon fishing. Were it not for a smallpox epidemic that broke out in the city and the effects of a world war, Tampico could have become one Grey's favorite fishing and writing haunts.

Grey could switch unpredictably from hunter to herdsman, and from a man of action to a man of contemplation. In another essay from *Tales of Southern Rivers* titled "The Great River of the Gulf,"

Grey holding Romer Grey at Lackawaxen ca. 1910, a year after he returned from the Santa Rosa River expedition.

Grey reveals his more placid side, as he probes the mystery of the Gulf Stream and its variety of fish.

In early 1924 Grey and R.C. returned to the fishing waters off Long Key. Grey had always been attracted to the Gulf Stream off Florida's coast, and on this occasion, he decided to investigate further its passage from the Gulf into the Atlantic Ocean. At first he was doubtful that an essay about the Gulf Stream should even be included in a book about "Southern Rivers." "It may be something of a poetic fallacy," he told his readers, "to call the Gulf Stream a river of the South, a flowing stream within the sea, but to me that is just what it is. As a matter of fact it is a current of blue water fifty miles or more wide, and it moves appreciably faster than the green ocean water that it divides."[3]

After a day sailing through intermittent squalls and sunshine, the two brothers encountered the demarcation line of the Gulf Stream:

> I saw the dark line of the blue water sharply defined against the green. There was now no ruffled current, as on windy days. The cloudy violet water merged irregularly into the green, raggedly and mistily, with streamers and ribbons, and thick bulks of solid color, and thin broken wandering lines. A low, heaving swell, just a perceptible movement of the water, made me think of the Pacific.
> . . . We turned and ran ahead of where [the sailfish] had showed, and trolled out baits over the spot and all around it, to no avail. Then we headed into the Gulf Stream.
> I climbed out on the bow, leaving R.C. to do the trolling, and took a position facing north so that I could command the water level ahead. It seemed rather remarkable that I could actually have a comfortable seat on a launch in the Gulf Stream. But it was a most pleasant fact.[4]

Predictably, Zane was prepared for several hours of good angling, but he was surprised by his own indolence:

> I took up my rod and, standing in the cockpit, I fished while at the same time I kept a keen lookout. That was the pleasure of roaming the sea. Indeed, seldom in twelve winter seasons off

Long Key had we ever had such comfortable water, so that we could enjoy looking for sea creatures. . . .

Sailfish showed in the transparent billows, long slim, sharp bronze fish, riding high on the swells and shooting down the curving slopes of the waves. We maneuvered the boat so that we got ahead of some of them, and drew our baits in front of their bills. They would follow the baits awhile, then shoot forward, to come even with the boat and pass it, not ten feet distant. This afforded a wonderful opportunity to see the sailfish close at hand, free, indifferent to the bait or boat. They had marvelous control over the the their native element, as much at home there as a frigate bird in the air. . . . I saw a purple and pink jellyfish, a globular ethereal creature, moving with its own life as well as the current of the stream. All I could remember was the rare color, the strange delicacy and abnormality of structure, the sucking bellows-like action that evidently propelled it, and the undoubtable fact of life. I had never before seen any other living thing like it and the chances were I never would again. Here is the fact that makes the ocean so supremely above other mediums of nature in fascinating possibilities, in unsolvable mysteries, in endless experience.[5]

As they drifted in the light chop of the Gulf Stream, Grey's attention was drawn to the other bow, where more creatures swam into view:

From time to time I espied a loggerhead turtle on the surface. . . . Every little while they lifted their huge blunt hawk-like heads to peer around. . . . Next to attract our attention were tiny flying fish. They flitted up like steely locusts and glinted in the sunlight and darted away a few yards, to fall back. They had no control over direction. Once I saw one close to the boat and high enough to be silhouetted against the sky. He was scarcely two inches long. I discerned wings and tail, tiny black eyes in a blunt little head. Except for the eye he appeared steely white in color. He popped out of a wave and blew with the gentle breeze.[6]

Moving deeper into the Stream, Zane and R.C. sighted an enormous school of sailfish. "Sailfish like rough sea," observed Grey. "They love to ride the swells, as do marlin swordfish." For an entire hour the brothers watched their antics, R.C. eventually tossing his line into the water. Zane snapped photos of one of R.C.'s attempts to land a sailfish. "We got three sailfish out of the school," Zane commented, "two of which were lightly hooked and which we let go."[7]

Grey added: "As far as the dimensions of a school of sailfish is concerned, this one was the largest I ever saw. But Captain Knowles said he had seen many larger ones, one notably that took hours to pass and extended on all sides as far as he could see. There must be millions of sailfish; and always there should be splendid sailfishing." However, Grey dryly concluded: "Unless some market use is discovered!"[8]

Tales of Lonely Trails features five of Grey's best essays on the American West, written over a period of twelve years: "Nonnezoshe"; "Colorado Trails"; "Roping Lions in the Grand Canyon"; "Tonto Basin"; and "Death Valley" (written in 1919, and the basis for *Wanderer of the Wasteland* and *Stairs of Sand*).

Written more than a year before "Tonto Basin," "Colorado Trails" is an action narrative, although it lacks the later essay's richness of characterization and variety of terrain.

In August 1917, Grey rendezvoused with R.C. in Denver, where Grey visited J. A. McGuire, the editor of *Outdoor Life,* presumably to interest the editor in buying his next adventure story. McGuire was elated to snare the writing expertise of Zane Grey. For nearly two decades the Denver-based *Outdoor Life* had been in competition with the New York–headquartered *Field and Stream.* Among the writers McGuire had collected into his writing circle were Rex Beach, James Oliver Curwood, and Chauncey Thomas, whose famous column "Campfire Talks" expanded Zane Grey's knowledge of the West. Between 1912 and 1919 "Campfire Talks" was a regular department in *Outdoor Life* and earned Thomas a national reputation.

McGuire also helped Grey acquire the services of Scott Teague of Yampa, who had a considerable reputation as a bear tracker and hunter. Teague, in fact, had authored an article titled "Jaguar Hunting in Old Mexico" (*Outdoor Life*, September 1913), so he quickly established a rapport with Grey. Grey and R.C. also called upon Professor Figgins of the Denver Museum of Natural History. Through Figgins, Grey arranged to have some specimens shipped to the museum after his hunt was completed. Zane and his party left in late August 1917 for their adventures, heading west through the Moffat Tunnel (Grey misspelled it Moffet), finally arriving in the mountain hamlet of Yampa on the western slope of the Rockies.

Yampa lay in a valley between the Flattop Mountains to the west and the Continental Divide to the east. The town, remarked Grey, had the appearance of being "old and forgotten"—reason enough that he "would like to live there awhile."[9] The Flattops, as their name suggests, were a distinctive, heavily forested tabletop ridge, containing a wealth of streams and the famous Trapper's Lake. The mountains to the east, where Grey and his party would end their travels, rose in serrated loops and were covered with September asters and great swaths of aspen and cedar. Between the ranges sat Yampa astride the Yampa River. Trickling out off the Flattops, the Yampa is merely a creek when it flows through the little town. However, forty miles to the west it becomes a rather formidable river. Near the Colorado border with Utah it joins the Green River, whose waters eventually flow into the mighty Colorado.

In Yampa Grey met his two local guides, Teague and Virgil. According to Grey, Teague was "a sturdy rugged man with bronzed face and keen gray-blue eyes," while Virgil looked as if he had stepped out of one of Grey's western novels. Bill, the cook, was "somewhat deaf" and spent most of the trip silently involved in his duties.

With their packhorses and wagons, they headed to Trapper's Lake, where they camped amid an amphitheater of ridges. Nationally known for its cutthroat trout, Trapper's Lake was situated in some of the most rugged and beautiful countryside in the Colorado Rockies. R.C. and Zane quickly found a spot near the outlet of the lake, and proceeded to cast their lines.

> "Got a whale!" [R.C.] yelled. "See him—down there—in that white water. See him flash red! Go down there and land him for me. Hurry! He's got all the line!"
>
> I ran below to an open space in the willows. In the white water I caught a flashing gleam of red. Then I saw the shine of the leader. . . .
>
> "Grab the leader! Yank him out!" yelled R.C. in desperation.
>
> He shouted that the water was too deep and for me to save his fish. This was an awful predicament for me. I knew the instant I grabbed the leader that the big trout would break it or pull free. . . . Nevertheless I had no choice. Plunging in to my knees I frantically reached for the leader. The red trout made a surge. I missed him. R.C. yelled that something would break. . . Another plunge brought me in touch with the leader. Then I essayed to lead the huge cutthroat ashore. He was heavy. . . . Near the shore as I was about to lift him, he woke up, swam around me twice, then ran between my legs.
>
> When, a little later, R.C. came panting downstream I was sitting on the bank, all wet, with one knee skinned, and I was holding his broken leader in my hands. Strange to say he went into a rage! Blamed me for the loss of the big trout! Under such circumstances it was always best to maintain silence and I did so as long as I could.
>
> After he had become . . . a rational being once more, he asked me:
>
> "Was he big?"
>
> "Oh—a whale of a trout!" I replied.
>
> "Humph! Well, how big?"
>
> Thereupon I enlarged upon the exceeding size and beauty of that trout. I made him out very much bigger than he actually looked to me and I minutely described his beauty and wonderful gaping mouth. R.C. groaned—and that was my revenge.[10]

As August waned, Grey and his retinue prowled the mountains surrounding the lake for deer, elk, and bear. Occasionally they rode down to the White River Valley, combing the river's edge for game, which they discovered was scarce. Climbing back up the mountain slope, Grey noticed many trees stripped by porcupines and aspens chewed by beavers. One morning they ascended a summit through "short, velvety yellow grass, like moss, spotted with flowers." At the top Grey remarked:

> Here at thirteen thousand feet the wind hit us with exceed-
> ing force, and soon had us with freezing hands and faces. All
> about us were bold black and gray peaks, with patches of snow,
> and above them clouds of white and drab, showing blue sky be-
> tween.
> . . . This grassy summit ascended in a long gradual sweep. . . .
> We rode out to the edge of the mountain and looked off. It was
> fearful, yet sublime. The world lay beneath us.[11]

Grey may have exaggerated or simply misjudged the altitude they were at, since the Flattops do not rise to that elevation. However, one thing is certain: it was the highest mountain he had ever climbed or would ever climb.

After days of poor hunting and damp, cold weather, Grey and his group rode eastward toward the Continental Divide, a distance of fifty miles. On the east slopes near Rabbit Ears Pass, they con-tinued their hunt for bear. It is not certain when Grey began to doubt his interest in hunting, but in late 1917 he seriously recon-sidered his motivations. "When a man goes out with a rifle," he re-marked to his readers, "he means to kill. He may keep within the law, but that is not the question. It is a question of spirit, and men who love to hunt are yielding to and always developing the primi-tive instinct to kill. . . . And that is to say if a man does not go to the wilds now and then, and work hard and live some semblance of the life of his progenitors, he will weaken. It seems that he will, but I am not prepared now to say whether or not that would be well. The Germans believe they are the race fittest to survive over all others —and that has made me a little sick of this Darwin business."[12]

Grey was devastated by the mass lunacy and the bloody ordeal of the Great War. In late 1917, at the time of the events in "Colorado Trails," the conflict was entering its fourth year. Instead of declining in intensity, it was actually escalating, due in part to America's recent entry into the war. Zane may simply have had enough of the death and barbarism on the Western Front, which may have caused his appetite for hunting to decrease substantially.

Whether because of the war or because Grey was looking at life from a new perspective, he was beginning to place less emphasis on the importance of hunting. Later in "Tonto Basin" this concern would intensify. However, in that essay, this shift in thinking did not affect the sense of adventure, diminish the vitality of the narrative, or curtail the apprehension of the hunt.

"Tonto Basin" and "Death Valley" reveal Grey's eye for detail, his sensitivity to the murmurings of nature, and his strong attraction to the outdoor life. "Tonto Basin" is divided into two parts, the first describing events in late September 1918, the second relating experiences of the following autumn. The essay follows Zane, his nine-year-old son Romer, R.C., and a group of companions as they journey from the Tonto Basin, Arizona, to the Natural Bridge, near the Mogollon Rim. (The Natural Bridge, now called Tonto Natural Bridge, should not be confused with the more famous Rainbow Bridge in Southern Utah.) Despite similarities to the trip in *The Last of the Plainsmen,* the one in "Tonto Basin" differs significantly in that Grey had nothing to prove. He was at the top of the best-seller lists, his reputation growing with each new novel. The narrative is gritty, crisp, matter-of-fact, avoiding the jeweled prose that characterized some of his first journeys west.

Of course the journey theme is central to Zane Grey's western novels, but in the nonfiction essay form he faced problems of length. The handwritten manuscript of "Tonto Basin" exceeds two hundred pages, making it unusually long for a narrative essay—more like the length of a book. Anthologies that include "Tonto Basin" frequently cut it to the bone and focus on the highlights. However, this is such a lovingly told story that it should be read in toto. "Tonto Basin" may be one of Grey's more meandering narratives, but it is one of the best essays of men in the western outdoors ever written.

Reaching the Natural Bridge was the group's first goal, but the journey itself is the basis for Grey's narrative. In additon to Zane, Romer, and R.C., the retinue included the veteran guide Al Doyle and his son Lee; Sievert Nielsen; the cook Joe Isbel; and Lee's dog "Pups," "a close haired, keen-faced canine," who spent most of his time barking, bounding ahead of the group, and treeing squirrels. Grey did not like him—too active and noisy, perhaps.

The Arizona interior has a unique blend of pine forest with mesas and plateaus, dropping quickly into the desert country. From the forests of Payson to the sands of Tucson, the land changes abruptly and dramatically. This land, south of Flagstaff and just east of Phoenix, became a second home to Zane. He loved its diversity and enjoyed pondering its vistas.

From Al Doyle's place in Flagstaff they departed on September 24, 1918, a few days before hunting season officially opened. Heading southeast, they encountered Mary Lake and Mormon Lake. The air was tinder-dry. Grey complained that his lips were so cracked that he could hardly drink or eat, let alone laugh at one of Lee Doyle's jokes. Camphor ice helped soothe his lips. Compared to the thick humidity around Tampico, this was arid indeed.

They traveled up into the pine and cedar forests, gradually making their way through the rugged mesa country. Several days later they reached the Natural Bridge, just northeast of Payson. Grey was mesmerized by unusual rock formations, perhaps because they were mute sentinels witnessing the passing of time. He was drawn to the sinuous canyons of Southern Utah, the immense arch of the Rainbow Bridge, the Grand Canyon, and the manmade cliff villages at Keet Seel and Mesa Verde.

A smaller version of the Rainbow Bridge, the Natural Bridge was "striking and beautiful. . . . It had a round ceiling colored gray, yellow, green, bronze, purple, white, making a crude and scalloped mosaic."[13] Al Doyle turned to young Romer Grey and told him that Apaches once occupied the caves on the upper part of the arch. It was all Zane could do to prevent his eager son from climbing up the side of the bridge.

The following day they left for Payson in the Tonto Forest. The deeper Grey penetrated the high country the better he felt. The group was soon joined by Richard Haught, bear hunter and raconteur. (Haught would later build Grey a cabin deep in the woods, which unfortunately burned to the ground in a forest fire in 1993.) Haught told countless stories of old Arizona, stories that Grey would tumble in his mind and use in later novels.

Although he liked the company of the men, he often sought solitude in the forest:

> Late in the afternoon I slipped off down the canyon, taking Haught's rifle for safety rather than a desire to kill anything. By no means was it impossible to meet a bad bear in the forest. . . . Like coming home again was it to enter that forest of silver-tipped, level-spreading spruce, and great gnarled, massive pines, and oak patches of green and gold. . . . What cool, sweet, fresh smell this woody, leafy, earthy, dry, grassy, odorous fragrance, dominated by the scent of pine. I felt a sense of deep peace and rest. This golden-green forest, barred by sunlight, canopied by the blue sky, and melodious with its soughing moan of wind, absolutely filled me with content and happiness.[14]

Grey liked the camaraderie of earthy men such as Haught and Doyle. In combination with the outdoors, they created some memorable times for Zane. On the trail, Zane generally trusted most of his companions—until they proved themselves unworthy of that trust. Over time Grey came to suspect Joe Isbel, the cook hired by Lee Doyle, of some dirty dealings. Zane thought Isbel was supplying portions of the group's food to other parties of wranglers and hunters. Grey even caught Isbel in the act one day, discovering him mingling with some strangers, "men of rough garb, evidently riders of the range."[15] Grey put the incident in the back of his mind and left camp to hunt. In the forest a few days later he found a solitary buck, which he passed on. Riding back to camp, and perhaps angry that he was empty-handed, he stumbled on Joe Isbel "eating an elaborate meal with three more strange, rough-appearing men." Cautiously, Grey eyed the hombres, the situation unfolding like a scene from one of his novels:

> Doyle looked serious. Nielsen had a sharp glint in his gray eye. As for myself this procedure of our cook's was more than I could stand.
>
> "Isbel, you're discharged," I said shortly. "Take your outfit and get out. Lee will lend you a pack horse."
>
> "Wal, I ain't fired," drawled Isbel. "I quit before you rode in. Beat you to it!"
>
> "Then if you quit it seems to me you are taking liberties with supplies you have no right to," I replied.
>
> "Nope. Cook of any outfit has a right to all the chuck he wants. That's western way."
>
> "Isbel, listen to this and then get out. You've wasted our supplies just to hurry and break camp. As for western ways I know something of them. It's a western way for a man to be square and honest in his dealings with an outsider. In all my years and in all my trips over the southwest you are the first westerner to give me the double-cross. You have that distinction."
>
> Then I turned my back upon him and walked back to my tent. His acquaintances left at once, and he quickly packed and followed.[16]

After Isbel and his bunch rode out of camp, Grey observed: "To travelers of the desert and hunters and riders of the open there are always hard and uncomfortable and painful situations to be met with. And in meeting these, if it can be done with fortitude and spirit that win the respect of westerners, it is indeed a reward."[17]

Soon thereafter, Grey and his party returned to the hunting trail,

Grey looking grizzled during the 1919 excursion into the Tonto Basin, Arizona. Grey typically never felt better than on a wilderness expedition.

which was one of their primary reasons for being there. Game was scarce, frustrating Zane. The group did manage to flush from a distant thicket a five-hundred-pound black bear, but none of them managed to land a shot. Although the hunting was dismal, the news that awaited them from one of Haught's neighbors was even more troubling.

The man rode up from the foothills, telling them of the epidemic of Spanish influenza that was spreading throughout the Southwest. At first Zane thought the man was exaggerating the situation, but the neighbor spoke of many victims both on the reservation and around Flagstaff. Grey, just recently settled in Los Angeles, became worried about Dolly and the children. Telling Haught that he would like to resume the hunt on the twenty-first of September the following year, Grey set off for home with Romer and R.C.

The second part of "Tonto Basin" picks up in September 1919, when Zane and R.C. planned to rendezvous in the Tonto Forest with Haught, Doyle, and his men. The Grey brothers arrived only four and a half hours late for the appointment.

When they entered the dappled sunlight of the forest, Grey was still suffering from fever and aching muscles. He was perhaps unknowingly carrying the influenza virus. He had been fighting the effects for several months before the journey, but Grey seldom if ever yielded to weakness and inertia. Exacerbating the situation was the stressful time he had writing *Wanderer of the Wasteland* and the marathon, eleven-hour battle he had recently endured with a swordfish. Like Theodore Roosevelt, he fought nervous strain with severe exertion, and he battled depression with strenuous outdoor exercise.

Meeting his old friends in the Tonto Forest, Grey and R.C. were ready for a new hunting season—but there were a few new looks to the expedition. In place of the rascal Joe Isbel, Grey brought along his personal cook, George Takahashi, who in Grey's estimation served up "the best supper anywhere." Takahashi would remain in Grey's employment for many years, traveling with him to Oregon, California, and the South Pacific. In addition to a fresh face at the chuckwagon, Grey also tried to get accustomed to his spirited new horse, Don Carlos.

In a horse—in a man—Zane Grey searched for the soul and strength to match his own. In Don Carlos, he got them both in spades. Grey first saw him while his movie company, Zane Grey Productions, was filming *Desert Gold* near Palm Springs. The chestnut was in high demand by film directors because of his stature, color, and splendid good looks. "High and rangy, with fine legs, broad chest, and a magnificent head," Don Carlos so impressed Grey that he bought him on the spot.[18]

Before taking his trip to the Tonto Basin in 1919, Zane shipped Don Carlos by train to Flagstaff, accompanied by Sievert Nielsen. After the train's arrival, Don Carlos, despite numerous pleadings, refused to descend the wooden ramp erected for him. Finally, after they removed the ramp, the great horse leaped the ten-foot distance to the platform, scattering the flock of spectators who had gathered for the occasion.[19]

In his fiction, Grey's heroes and their steeds have a virtual symbiotic relationship. In reality, however, the famous author and his wonder horse had a somewhat different partnership. On the trail heading east out of Flagstaff, Grey discovered that "nineteen miles on Don Carlos reduced [him] to a miserable aching specimen of manhood." Grey's loins, legs, and back throbbed. Despite his agony, Grey rode with his companions as if he were unaffected.

The heat intensified as they proceeded into the Painted Desert. Dust-devils whirled into their midst. Zane and his horse plodded along with difficulty: "As he was nearly seventeen hands high, and as I could not get my foot in the stirrup from level ground, to mount him in my condition seemed a little less than terrible. I always held back out of sight when I attempted this. Many times I failed. Once I fell flat and lay a moment in the dust. Don Carlos looked at me in a way I imagined was sympathetic."[20]

"In the middle of winter," the French writer Camus once observed, "I discovered that there was in me an invincible summer." For Grey, such extreme exertion cried out to his very manhood. He endured the exhausting trail ride on Don Carlos, even though his body was giving out. Somehow, he avoided abandoning the trip. Eventually, they headed up into the tall grass and sweet-smelling cedars of the mountains. When they camped, Grey fell from the saddle, bone-weary. Over the next few days, he gained strength and felt firmer in the saddle.

George Takahashi turned out to be as wonderful a companion as he was a cook. Grey admired his generosity, hard work, and his frugality in camp. Before he worked for Grey, Takahashi picked cantaloupes in the searing Imperial Valley, where he commanded the highest pay and the deepest respect. He saved religiously. By the 1920s he was, by Japanese standards, a wealthy man. Grey and Takahashi often good-naturedly talked of their hunting experiences. Once, Grey told him that his father had been an expert squirrel hunter in his day. Lewis Gray, according to Zane, could "bark" a squirrel, which involved shooting a bullet and hitting the bark just below the animal. The stunned squirrel would then fall from the tree as if dead. Takahashi exclaimed: "Aw my goodnish—your daddy better shot than you!" After swallowing hard, Grey admitted: "Yes, indeed he was."

Grey's descriptive talents served him well in this narrative essay. Although his evocations of the rich Arizona landscape are amply demonstrated, his attentions throughout the second part are clearly on the hunt and its attendant excitement. The party looked for deer, elk, and turkey, but their keenest eye was saved for the bears— brown, black, and grizzly—who prowled the Tonto Basin.

Nothing could rouse Grey from his sickbed or his cot like the prospect of the hunt. And certainly nothing, with the possible exception of his western novels, provided him so much enjoyment and distraction from reality. But Grey was an ethical hunter, and always savored the months of preparation, the assembly of the horses and hounds, and the autumn snap in the air as much as he enjoyed pulling the trigger.

As one of the major writers for *Field and Stream* and *Outdoor Life,* Zane Grey canvased North America and later the world for outdoor experiences. By the time of the writing of "Tonto Basin" (1919), he was becoming deeply conflicted about his participation in hunting. Toward the end of the essay he delivers a ten-page treatise defending his role as a hunter. It is a long and often specious argument, filled with the customary Grey idealism. Two years before, in 1917, he had admitted in "Colorado Trails" that "the more I hunt the more I am convinced of something wrong about the game."[21] In Arizona, his ambivalence is rendered through overstatement:

> Hunting is a savage primordial instinct inherited from our ancestors. It goes back through all the ages of man, and farther still—to the age when man was not the man, but hairy ape, or some other beast from which we are descended. To kill is in the very marrow of our bones . . . no instinct is ever wholly eradicated. . . . By brute strength, by sagacity, by endurance he killed in order to get the means of subsistence. If he did not kill he starved. . . .
>
> We cannot escape our inheritance. Civilization is a veneer, a thin polish over the savage and crude nature. Fear, anger, lust, the three great primal instincts are restrained, but they live powerfully in the breast of man. Self preservation is the first law of human life, and is included in fear. . . . The secret now of the instructive joy and thrill and wildness of the chase lies clear.[22]

In his essay he cites other hunters such as Stewart Edward White and the far better known Theodore Roosevelt as proof that he is not alone in his convictions. Grey certainly knew of Roosevelt's reputation as a naturalist, conservationist, and hunter, and that combination seemed to support Grey's beliefs that a civilized man could also be a sportsman.

However, Grey's fervent defense of blood sports in "Tonto Basin" proved to be something of an omen. Although he continued to hunt throughout the 1920s, the "joy and thrill and wildness" of the sport began to diminish. By 1930, he abandoned his hunting cabin in the Tonto wilderness, lost interest in his rifles, and refused to hunt for the rest of his life.

After the official closing of the frontier in 1890, writers were beginning to regard the Southwestern desert as something more than just a wasteland between civilization and the orchards of California. In addition to Zane Grey, nature writers such as Mary Austin (*The Land of Little Rain*), John Van Dyke (*The Desert*), and George Wharton James (*Wonders of the Colorado Desert*) examined some of the mystic secrets of this wide and vacant land. Van Dyke, for instance, could sound very much like Zane Grey: "Nature neither rejoices in the life nor sorrows in the death. She is neither good nor evil; she is only a great law of change that passes understanding." George Wharton James in his *Wonders of the Colorado Desert* of 1906 echoes some of Grey's major themes: "The desert is nothing if it is not sincere. It is sincere to brutality. Open, bare, exposed it lies, and yet it is not dead. It is alive with a fiery aliveness that takes you into its heart and compels you to be as it is, open, frank, sincere." Like several of Grey's fictional heroes, George James discovered the healing qualities of the desert after relinquishing his career as a minister.

After the 1918 hunting season in the Tonto Forest, Grey and Sievert Nielsen headed north of Los Angeles to Death Valley, where they spent most of the spring of 1919. From that experience came the short but insightful essay, "Death Valley." Also, Grey's observations would form the basis of the western novels *Wanderer of the*

Wasteland and *Stairs of Sand*. Along with "Nonnezoshe" and "What the Desert Means to Me," "Death Valley" contains some of Zane Grey's most introspective thinking on his relationship to nature and God. The desert figures prominently in such novels as *Desert Gold, The Rainbow Bridge,* and *Wanderer of the Wasteland,* but in his essays his narrative voice is more leisurely, more concentrated, and at times more evocative.

First published in *Harper's Magazine* in April 1920, the essay was reprinted in *Tales of Lonely Trails* in 1922. Although Grey did not have the patience and sensitivity of a great nature writer, he did possess a keen sense of observation. And sometimes in the desert, because he was not distracted by hunting or other activities, his attention could be focused on life and death, sand and sky, and his own spiritual yearning.

At the heart of a Grey narrative essay is usually a strong, colorful companion figure—in this case Sievert Nielsen. Zane acquired Nielsen's friendship in an odd fashion. After reading *Desert Gold* and its story of a lost gold mine, Nielsen wrote Grey a letter in which he offered to help the author find the mysterious mine. Although Grey's story was completely fictitious, the naive Sievert Nielsen was convinced of its authenticity. Grey was amused by and attracted to Nielsen from the beginning. He invited Nielsen to Avalon, and was surprised when he showed up. Looking like a viking god, Nielsen was around thirty-five years of age, five-feet ten, and barrel-chested. Grey liked his direct, honest, and gentle manner. Thus began a friendship that lasted several years and was tested in the deserts of California and the forests of Arizona. On one occasion in the Tonto Forest, Nielsen saved Grey's life in a hunting incident, an act of bravery which Zane never forgot and referred to throughout his life.

Nielsen's role on their trip to Death Valley in 1919 was to help with the camping gear and drive the mule team. First Grey and Nielsen took a train to Death Valley Junction, where they were awed by the sunset: "a weird, strange sunset in drooping curtains of transparent cloud, lighting up dark mountain ranges. . . . [S]ome peaks [were] clear and cut black . . . others [were] white with snow."[23] The contrast in colors and features was the initial sign that they were entering a strange new world, a world that Grey both feared and loved.

Grey had always been attracted to the idea of the Valley of Death. Historically, it was rich in bizarre incidents of grim survival, bravery, and cowardice. A Mormon party of seventy people once stumbled into the valley during the Gold Rush. Thirst-crazed, they wandered from sinkhole to sinkhole, while a throbbing sun destroyed their minds and spirits. Only two survived, and the notoriety of Death Valley was assured.

Such calamities only spurred Grey to see Death Valley for himself. While Nielsen attended the wagon, Grey toured the famous borax mill, which in its heyday in the 1890s produced twenty-five hundred sacks a day. Zane was naturally drawn to the workers who toiled in the intolerable conditions of the mill. "These laborers of the borax mines," he wrote, "like the stokers of ships, and coal-diggers, and blast furnace-hands—like thousands and millions of men, killed themselves outright or impaired their strength . . . and as the years go by my respect and reverence and wonder increase for these men of elemental lives . . . these uncomplaining users of brawn and bone, these giants who breast the elements, who till the earth and handle iron, who fight the natural forces with their bodies."[24]

Beyond the gypsum-white hills and hardscrabble ridges lay the heart of the valley, capped by the sawtooth edge of the Funeral Range. He wandered in this region, sometimes alone, at times accompanied by Nielsen. He began to formulate and struggle with some of the philosophical issues he would advance in his novel *Wanderer of the Wasteland*. Although his essay "Death Valley" contains the sketches of such inquiry, he needed the larger canvas of the novel to portray them more completely.

In Monument Valley, Grey wanted to feel the presence of eternity; here in the desert he wished to feel the presence of death. He found in this "ragged rent of the old earth" some the vestiges of people's connection to the ancient past: "Why had I longed to see Death Valley? What did I want of the desert that was naked, red, sinister, sombre, forbidding, ghastly, stark, dim and dark and dismal, the abode of silence and loneliness, the proof of death, decay, devastation and destruction . . . ? The answer was that I sought the awful, the appalling and terrible because they harked me back to a primitive day where my blood and bones were bequeathed their heritage of the elements."[25]

Death and the primordial elements may have pervaded the scene, but the valley was not barren of life. Grey and Nielsen met a rancher named Denton, a taciturn hermit who related the grim details of this remote and burning place to his eager guests. According to Denton, the temperature hovered at 125 degrees in the daytime; the valley was fatal to white women, meat-eaters, and alcohol drinkers; and only people with robust heart and lungs could survive. Later, the two desert explorers met a prospector, who liked to talk to burros. He explained that once in Death Valley he almost died from thirst. He lost his mind and his senses in a battle with the sun, heat, and desert birds. His burros ultimately saved him, and he was grateful. Grey and Nielsen also conversed with a band of Shoshone Indians, who showed them their dusty tents near the fields that they worked for the rancher Denton. From the Indians, the prospector, and Denton, Grey gleaned the history, culture, and folklore of Death Valley. Even in the most inhospitable place, there were reminders of the persistence of life.

Sometimes Grey and Nielsen saw evidence of this in the most unlikely places. On a ridge "swept clean and packed hard by the winds," they found a flower so small that it almost defied detection. For a moment, Grey focused on its color and brilliance. "That desert flower of a day," he remarked, "in its isolation and fragility, yet its unquenchable spirit to live, was as great to me as the tremendous reddening bulk of the Funeral Mountains looming so sinisterly over it."[26] In Death Valley Grey found moments of light and darkness, peace and turmoil, tragedy and hope, captivity and deliverance. "Death Valley" may be his darkest and most existential essay. As he pokes the sands of the valley, he is really probing the mysteries and agonies of his own inner self. He raises an important question. Is there any link between surviving the elements in Death Valley and surviving the deserts of our emotional lives? If one knows how to prevail in the former, can he or she therefore survive the latter? For Grey, the answer lies in being constantly connected to his feelings rather than to his intellect. Through his emotions, as raw and ugly as they are apt to get sometimes, Grey finds the clear routes to the past, from whence he draws his energy and knowledge. Death Valley resists civilization, reason, and intellect. It is the ultimate state of nature, primitive, remote, indifferent, elemental, rugged, and time-less, and Grey rejoices in its wisdom.

Grey further asserts that even in our modern age there must al-ways be a necessity for places like Death Valley: "It had been set apart for the hardy diggers for earthen treasure, and for the wan-derers of the wasteland—men who go forth to seek and to find and face their souls. Perhaps most of them found death. But there was a death in life. Desert travelers learned the secret that men lived too much in the world—that in silence, and loneliness, and deso-lation there was something infinite, something hidden from the crowd."[27]

CHAPTER SIX

🐟 🐟 🐟

The Sea Gypsy

Who ordered that their longing's fire
Should be, as soon as kindled, cooled?
Who renders vain their deep desire?
A God, a God their severance ruled!
And bade betwixt their shores to be
The unplumbed, salt, estranging sea.

— MATTHEW ARNOLD

WHEN *Tales of Fishes* appeared in 1919, Zane Grey was famous for his western novels, but only a small segment of the population knew of his fishing acumen. Within two years, many American readers did.

Published just after the world war ended, *Tales of Fishes* provided welcome relief from the drudgery of the war years in America. By using a simple title, Grey seemed to say: this book is about fishing; take it or leave it. Readers not only took it, they snatched it up, making it one of Grey's most popular outdoor books.

The twentieth century saw some notable novelists of the sea, including Jack London, Joseph Conrad, Nicholas Monserrat, Ernest Hemingway, and Herman Wouk. Few nonfiction books have ever challenged the work of these authors. One of the exceptions is Grey's *Tales of Fishes,* which is all the more remarkable because it deals with Grey's personal experiences on the water.

Tales of Fishes covers Zane Grey's fishing and boating experiences between the years 1905 and 1918, beginning with one of his first Mexican adventures and ending with his enchantment with Avalon harbor. Intermingled are Zane's exploits in Long Key, Florida, where, at the time of the book's publication, he was president of the Long Key Fishing Club.

In the thirteen essays that comprise *Tales of Fishes*, Grey moves quite easily between the aesthetic and the practical, the cerebral and the visceral. He rarely, if ever, sentimentalizes the ocean. He never worships the sea at the expense of direct, concrete reporting.

Grey's adventures in Mexico are related in the first two essays, "Byme-by Tarpon" and "Island of the Dead" (*Everybody's,* September 1909). In the brief "Byme-by Tarpon" (discussed in chapter 3), Grey describes his association with his Mexican guide Attalano and their search for the fabulous tarpon of Tampico. "Island of the Dead" is one of Grey's best lyrical essays, featuring some of his most sensitive and poignant descriptions of the southern Caribbean. Traveling on board the *Monterey* from Cuba to the Yucatan Peninsula, Grey heard of the nearby Alacranes Reef, "where lighthouse-keepers went insane from solitude," and of Isla de la Muerta, where strange seabirds called rabihorcados swooped down to prey on smaller birds called boobies. Chartering a boat from the mainland, he set off for the island. During the short voyage, he witnessed the majesty of a Caribbean sunrise: "Sunrise on the Caribbean was glorious to behold—a vast burst of silver and gold over a level and wrinkling blue sea."[1] On the island, he climbed the lighthouse steps. Two previous lighthouse keepers had indeed gone mad, but the current one was quite sane, and received Grey like an honored guest. From the lighthouse, Zane saw the sun-washed beaches below: "Ridges of white and brown showed their teeth against the crawling, tireless, insatiate sea. Islets of dead coral gleamed like bleached bone, and beds of live coral, amber as wine, lay wreathed in restless surf. From near to far extended the rollers, the curving channels, and the shoals, all colorful, all quivering with the light of jewels."[2]

For a few days Grey felt the solitude of a Robinson Crusoe, admitting that "the loneliness of the coral reef haunted me. The sound of the sea, eternally slow and sad and moaning, haunted me like a passion. Men are the better for solitude."[3] He later witnessed the rabihorcado's assault on the boobies of the island. As armies of boobies brought fish back from the sea, the fierce rabihorcados chased and attacked them, forcing the boobies to drop their catches. The rabihorcados soon made feasts of the boobies' fish. To Grey, a proud Darwinist, it was proof that in nature, as in life, there were pursuers and the pursued; there were those who prevailed and those who submitted.

Grey's travels in Mexico occurred before he became a household name. As he became famous, he combed the fishing grounds near Long Key, Florida, where he not only wrote some of his best fiction, but also some of his best narrative essays. The "Long Key" essays in *Tales of Fishes* include "Sailfish," "Gulf Stream Fishing," "Bonefish," and "Some Rare Fish." For action, for technical knowledge, for color, light, and movement, they have rarely been equaled in literature.

Long Key—that southern jewel in the necklace of islands dangling from Florida's south coast—mesmerized Grey with its abundance of fish and dazzling tropical light. He wondered at times why Long Key was so special to him. In the essay "Sailfish" he reasoned that it was "not the fish alone that drew real sportsmen to a place. . . . It was the spirit of the place—the mystery, like that of the little hermit crab, which crawls over the coral sand in his stolen shell . . . sunshine . . . and the wind in the waving palms; and the lonely, wandering coast with the eternal moan out on the reefs, the sweet, fresh tang, the clear antiseptic breath of salt, and always by the glowing, hot, colorful day or by the soft dark night with its shadows and whisperings on the beach, that significant presence—the sense of something vaster than the heaving sea."[4]

One of Zane Grey's significant achievements in *Tales of Fishes* is the action scenes. Any writer can describe simple action, such as a person walking across a room, drinking a cup of coffee, folding a letter, and so on. However, it takes a gifted writer to depict complicated action, such as tracking, catching, and hauling in a sailfish. Here the prose must move effortlessly and seamlessly between describing the ship, the angler, the fish, and the sea. Grey frequently manages this flawlessly. He may have been assisted in this process by watching motion pictures and seeing how different shots and angles were spliced together to make one continuous scene. During one pursuit, Zane recorded the action this way:

> This fellow came up two hundred yards from the boat and slid along the water with half of his body raised. . . . He went down and came up in a magnificent sheer leap, with broad sail shining in the sun. Very angry he was, and he reminded me of a Marlin swordfish. Next he went down, and came up again bent in a curve, with the big sail stretched again. He skittered over the water, going down and coming up, until he had leaped seven times. This was a big, heavy fish, and on the light six-ounce tip and nine-thread line I had my work cut out for me. We had to run the boat toward him so I could get back my line. Here was the advantage of having a fast boat with a big rudder. Otherwise I would have lost my fish. After some steady deep plugging he came up again and set my heart aflutter by a long surface play in which he took off one hundred yards of line and then turned, leaping straight for the boat. Fortunately the line was slack and I could throw off the drag and let him run. . . . After that he went down into the deep water and I had one long hour of hard work in bringing him to the boat. . . . Six hours later [at the dock] he weighed fifty-eight and a half pounds . . . the largest sailfish I know of caught on light tackle.[5]

Zane Grey's descriptions of the simple lives of Gulf Stream fishermen had a profound effect on twenty-year-old Ernest Hemingway, who claimed *Tales of Fishes* as one of his early bibles. Grey's pruned sentences and vivid angling sequences not only assisted the young Hemingway in his own struggles with writing, but also expanded his fishing knowledge. Like Grey, Hemingway was attracted to the

Florida Keys. He also shared a belief with Grey that fishing and hunting brought a man closer to his primordial past, and that killing a noble fish ennobled the angler. In his 1952 novella *The Old Man and The Sea*, Hemingway developed some of the same themes that Grey struggled with years earlier.[6]

Whether Grey actually had any significant influence on the later Hemingway—particularly on the writing of *The Old Man and the Sea*—remains debatable. Grey personally shared many traits with the Hemingway hero. Certainly there are also numerous similarities between the two writers and their themes of the sea, but whether there is any direct connection is undocumented. However, consider this observation by critic Clinton S. Burhans from his essay "Hemingway's Tragic Vision of Man" (1961):

> Santiago comes to feel his deepest love for the creature that he himself hunts and kills, the great fish which he must catch not alone for physical need but even more for his pride and his profession. The great marlin is unlike the other fish that the old man catches; he is a spiritual more than a physical neccessity. He is unlike the other fish, too, in that he is a worthy antagonist for the old man, and during his long ordeal, Santiago comes to pity the marlin and then to respect and love him. In the end he senses that there can be no victory for either in the equal struggle between them, that the conditions which have brought them together have made them one. And so, though he kills the great fish, the old man has come to love him as his equal and his brother; sharing a life which is a capricious mixture of incredible beauty and deadly violence and in which all creatures are both hunter and hunted, they are bound together in its most primal relationship.[7]

Grey's motivation seems similar to Hemingway's humble Cuban fisherman. Grey felt extraordinary indentification with any fish he pursued. The more prolonged the combat, the more this feeling intensified. Frequently he felt remorse after the catch, as if this were part of a compulsive ritual. After catching a beautiful fish, he remembered the sensation this way: "It gave me pang—that I should be the cause of the death of so beautiful a thing."[8] Or, upon seeing a fish lying in a boat or helpless on the moss, he admitted that he was "always sorry, and more often than not let the fish go alive."

Later, Hemingway claimed that Grey was simply after self-glorification as an angler. In 1930, when Hemingway enjoyed international stature, Grey wrote him a letter inviting Hemingway to accompany him on a world fishing cruise. Hemingway declined. He reasoned, perhaps unfairly, that Grey might take the opportunity to cash in on Hemingway's popularity.[9]

At Long Key Grey fished for sailfish, bonita, barracuda, and the homely but spirited bonefish—the "gamiest fish of all," according to him. Bonefish, or *Albula vulpes,* was virtually an unknown fish until Zane Grey popularized it in the 1910s and 1920s. In one of his best essays at Long Key, simply titled "Bonefish," Grey mixes his philosophy of ocean fishing with vivid description and a strong character study. Grey set the tone of the essay from its outset: "Surely the longer a man fishes the wealthier he becomes in experience, in reminiscence, in love of nature, if he goes out with the harvest of a quiet eye, free from the plague of himself."[10] Grey claimed that the amazing bonefish was the "wisest, shyest, wariest, strangest fish" he ever studied, further characterizing it as having "phantom speed" and "utterly baffling" cunning.[11] After reviewing his list of superlatives, he announced to his readers: "I am prepared to state that I feel almost certain, if I spent another month bone-fishing, I would become obsessed and perhaps lose my enthusiasm for other kinds of fish."[12]

In "Bonefishing" Zane is once again accompanied by the redoubtable R.C. Grey. (He was financially secure, allowing him to accompany Zane on travels in America, and later, around the world.) Zane described one fishing sequence in which he and R.C. saw the tail of a phantom bonefish:

> At last I made a cast, but did not see him anymore. The wind was across my line, making a curve in it, and I was afraid I could not tell a bite if I had one. . . . I swept my rod up and back, hard

The three Grey brothers about 1916 at Lackawaxen. Ellsworth, called Cedar (right), frequently joined his brothers for fishing expeditions in Pennsylvania; R. C. (middle) followed Zane around the world.

as I dared. The line came tight, I felt a heavyweight. . . . I had hooked him. The thrill was remarkable. He took a short dash, then turned. I thought I had lost him. . . . Frantically I wound the reel, but could not get in the slack. I saw my line coming, heard it hiss in the water, then made out the dark shape of the bonefish. He ran right at me—almost hit my feet. When he saw me he darted off with incredible speed. . . . He ran four hundred feet in the dash, and I ran fifty. Not often have I of late years tingled and thrilled and panted with such excitement. It was great. It brought back the days of my boyhood.[13]

As Grey discovered, bonefishermen were a unique and reclusive breed, "loathe to tell anyone about their methods." The more Zane inquired about the species, the more the bonefishermen tried to ignore him. The old bonefishermen, observed Grey, "will avoid a bonefishing ground while others are there, and if they are surprised there ahead of others, they will pull up anchor and go away."[14] Grey's account of his failure to drag information from some of the old bonefisherman is one of the highlights of the essay, and further underscores that one of his strengths as a narrator is his willingness to be the inquisitive student.

Zane developed the deepest affection for these bonefishermen, whom he collectively called "the Bonefish Brigade." Often these bonefish anglers were wealthy and influential men from New York and Boston, who periodically dropped out of polite society to vacation in Long Key. Here they rolled up their pantlegs and fished like teenagers for the homely bonefish. Grey described their often clandestine movements this way:

> Usually after a day or two of rest three or four of these gentlemen would don the most disreputable clothes, and armed with an old bag and bucket they would sally forth on some errand most strikingly and obviously important. It puzzled me. I used to watch them wonderingly and and half with pity and amusement . . . the bag and bucket made me suspicious. Could it be possible that this gang, among whose number were Standard Oil magnates and other kinds of millionaires, was going to catch bait? The idea was preposterous . . . but when they came back wet, tired, dirty, and happy, with the bag and bucket full of something manifestly precious, I had a shock. Actually these men had been after bait! R.C. shared my amaze and discomfiture; and thereafter we spied upon these men who had our secret of harking back to boyhood.[15]

Grey knew these bonefishermen by their nicknames. "Fishermanz" was the chief of the brigade and was famous for sitting in his camp chair the whole day, absent-mindedly staring at the tide. "Much as I studied him that first visit of mine at Long Key," Grey commented, "I never saw him get even a bite. He seemed to dream and that made me jealous. I can stand a man to be a better angler than I am—which is hard to be—but as far as the dreamer end of it I claim distinction."[16]

In addition to "Fishermanz" there was also "Bumfeller," who used to "anchor a skiff some fifty feet offshore and sit all day, motionless as an Indian fisherman." "Loosfish" was a "slight, serious-faced man in the morning," but after returning from fishing became suddenly "energetic, violent, and exceedingly profane." Grey assumed that he "could not do anything but lose fish."[17]

Another member of the oddball bonefish gang was "Crownshanks," whose forte was strolling the beach. Grey acerbically noted that Crownshanks was as good a beachcomber as he was. Crownshanks's genius, however, was his facility with a cigarette:

> He always had one in his mouth—no, not exactly that, for the end of the cigarette was pasted on under the edge of his left incisor tooth. It hung there. It performed miraculous feats. It never fell. That was the mystery to me. Crownshanks never smoked it, that was sure. . . . This genial and intellectual man could discourse with you for many hours on any subject, though he preferred fishology, and he was equally well-versed in business, politics, religion, literature, socialism, metaphysics, psychology, altruism, and prizefighting. But I was always so bewitched and bewildered by the sight of his everlasting cigarette—by my irresistible gamble on whether it should stick there longer or not—that I could never concentrate on what he was talking about.[18]

Grey remained perplexed as to why bonefishing was "the fullest, the most difficult, the strangest and most thrilling, the lonesomest and most all-satisfying of all kinds of angling." He concluded that the sport had "all the finesse, the delicacy, the skill, the incomprehensible vagaries, the test of endurance that salmon fishing had. And more! For in bonefishing there is more of a return to boyish emotions than in salmon fishing. Perhaps that is the secret."[19] Grey became a fierce advocate of the bonefish, declaring that "the man who named them bonefish should have had half of that name applied to his head."[20]

✨ ✨ ✨

Although bonefishing and sailfishing consumed most of Zane's time at Long Key, he also angled for wahoo and dolphin. In "Some Rare Fish" Grey described his first encounter with a wahoo. While trolling near Tennessee Buoy, he and his boatman, Captain Sam Johnson, thought they had caught a sailfish running alongside the hull. For the next few moments, however, the fish, darting and changing speed, confounded the two experienced fisherman. "That fish," Grey wrote, "made me seem like an amateur. . . . The fact was he had so much speed that I was unable to keep a strain on him. I had no idea what kind of fish he was. And Sam likewise was nonplussed."

Soon, Grey hauled in his first wahoo—"a wild, strange graceful fish . . . his color appeared to be blue, green, silver crossed by bars . . . and his head sharper, more wolfish than a barracuda."[21] Grey went about his routine of researching the wahoo, questioning mentors, casual acquaintances, and fellow beachcombers, and digging through journals. He did this for both the wahoo and the dolphin. Of the latter he told his readers: "Dolphin seems a singularly attractive name. It always made me think of the deep blue sea, of old tars, and tall-sparred, white-sailed brigs. It is the name of a fish beloved of all sailors. . . . I suspect that is because the dolphin haunts ships and is an omen of good luck, and probably the most exquisitely colored fish in the ocean."[22]

Zane Grey loved the Atlantic, Gulf, and Pacific waters for different reasons. Long Key, with its varieties of fish and plant life, was closer to his home at Lackawaxen, providing a winter getaway from the snow and cold. Avalon and Santa Catalina Island, however, possessed a special magic. In Arthurian legend Avalon was the island in the west where dead knights were buried. Grey's Avalon, however, was full of more lively heroes—mostly robust, aging fishermen who gathered at the Catalina Tuna Club to smoke cigars, swap

Grey at Avalon, Santa Catalina Island, in the early 1920s. Zane loved the climate, and of course, the fishing of this West Coast paradise.

stories, and boast of the dimensions of their various trophies. After moving to California, Grey spent more and more time fishing in Pacific waters. In Long Key he fished for bonefish, wahoo, and sailfish; in Avalon he tracked swordfish, striped marlin, and tuna.

Seven of the essays in *Tales of Fishes* recount Zane Grey's adventures in the islands off the coast of Southern California, particularly on Santa Catalina and San Clemente Islands. These "Catalina" essays include "The Royal Purple Game of the Sea," "Two Fights with a Swordfish," "Swordfish," "The Gladiator of the Sea," "Seven Marlin Swordfish in One Day," "Big Tuna," and "Avalon, the Beautiful."

Depending on the year, the place, and his frame of mind, Grey's favorite sporting fish often changed quickly. In California, he preferred fishing for tuna. Gradually, he developed a respect for the fighting spirit of the swordfish, or *Xiphias gladius,* "the noblest warrior of all the sea fishes." He proudly proclaimed that in the twenty-two-year history of the Catalina Tuna Club only five anglers had earned the gold-and-white broadbill swordfish button. He was honored to be one of them.

For more than a century the Catalina Tuna Club, that bastion of saltwater angling, has stood proudly in the great half moon of Avalon Harbor, the reflection of its while facade dissolving in into the blue waters of the Pacific. On June 1, 1898, Dr. Charles Holder landed a 183-pound blue-fin tuna with a Tycoon rod and Fin-Nor reel. A month later the Catalina Tuna Club was founded and quickly became a major center of West Coast fishing. The twenty-four members of the original founding body had all taken a fish over a hundred pounds. From that point forward, anglers who accomplished similar feats were awarded the club's famous Blue Button label pin.

By summer 1914, when Grey arrived to prove his angling skills, Avalon and Catalina Island were humming with activity. Although both tuna and swordfish lured Grey to Avalon, it was tuna that first grabbed his imagination. Zane observed that tuna "rushes his prey and literally smashes the water white. His speed, his power, his savage spirit are indescribable."[23] In the essay "Big Tuna" (*Field and Stream,* May 1919) he remarked that it took him five seasons to catch a giant tuna, so evasive were the fish's movements. By the summer of 1918, Zane was frustrated and heart-sick over watching other fishermen bring in catches of a hundred pounds and more. He resolved that summer to land his big tuna. On a boat piloted by Captain Danielson—called Captain Dan—Grey set out into Catalina waters. After a few hours, with the sun glinting off the sea, Captain Dan and Zane sighted a school of tuna:

> The ambition of years, the long patience, the endless efforts, the numberless disappointments, and that never-to-be-forgotten day among the giant tuna—these flashed up . . . and roused in me emotion utterly beyond proportion or reason. This happened to me before, notably in swordfishing, but never had I felt such thrills, such tingling nerves, such oppression on my chest, such a wild eager rapture. It would have been impossible, notwithstanding my emotional temperament, if the leading up to this moment had not included so much long-sustained feeling.[24]

After Zane hooked a large tuna, he and Captain Dan prepared for a long, sustained battle:

> "I'm afraid of sharks," said Dan.
> Sharks are the bane of tuna fishermen. More tuna are cut off by sharks than are ever landed by anglers. This made me redouble my efforts, and in half an hour more I was dripping wet, and burning hot, aching all over, and so spent I had to rest. Every time I dropped the rod on the gunwhale the tuna took line—zee—zee—zee—foot by foot and yard by yard. My hands were cramped; my thumbs red and swollen, almost raw. I asked Dan for the harness, but he was loathe to put it on because he was afraid I would break the fish off. So I worked on and on, with spurts of fury and periods of lagging.[25]

Three hours later Grey was in "bad condition. . . . Where before

I had sweat, burned, throbbed, and ached, I now began to see red, to grow dizzy, to suffer cramps and nausea and exceeding pain." Captain Dan finally got Grey into the harness, where he finished the struggle. The tuna had taken them fifteen miles off course. With some finality, Grey wrote: "There the tuna was, the bronze-and-blue-backed devil, gaping, wide-eyed, shining and silvery as he rolled, a big tuna if there ever was one, and he was conquered." After Grey and the Captain hauled in the 138-pound tuna, Zane got his breath: "Three hours and fifty minutes! The number fifty stayed with me. As I fell back in my chair, all in, I could not see for my life why any fisherman would want to catch more than one large tuna."[26]

During some of his first days in Avalon, the often cocky Zane Grey stopped in to see Mr. Parker, a renowned taxidermist. He told Parker how he would like his swordfish mounted. Parker stammered, "Say, young fellow, you want to catch a swordfish first!" Grey eventually did, becoming one of the more famous salts around Catalina.[27]

Grey recorded his initiation into the pursuit of swordfish in "The Royal Purple Game of the Sea" (first published in *Recreation,* December 1915). At first it was a disappointing season with many sightings and futile chases around San Clemente Island. He continued the pursuit, however, in typical Grey fashion: "Day after day, from early morning till late afternoon, aboard on the sea, trolling, watching, waiting, eternally on the alert, I kept up the game. My emotional temperament made this game a particularly trying one. And every possible unlucky, unforeseen, and sickening thing that could happen to a fisherman had happened. I grew morbid, hopeless. I could no longer see the beauty of that wild and lonely island, nor the wonder of that smooth, blue Pacific, nor the myriad of strange sea-creatures. . . . Only by going at it so hard, and sticking so long, without any rests, could I gain the experience I wanted."[28]

The following year, 1915, he returned. On a boat piloted by

Captain Dan, they trolled the waters off Santa Catalina and San Clemente. He caught several swordfish over a hundred pounds, and later in the expedition landed one at three hundred and sixteen pounds "on faulty scales at Clemente," Grey reported. "He very likely weighed much more."[29]

On San Clemente, Catalina's sister island lying forty miles south-southwest, Grey found an abundant fishing ground and a coastline that he came to venerate. "The promontories," he wrote, "run down into the sea, sheer, black, rugged, bold and mighty. The surf is loud and deep and detonating, and the pebbles scream as the waves draw them down. . . . Wild and beautiful Clemente—the island of caves and canyons and cliffs . . . with wild goats silhoetted against the bold skyline!"[30] Grey explained that a man named Al Shade kept the only fishing camp on the island. For Grey it was "a clean, comfortable, delightful place. . . . Shade lives a lonely life there ten months in the year. And it is no wonder that when a fisherman arrives Al almost kills himself in his good humor and kindness and usefulness. Men who live lonely lives are always glad to see their fellowmen. But he loves Clemente Island. Who would not?"[31]

In addition to Clemente's wild coast and wonderful isolation, it also possessed great swordfishing. On one occasion Captain Dan alerted Zane that a significant day was at hand. "The sea's alive with swordfish! It's the day!" Their boat soon closed in on a "monster" swordfish. They both prepared their cameras as well as Grey's rod and reel:

> He came up, throwing the water in angry spouts. If he did not threaten the boat I was crazy. He began an exhibition that dwarfed any other I had seen, and was so swift that I could scarcely follow him. Yet when I saw the line rise, and then the wonderful, long, shiny body, instinct with fury, shoot into the air, I yelled the number of the leap, and this was the signal for the camera-workers. They held the cameras close, without trying to focus, facing the fish, and they snapped when I yelled. It was all gloriously exciting. I could never describe that exhibi-

tion. I only know that he leaped clear forty-six times, and after a swift, hard hour for me he got away. Strangely, I was almost happy that he had shaken loose, for he had given such remarkable opportunities for pictures.[32]

Thus began Grey's obsession with swordfish, which he describes vividly and in great detail in the Catalina essays. Four- to six-hour battles were common; so were the aching joints and back, the blistered hands, the chapped lips, and the throbbing head. Sometimes he was so exhausted fighting a swordfish that he collapsed in the boat. The next day he would be up at five and back on the sea, searching the rolling horizon.

In "Swordfish" (first published in *Field and Stream*, March 1919) Grey discusses the habitats, sizes, palatability, and some of the history of the warrior fish. He demonstrates his facility to blend background information, insight, subtle humor, and the romance of the sea. As if he were training for a boxing match, Grey thoroughly prepared himself by researching his opponents' strengths and weaknesses. In "Gladiator of the Sea" (*Field and Stream*, April 1918) he applies his knowledge in combat with several swordfish. In this adventure Captain Dan is back at the helm, as the Ahab-like Zane Grey chases the darting swordfish. In the action sequences, Grey is simply brilliant. Even in more relaxed moods, reclining on the deck of the ship, his diction is gorgeous: "The sea was like a beveled mirror, oily, soft, and ethereal, with low swells barely moving. An hour and a half later we were alone on the sea . . . with the sun faintly showing, and all around us, inclosing and mystical, a thin haze of fog. . . . Alone, alone all alone on a wide, wide sea! This was wonderful, far beyond any pursuit of swordfish."[33]

Through many seasons at Avalon Zane developed an unusual bonding with the swordfish. He explained this closeness this way:

> The pursuit of swordfish is much more exciting than ordinary fishing, for it resembles the hunting of large animals on the land and partakes more of the nature of the chase. . . . The

swordfish is a powerful antagonist sometimes, and sends his pursuers' vessel into harbor leaking, and almost sinking, from injuries it has inflicted. I have known a vessel to be struck by wounded swordfish as many as twenty times in a season. . . . One of Captain Ashby's crew was severely wounded by a swordfish which thrust his beak through the oak floor of a boat on which he was standing, and penetrated about two inches in his naked heel. The strange fascination draws men to this pursuit when they have once learned its charms. An old fisherman, who had followed the pursuit for twenty years, told me that when he was on the cruising-ground, he fished all night in his dreams, and that many a time he has rubbed the skin off his knuckles by striking them against the ceiling of his bunk when he raised his arms to thrust the harpoon into visionary monster swordfishes.[34]

Grey's unrelenting hunt for swordfish and tuna may leave some readers wishing to remain in the harbor. His angling objectives sometimes border on the maniacal, as he satisfies his lust for the capture. This frenzy might annoy, perplex, offend, or even shock readers who are not as driven in pursuit of their goals, let alone those who are not dedicated anglers.

The one exception in *Tales of Fishes* to this emphasis on the chase is the cautionary and lyrical essay "Avalon, the Beautiful," which concludes the book. In Avalon Grey discovered the irresistible combination of a remote fishing paradise, a Mediterranean climate, and an enchanting village. Later he found that it was also threatened by civilization. In the essay Grey warns of the dangers of overfishing and criticizes people's misunderstanding of the fish that populate the waters surrounding Santa Catalina Island. "Their doom has been spelled," Grey laments. "That is why I say to fishermen . . . they must go soon to Catalina before it is too late."[35] He also cites the Japanese and other foreign fishermen, "the canneries and the fertilizer plants . . . greed and war" as having cast "their dark shadow over beautiful Avalon."

At the time of the writing of "Avalon, the Beautful" (1918), Grey reached the painful realization that the great secret of California fishing—indeed the aura of California itself—was becoming known to the rest of the world. "Clemente Island, the sister island to Catalina," he remarked, "was once a paradise for fish, especially the beautiful gamy yellowtail. . . . But there are no more fish there . . . the boiling schools of yellowtail are gone." Part of the blame he leveled at the American war effort, which kept the fish canneries working day and night. But mainly he criticized the plundering of the environment by exploitive foreign nations and ignorant American fishermen. "Let every angler who loves to fish," Grey asserted, "think what it would mean to him to find the fish were gone. The mackerel are gone, the bluefish are going. . . . We must find ways and means to save our game fish of the sea."[36]

However, fishing was not the only thing that Grey wanted to preserve in Avalon. He concluded his essay by trying to capture the watery enchantment of his island. "Happily," he gloated, "neither war nor business nor fish-hogs can ruin the wonderful climate of Catalina." He loved the "dazzling white hot days and cool foggy nights." He was also grateful that Catalina Island was "the only place where the omnipresent, hateful, and stinking automobile does not obtrude on real content." Although entranced by Avalon's "fragrant salt breath of the sea, its music and motion and color and mystery and beauty," Grey ended his essay and his book with a note of urgency: "Go to Avalon before it is too late."[37]

If Avalon was sometimes too crowded and too threatened by foreign fishing boats, San Clemente resisted most attempts at domestication. Sometimes Grey would sail to Clemente just to experience the isolation and wild beauty of the slopes. As recorded in "Seven Marlin Swordfish in One Day," Grey described the island's enchanting fascination:

> I rested high up the slope, in the lee of a rugged rock, all rust-stained and gray-lichened, with a deep cactus-covered canyon to my left, the long, yellow windy slope of wild oats to my right,

and beneath me the Pacific, majestic and grand, where the great while rollers moved graceful heaves along the blue.

Lazily and dreamily, Grey watched as Clemente revealed its mysteries:

> A big black raven soared by with dismal croak. The wind rustled the oats. There was no other sound but the sound of the sea—deep, low-toned, booming like thunder, long crash and continuous roar. . . . How wonderful to watch eagles in their native haunts! I saw a bald eagle sail by, and then two golden eagles winging heavy after him. . . . They circled and flew in and out of the canyon, and one let out a shrill, piercing scream. . . . Life is beautiful, particularly elemental life. Then far above I saw the white-tipped eagle and I thrilled to see the difference now in his flight. He was monarch of the air, king of the wind, lonely and grand in the blue. He soared, he floated, he sailed, and then, as swift as an arrow, to slow and circle again, and swoop high and higher, wide-winged and free, ringed in the azure blue, and then like a thunderbolt he fell, to vanish beyond the crags.[38]

The island, Grey explained, lay beyond any visitation by ships and was mainly inhabited by Mexican sheepherders. Windswept and barren, it seemed "consecrated to sun and sea." In the day the island was "an empire of the sun. But at sunset fog rolled up from the outer channel, and if sun blasted the life on the island, the fog saved it." At the east end of the island Grey found a striking promontory, where he could look at the plunging cliffs below: "I loved to watch a great swell rise out of the level blue, heave and come, slow-lifting as if from some infinite power, to grow and climb aloft till the blue turned green and sunlight showed through . . . and rising sheer, the whole swell, solemn and ponderous and majestic, lifted its volume in one beautiful instant, then curled and rolled in with a thundering, booming roar, all the curves and contours gone in a green-white seething mass that climbed the reefs and dashed itself to ruin."[39]

In the years following the publication of *Tales of Fishes,* Grey returned repeatedly to both Avalon and Long Key. Avalon became a bustling tourist village and continued its renown as an angler's paradise. Zane Grey became one of its more famous citizens, but there were also increasing numbers of movie stars taking up residence. The Grey hilltop home later became the Zane Grey Pueblo Hotel, which is still in operation. Long Key did not fare as well. Virtually destroyed by the disastrous hurricane of 1935, Long Key Fishing Camp was nearly abandoned as an important fishing center. Today, deep sea fishing has returned, although not with the same glory as when Zane, R.C., and their friends plied the waters searching for barricuda and bonefish.

Praise for *Tales of Fishes* often came in strange forms. A few years after publication of the book, Zane and R.C. happened to be vacationing in Long Key. Also relaxing in the sunshine was John Wanamaker, the retailing tycoon and owner of the famous Wanamaker Store in Philadelphia. Wanamaker had sailed down to Florida on his luxurious yacht, and unbeknownst to Zane, was engaging in his own passion for fishing. One day in Long Key Zane received a message that Wanamaker wished to see him on the latter's yacht. Zane dressed in his best clothes—or the best he had with him—and headed the short distance to Wanamaker's ship. When Zane entered the tycoon's plush quarters, he noticed a copy of his *Tales of Fishes* on the desk. Soon, the distinguished, white-haired Wanamaker entered and introduced himself. He placed a cordial hand on Grey's shoulder and said: "Zane Grey, you are distinctively and genuinely American. . . . I have given away thousands of your books and I have sold hundreds of thousands in my stores. The good you're doing is incalculable. *Never lay down your pen!"* Tongue-tied and embarrassed, Grey muttered some words of thanks. After leaving Wanamaker's yacht, he returned to the beach and the company of R.C., although he never mentioned a word to his brother about this encounter until years later.

Tales of Fishes—Grey's 1919 paean to the beauty of angling—remains a fresh sea breeze to hearts becalmed by worry, stress, and lethargy. Although Zane Grey did not write a great fiction work about the sea, he perhaps accomplished something more colorful, enthralling, and enduring. Among his later fishing works are *Tales of Tahitian Waters* and *Tales of Swordfish and Tuna*, but it would be difficult to find one to equal the vigor and grace of *Tales of Fishes*.

The year 1919 was a bonanza for Grey. Besides publishing *Tales of Fishes*, Harper issued *The U.P. Trail*, which quickly soared to the top of the best-seller lists. In the summer he quietly slipped away to the Pacific Northwest, secure in the knowledge that his name was one of the most recognized in American letters. Dolly accompanied him on the motor trip, as did R.C. Grey.

They headed for Crater Lake in Oregon, whose azure blue surface Zane described as "exquisite, rare, unreal." "This rare blue," he continued, "is not of this earth." As with most bodies of water, Grey was at first awestruck by its beauty, then eager to drop his hook in the water as soon as possible. The steep path to the lake, however, still clogged with ice and snow, looked particularly treacherous. Back at the hotel and dressed in his rough clothes, Grey bumped into a rather terse hotel custodian, remarking to him that he wanted to fish in the lake but was concerned about the seemingly impassable route. "It ain't no boulevard," said the man. "Any boats down there?" asked Zane. "No," came the reply. "They was all smashed by snow-slides." "Say," concluded the man, "I reckon if you start down you'll get down quicker'n you'll climb up." Considering the conversation "asinine," Grey walked away and talked things over with R.C. and Dolly.

Dolly thought the slope much too dangerous, and R.C. concurred. "Do you take me for a Swiss ski-runner?" stammered R.C. Grey was used to arm-twisting, cajoling, and employing some good old-fashioned charm in such situations. He told R.C. that no one was better on bad trails. R.C. finally capitulated. "Aw, come on," he said, "If you start to slide and I don't see you any more I'll come back."

Leaving Dolly at the hotel, the brothers made their icy descent to the lake. They agreed it was the most precipitous slope they had encountered in their travels. They made their way down the path bearing their knapsacks and fishing gear. Fifty yards down the trail the footing got worse. Zane wanted to turn back, but R.C. because of the ice could not turn on the path. Zane saw a sturdy bush ahead of them, picked his way toward it, and finally grabbed a branch. He urged R.C. forward, extending his fishing rod for him to grasp. As they both clung to the bush, R.C. reflected: "Some place—that! I thought of the time when we were kids—coasting down Maple Hill —and my sled went over the bank—breaking my arm in two places. Do you remember? Funny what a fellow thinks of."[40]

After they had rested, they gingerly climbed down through the brush dotting the slope. They reached the lake and Zane stared into the shallow, opal-blue waters. He counted nine very large trout "swimming aimlessly around in less than two feet of water." He told R.C.: "That's a sight worth sliding down the snow to see, hey?"

Zane proceeded to cast his line as R.C. walked a brief distance up the shoreline. Grey described his experience fishing in Crater Lake this way:

> I sat down to change my flies for a spinner. I selected the largest and gaudiest I had. While I had this on, I saw R.C. catch another trout, a smaller one, that appeared to be landed in short order. By this time I was curious about these Crater Lake rainbows. They acted and looked rather queer to me.
>
> Then I got up to try my hand again. All I succeeded in doing was to scare away the bunch of trout in that particular spot. I moved upshore. More or less trout would be passing up or down, some in close, others far out. As they did not seem to mind me, I got over trying to be careful, to keep out of sight. I stepped out

boldly. And I cast that spinner in nine hundred different ways. No good! I heard R.C. yell, and then I heard him yell again. I was too busy and mad to watch him catch fish. . . .

Presently R.C. showed up, dragging trout that under normal fishing conditions would have made my eyes bulge. We exchanged views. He had arrived at my conclusions, and he added that he did not believe the crater of an extinct volcano was a natural environment for trout.[41]

Grey's angling experience at Crater Lake proved to be more arduous than pleasurable. But this time he was willing to let the austere beauty of the setting take precedence over his dismal outing on the lake. However, he was so impressed by the Pacific Northwest that two months later he returned—this time to the western coast of Canada.

When the Great War ended in Europe in November 1918, Canada, like many nations, was exhausted both emotionally and economically. It had sent a large contingent of troops to support the British Expeditionary Force, serving gallantly on such hallowed, bloodstained battlegrounds such as Paschendale, Ypres, and Flanders.

Even before the war, American outdoor periodicals were promoting the scenic wonders and abundant wildlife of Canada's interior and coastline. Returning veterans were lured northward by tales of superb fishing and hunting. Grey, however, never really embraced Canada as he did the South Pacific cultures. For one thing, he was unfamiliar with Canadian authors, history, and issues. He loved the promise of the rugged, dangerous trails, but he did not surrender to the mystique of the great north.

Grey generally used two criteria for scouting new fishing spots. The first was an article in a major angling journal. The second was word-of-mouth recommendation. It was often the latter that he trusted the most. For many years he had heard of the challenging salmon run on the Campbell River in the northern part of Vancouver Island.

In Vancouver in mid-August Zane and R.C. boarded the steam-ship *Princess Pat* bound for Nanaimo on the eastern coast of Van-couver Island. There they would proceed overland by car to the port of Campbell River. In Nanaimo Grey discovered that their driver could not make more than six miles an hour. They fired him in the first town, securing another driver who barreled along so fast they "could hardly keep him in sight."

They passed through wooded, mountainous countryside. Dark clouds drifted over the hills, and mist hung in the treetops. At Fort Campbell they found a "bleak and dreary" settlement composed of "a tavern and some weather-beaten houses." In the tavern Zane and R.C. heard the locals and visitors discuss the fishing possibili-ties for the area. One, a vacationing New Yorker, declared that the Campbell River was "fished out long ago." "The net boats," he con-tinued, "have ruined what was once the greatest fishing in British Columbia."[42]

Although discouraged by the reports, Zane and R.C. had trav-eled over five hundred miles to fish for tyee salmon and were not about to quit now. Characteristically, Grey unpacked his bag, made some notes in his journal, went to bed, and rose at five in the morn-ing. Surrounded by a magnificent forest, "the richest, greenest, and most verdant" he had ever seen, he and R.C. plunged into the Campbell River and proceeded to fish for the renowned salmon. Results came quickly. "The method of fishing for tyee salmon," Grey wrote, "was to troll with a specially-made spoon that in size, silver color, and motion resembled a herring. This spoon trolled on its edge and imparted a singularly life-like motion." He soon pulled several thirty- and forty-pound salmon from the cold waters of the river.

While Grey concentrated on his fishing technique, he was con-stantly aware of his surroundings. Perhaps because he was in a new country, his senses were particulary sharp. Of the the dark-green Canadian backdrop, he wrote: "Toward sunset the light changed and there were a few moments of exquisite beauty. A vivid sundog gleamed among the creamy white clouds of the south. It was a strange mixture of colors, rose and gold-green, and faint purple, and lesser hues . . . but the sunset in the gap of the mountains held my gaze. It was a bright open space in all the angry mass of cumulus clouds, a stormy flare of fire against white clouds like rolling smoke."[43]

Grey was confounded by the reported demise of the Campbell River and the evidence of his own good luck. "What a strange, ancient, worn-out place this Campbell River! Once it had been the most famous of English fishing resorts." Perhaps what bothered him the most was the voice of the river. Even while he was having success fishing, he heard the cold roar of the water:

> One of the most striking features at Campbell River was the sound of the water out in the channel. It must have been a rip tide. All I could see was a roughened line of tiny whitecaps. But the sound was menacing. It did not resemble the sound of the sea across a bar, nor the low sullen roar of the river rapids, but it gave me a deep and haunting thrill. Nearly all the time, and especially at night, I was aware of this strange, weird murmur of chafing waters. It held a cold note of the northland. It suggested the contending tides of the dark green Arctic seas. Not a welcome sound for an angler![44]

In the end, however, Grey claimed that his experiences in Canada were among his most memorable and declared that the tyee salmon was the "most magnificent, versatile fighter." Moreover, he maintained that he wanted to return to the great north. Next time he intended to "journey northward, far beyond Vancouver [Island], and find a river where the tyee run large and many." In his imagination he could visualize such a place: "a broad swift river, sliding out of the forest into a green channel, with glancing, cold lights from the setting sun, with shadows of the bold wild mountains, and in the eddying tide where fresh and salt water meet, the riffle and splash and surge of the beautiful green-backed tyee."[45]

After Zane and R.C. left Vancouver Island and before they returned to the bountiful swordfish run on Catalina Island, they sojourned briefly in the Klamath River country of southern Oregon, where they resumed the fierce competition that typified most of their angling adventures. At forty-four, R.C. Grey still maintained the spunky nature that he developed on the baseball diamonds of Ohio.

Zane by this time was so fanatical about fishing that he often had to remind himself of his writing responsibilities. As the decade closed and the beginning of a new one approached, he was about to enter one of his most prolific periods. It was also a time that he began developing more exotic escape routes from an American culture that he increasingly viewed as hostile, corrupt, and generally immoral.

꒷ꂃ ꒷ꂃ ꒷ꂃ

The Barefoot Adventurer

There's a race of men that don't fit in,
    A race that can't stay still;
So they break the hearts of kith and kin,
    And they roam the world at will.
They range the field and they rove the flood,
    And they climb the mountain's crest;
Theirs is the curse of the gypsy blood,
    And they don't know how to rest.

— ROBERT SERVICE

In his 1846 novel *Typee,* a then unknown Herman Melville described his arrival in the Edenic South Sea island of Typee. After disembarking from the whaling ship named (ironically) *Dolly,* Melville and his fellow crew members soon burrowed into Taipian culture, witnessing how this resilient people transcended society's modern evils. There were no laws or crime. There was no emphasis on private property, possessions, or religion. Warfare was nonexistent. The men were handsome, fearless, and strong. The women were friendly, beautiful, and vivacious. By all accounts, including Melville's, they were the happiest and most resourceful people in the Marquesas Islands—perhaps in the South Pacific.

Since Melville's time, many Europeans and American writers and artists have been drawn to the South Pacific, particularly to places like the Marquesas, the Solomons, Tahiti, New Zealand, and Australia. In Melville's footsteps came the painter Paul Gauguin and writers such as Robert Louis Stevenson, Jack London, and Zane Grey, lured by the light and the prospect of a sensual paradise. "A fisherman has many dreams," wrote Grey, "and from boyhood one of mine was to own a beautiful white ship with sails like wings and sail into lonely tropic seas."[1]

Of course, Zane Grey had always been a barefoot vagabond. From his days in Zanesville and Columbus to his numerous excursions through the American West, Grey was always ready for a fresh adventure or prepared to tilt at a new windmill. In 1924, however, his quest took a more radical and signficant turn when he purchased his "beautiful white ship" and began to sail farther from home. Physically, he was fully prepared. He was fifty-two years old. With his sapling frame and shock of steel-gray hair, he was as fit as at any time in his life. His leathery hands and wind-burned cheeks spoke of many hours in the outdoors. Professionally, he was at the top of his game. Following a string of publishing successes, including *The U.P. Trail, Man of the Forest,* and *Wanderer of the Wasteland,* he was arguably the most popular writer in America. Zane, however, wanted more.

In Nova Scotia, Canada, Grey found his mentor of the sea, Captain Laurie Mitchell, a thoroughly British version of Buffalo Jones and Al Doyle. A retired army officer and remittance man, Mitchell came to Nova Scotia to fish and soon was setting world records for bluefin tuna, records much admired by Zane Grey. Grey met him briefly after the war on a fishing trip to Nova Scotia. After some correspondence between them, Grey arrived in Liverpool, Nova Scotia, for a more extended sojourn in the summer of 1924.

Laurie Mitchell was nearly five-foot ten, slender, with a roguish glint in his eye. He smoked a pipe that usually dangled from the side of his mouth. Normally clean-shaven, Mitchell at one time challenged Zane to a beard-growing contest on a voyage. After measuring their stubble and receiving the opinions of their shipmates, they agreed to call it a draw. In another instance, Grey invited Mitchell to his cabin at Winkle Bar, Oregon, on the Rogue River.

After making the arduous three-hour horseback ride, Mitchell, either from fatigue or too much liquor, promptly fell out of his saddle. The irrepressible R.C. stared down at him and joked: "Well, Cap, this little Z.G. jaunt wasn't anything. Wait till we strike out for the Tonto Basin and the bear hunt." Mitchell declared: "By gad! you'll have to bury me if you ever put me on another saddle like that." He swore that he would never ride a horse again—and he kept his word.

Laurie Mitchell's fishing accomplishments were impressive. The toast of Nova Scotia, he once landed a 710-pound bluefin tuna. The record held until Zane Grey, on August 22, 1924, reeled in a world-record 758-pound bluefin, a catch that Mitchell acknowledged somewhat grudgingly. Grey went on to set four world fishing records that year.

While strolling through Liverpool harbor one day, Grey spied a 190-foot-long, three-masted schooner named *Marshal Foch*. He thought it was the perfect ship to actualize his dreams of a South Seas voyage. He bought it for $17,000 and renamed it *Fisherman*. Grey proceeded to have it reconditioned for ocean travel, sinking another $40,000 into the ship for this purpose—a princely sum in the mid-1920s. When the changes were completed three months later, she was a handsome ship indeed.

Zane spared no expense on *Fisherman*. Below decks, there was a dining room, salon, four bathrooms, a photographic darkroom, and six staterooms. *Fisherman* was powered by four Fairbanks-Morse engines, plus several auxiliary engines, generators and pumps. In the forecastle, there was an engine for hoisting sails and anchors, plus lathes, a tool bench, a forge, and a carpenter shop for repairs. On deck, *Fisherman* sported three launches, especially designed for deep-sea fishing. "For catching fish and battling the monsters of the tropic seas," Grey proudly noted, "we had every kind of tackle that money could buy and ingenuity devise."[2]

As *Fisherman* was being reconditioned, Grey asked Mitchell to accompany him on a trip to the Pacific Ocean. Mitchell agreed, perhaps because his livelihood in Nova Scotia was not as secure as Grey had at first thought. The ship's changes required three months of labor. Since Grey did not wish to wait through the Canadian winter, he drew up a plan. He would return to the West Coast and rendezvous with his new ship in January in Balboa, the western port on the Panama Canal. From there he, his friends, and his crew would sail, fish, and vacation in the waters around Central America and Mexico.

He hand-picked his crew for the voyage to the Caribbean and through the Panama Canal. Most of the crew proved equal to the task of sailing *Fisherman* through the Atlantic gales, but the sailing master (who was not Mitchell) was an abysmal choice. After leaving Nova Scotia in December 1924, *Fisherman* headed to Jamaica and the western Caribbean. Between Jamaica and Panama, in an attempt to run through some shoals, the ship ran aground. Caribbean natives tried to loot the ship as it rested immobilized. Only an alert crew with rifles scared them off. When *Fisherman* reached Colon, a close inspection revealed that her keel had been stripped.

After a rocky maiden voyage, Grey's honeymoon with his new ship was just beginning.

The two happiest days in a sailor's life, as the adage goes, are the day he buys his yacht and the day he sells it. For Zane Grey the first days aboard his new vessel were pure joy, as they meandered through the Pacific waters. They sailed from Balboa at the end of January 1925, heading for Cocos Island, five hundred miles to the southwest. Grey had assembled a rather diverse entourage for his inaugural voyage. On board were his son Romer and R.C.; Laurie Mitchell, whom Grey called "Cappy"; Jess Smith, a cowboy friend, and his wife; Johnny Shields, a friend of Romer's; Bob King, a fishing buddy of Grey's; Chester Wortley, a movie cameraman with Lasky Studios; Mildred Smith, Grey's secretary; and George Takahashi, the indispensable cook. The new skipper was Sid Boerstler, or "Captain Sid," whom Grey trusted more with each fresh day. As honorary captain, Grey got to tinker with his impressive new ship, while his crew managed the logistical and navigational aspects.

Out on the open sea, Grey was at first unaccustomed to the motion of the *Fisherman*. "How slow and stately she rose and fell, and rolled!" he wrote. "The great tall spars with their huge sails seemed to reach the skies. I walked the lonely deck and sat here and there, always looking." All his dreams of owning a ship and sailing into the lonely wastes seemed to be coming true: "The worries and troubles incident to this long-planned-for trip began to slough off my mind and leave me. . . . I was going down the grand old Pacific; and there was promise of adventure, beauty, and discovery."[3]

The choice of Cocos Island was carefully planned by Grey. It was reputed to be the hideout of the notorious British pirate Davis, who plundered ships and brought his stolen booty back for burial on the island. The remote island became the inspiration for Stevenson's *Treasure Island,* which Grey had read countless times. Cocos Island rises steeply from the water, affording few anchorages. From the *Fisherman* Grey and his crew saw the undulating coastline that was studded with caves and caverns concealed by matted foliage. Grey was drawn to the idea of treasure, but he knew most of the island was inaccessible. He decided to sample the fishing instead.

R.C. as it turned out had better luck than Zane, reeling in a twenty-pound yellowtail. Romer and Johnny, from one of the launches, sighted sharks. Grey decided to try to land one, but came up only with a broken line. Since R.C. was not having any more fortune after his first success with the yellowtail, the brothers agreed to go ashore. At a place called Wreck Bay, they found a palm-lined stretch of beach. On rocks near the shore they found names and dates of early sailors, one dating back to 1817. Farther down the beach they found the skeletal remains of a Spanish galleon. Romer and Johnny, inspired by the romance and adventure of the setting, left the party and headed inland to explore more of the island. Zane, however, was content to remain on shore and savor the historical intrigue, the water, the bright sky, and marauding gulls as they dove over the coast.

When they returned to the *Fisherman,* Grey was concerned by the shark infestation around the ship. They thrashed around and butted the hull, preying on the tuna and yellowtail. Grey immediately became fearful of his family's and friend's lives; any minor error could send someone to certain death. "We saw a yellowtail and amberjack swim among the sharks," Grey remarked, "but the instant we hooked [one] he was set upon by these voracious monsters. They fought like wolves."[4]

The sharks' ferocity became apparent shortly thereafter. R.C. and Bob King went out in one of the launches. After a short spell of fishing, King began shouting, waving his arms, and pointing at R.C. Zane's brother was hunched over a taut line, fighting madly with a tuna. Bob King reached down and pulled on the leader. The tuna's head broke through the water, along with a shark who was in the process of devouring the tuna. R.C. had caught both the shark and the remains of the tuna! Other sharks milled in the water, ready to join in the kill. R.C. wrestled furiously with the line, but the shark would not release the head of the tuna. Bob King, helping R.C., fell back into the boat. Finally, the shark's jaws clamped shut. The tuna's head bobbed on the line, and the shark swam away. As the water subsided, a dozen other sharks fought Bob King for the beheaded tuna. By that time, R.C. and King were exhausted, and the water was frothy and scarlet.

Although Grey fished for a few more days, he chafed to leave Cocos Island and head for their next destination, the Galapagos Islands, off the coast of Ecuador. As the *Fisherman* departed, he could only imagine the conflict that went on below the serene surface of the Pacific.

> Strife in this hot ocean was intensely magnified, in proportion to the enormous number of fish. Nature had developed them to be swifter, fiercer, stronger than fish in northern seas. It struck

me strangely that there had not been any sign of fish feeding on the surface, such as was so familiar to our eyes in Florida, California, and Nova Scotia waters. Yet here there are a million times more fish, little and big. The upper stratum of water was hot, and all species of fish remained below it, until something unusual brought them up. Tremendous contending strife went on below the beautiful blue surface of the Pacific. It seemed appallingly deceitful. The beauty was there to see, but not the joy of life.[5]

As for the buried treasure not yet lifted from the island, he hoped that it would be unearthed by "some honest, needy fisherman."

Before leaving the immediate area, the *Fisherman* cruised the waters of the Gulf of Panama, finding some tiny islands huddled together. Grey was amazed by the abundance of life flourishing in these isolated islands in the Pacific. And too, he was quite happy to roam leisurely on his new ship and investigate islands as they came into view. "The outermost island of the group was a long, low black ledge absolutely covered with pelicans. Perhaps this rock island was half an acre in extent and rose twenty feet or so above the current. . . . There was rip tide that set in from the open sea, and which met the offshore current just around the corner of this island." In the rip tide he discovered huge schools of red snapper. "There were thousands of them. And when we ran into the current the crimson patch disintegrated and appeared to string out after our boats. The red snapper followed us. Each angler was playing a fish at the same time, while hundreds of great red-golden fish, hungry and fierce, almost charged the boat!"

As they circled the islands, they were descended upon by armadas of seagulls. "Over our heads," Grey observed, "while the anglers trolled . . . and the boatmen handled wheels and and levers, the screaming wild fowl sailed to and fro. . . . It was a wonderful place and I had to force myself to leave it, though I had not laid a hand on my rod. Some privileges should be respected. And as we ran away from that white-wreathed and bird-haunted rock, I knew another marvelous fishing place had been added to my gallery of pictures."[6]

★ ★ ★

While the fierce winter of 1925 raged back in America, Grey and the *Fisherman* cruised down to the Galapagos archipelago in eighty-degree weather. After a few brief squalls, the ship plied the molten sea under a brilliant, cloudless sky.

Like most students of history, Zane Grey yearned to tread in the footsteps of his heroes. One of Grey's major teachers, if not the guiding spirit behind the spare naturalism of his fiction, was Charles Darwin, whose investigations of the islands were recorded in his famous *Voyage of the Beagle*. For Grey, coming to the Galapagos Islands was like perusing his professor's laboratory. As Marchena Island, the first of four islands in the group, came into view, Grey likened its windswept surface to parts of Arizona. Sailing farther into the straits, the *Fisherman* encountered Santa Cruz Island with its serrated volcanic peaks and veins of red lava. Attracted by the scenery and the mystery of the island, they steered for Conway Bay, where they dropped anchor in February 1925.

Going ashore, Grey and his party were overwhelmed by the density of the forest, the abundance of plant life, the stifling heat, and the rather spirited—and ubiquitous—desert flies. Grey did not have to walk more than fifty yards from shoreline to see iguanas, crabs, seals, and the renowned tortoises of the islands. Zane and R.C. were fascinated by the "infinitely strange" varieties of animal and vegetable life on the island, and often hours of mute contemplation replaced the moments normally reserved for angling in the bay. The group stayed and fished at Conway Bay for several days. Zane caught a fifty-one-pound dolphin from the deck of the *Fisherman*, while R.C. reeled in a cumbersome needlefish, which, unfortunately, flopped over in the launch and sank its jaws into Bob King's leg. Without a trained physician on board, "Doc" Zane Grey did most of the first aid himself. Such responsibility began to wear on Grey. Realizing that they were hundreds of miles from civilization, he fretted constantly over his friends' and the crew's welfare.

From Conway Bay they sailed the eight-hour stretch to Darwin Bay, nestled near Tower Island. Once dubbed "Nightmare Island" by Spanish explorers, the volcanic atoll with its dangerous reefs and man-eating sharks provided Zane some vexing moments and troubled dreams. Nothing angered Grey more than someone, let alone an uninvited shark, trying to steal his fish. Once on the *Fisherman* in Conway Bay he was grappling with a six-foot wahoo when a monstrous shark came out of the depths and swallowed up his catch. Grey was so infuriated he switched from trying to reel in wahoos to baiting sharks. His heavy tackle worked temporarily. However, the fifteen-foot sharks quickly devoured his copper-wire leaders and swam away.

One night as the *Fisherman* lay at anchor in the bay, a brief but powerful storm nearly swamped the boat and its launches. The rain and wind pelted the helpless ship, as Grey and crew first thought it advisable to head into open water and leave the launches behind. After a quick council they decided to wait out the storm in the harbor, rather than trying to finish their expedition without their precious fishing boats.

On their return voyage to the coast of Panama, the *Fisherman* encountered a more vicious storm, prompting Grey to call the experience "the most harrowing" of his life. Piloted by Captain Sid, the *Fisherman* entered the teeth of the gale at night. Grey, standing on the rolling deck, could barely see the bowsprit, as darkness, rain, and wind descended on the ship's rigging. Adding to their alarm were the reports of a steamer in the vicinity. Since visibility was near zero, Grey and the crew became fearful not only of being swamped by the vomiting sea, but also of colliding with the phantom steamship.[7]

One of Zane Grey's great fears was loss of control, and this experience reinforced his sense of vulnerability. Hours passed as the storm deluged his ship. Nearly paralyzed by fright, Grey finally stumbled toward the bow, where he encountered the Canadian lookout. The man peered straight ahead into the dripping, windy darkness, seemingly unaware of Grey's presence beside him. Grey knew the man was a veteran of such storms, and being near him brought Grey some comfort. At length, the lookout simply muttered: "Men who go down to the sea in ships must be prepared." His words soothed Zane, and the fear subsided.[8]

The next day the sun shone and the wind dropped, as they sailed nearer to Panama Bay. On the horizon there was no sign of the steamer, only the flights of boobies drifting on the breeze. Grey never forgot the moment when another person's words meant so much to him.

Just after the spring equinox, the *Fisherman* dropped its anchor in Zihuatanejo Bay, Mexico, where for several days the party toured the village and fished for marlin in the sapphire-blue waters. Ashore they collected baskets, leatherwork, and the usual assortment of tourist souvenirs. On the bay, Grey wrestled for four hours with a black marlin, which left his hands lacerated and bleeding, his head dizzy, and his lungs gasping for air. Just as he was about to bring the marlin aboard, the line snapped. Not willing to remain vanquished too long, Grey went out and chased a sailfish. Chester Wortley, the professional motion-picture photographer on board, filmed Zane battling the sailfish from another launch. Later, when Grey watched the film, he counted forty-three leaps the fish had made through the air before surrendering.

After leaving Zihuatanejo, they sailed to the northwest and through the waters around Cabo San Lucas. They were homeward bound, hoping to arrive in Avalon harbor by the end of April. Under the hot pour of the Mexican coastal sun, Grey spied off the bow of the *Fisherman* an armada of frolicking porpoises. As the ship drew nearer to them, Grey's focus became more intense, sensing in their playful freedom some of his own: "What action, life, rhythm! How the black backs and silver sides flashed! The roar . . . was so loud we had to shout to hear each other." Soon, the *Fisherman* was alongside the leaping porpoises. Grey resumed his feverish scrutiny:

> In a few moments we were surrounded by splashing, puffing, leaping gray bodies. Tiny baby porpoises leaped alongside huge plump ones, presumably their mothers. The roar of the splitting water filled my ears. Sometimes a row of twenty would leap right in front of me. I would be looking down on their glistening backs. The slapping of flat tails mingled with the roar.
>
> They drew away from us, and sheering east, headed in the track of the sun. To our right came the other half of the school, soon to join those we had followed. Then we were afforded a scene of extraordinary beauty and life. The sunlight now was strong, the sea like a sheet of burnished silver, and the porpoises became black as ebony. What vigor, what strange freedom, what glittering incessant action! Above the white splashes showered millions of sparkling drops, bright as diamonds. Thus the maelstrom distanced us and swept on into the glare of the sun.[9]

After a marathon fight with an unusually testy whale shark, the crew headed to California. Perhaps the greatest bounty of Grey's voyage was the number of important photographs—both still and motion—that the party collected. For instance, Grey possessed rare footage of leaping sperm whales. Additionally, they had significant shots of whales cavorting before they took their plunges into the deep. Photographs and footage of Grey's and R.C.'s angling experiences rounded out the collection. Upon arrival home, Grey promptly wrote up the notes of his journey, which Harper's published under the title *Tales of Fishing Virgin Seas.* Appearing the same year as his journey, the book was the third in the list of Grey's phenomenally successful angling titles, further diversifying his writing career and securing his reputation as an international adventurer, explorer, and sportsman.

⋙ ⋙ ⋙

In the 1920s Zane Grey thought that the Rogue River in Oregon was just about the wildest, best-fishing river in America. Although the sea constantly lured him, the Ohio boy of summer never really forgot his love of freshwater angling. In the mid-1920s Grey bought a remote cabin at Winkle Bar, Oregon, near the Rogue River. In summer 1925, just after his return from his Galapagos excursion, he journeyed to Grant's Pass, Oregon, with a group of friends to inaugurate his next adventure.

Grey's entourages, which often in scale resembled Mount Everest expeditions, were becoming legendary. They ranged from two to twenty people in Grey's immediate party; additionally there were local guides, numerous pack horses, several spirited canines, and anyone else they might collect along the way. Although Grey was first and foremost a solitary man, he also believed in the sharing of the feast.

The Winkle Bar retreat became a favorite with Grey and Dolly, replacing Arizona as a place they could both enjoy. After the first year, the Grant's Pass newspaper, the *Daily Courier,* anticipated the annual invasion of Grey's retinue and dispatched a reporter to cover their activities. Having Zane Grey camped out on the Rogue became a major advertisement for southern Oregon.

This particular trek to the Rogue River (first published as "Shooting the Rogue," *Country Gentleman*, April–May 1926) included Grey, Romer, and George Takahashi, who had become a fixture in Grey's traveling scullery. Also on the trip were Cappy Mitchell, who saw the Pacific Northwest for the first time; Grey's drivers, Ken and Ed; and "Lone Angler" Wiborn and his wife.

Grey and Wiborn had been friends since attending the University of Pennsylvania. Wiborn went on to become a physician, but gave up his occupation due to ill health. He eventually chose a life in the outdoors, becoming a nationally recognized fisherman. Adamantly a solitary man—hence the sobriquet "Lone Angler"—he accompanied Grey on numerous fishing expeditions.

Grey's main interest in the Rogue River country was steelhead fishing. However, on this occasion he decided to follow the river in boats from Whiskey Creek in south-central Oregon due west to the delta at Gold Beach, Oregon, a journey of about 120 miles. In volume and ferocity, the Rogue is not even a miniature Colorado River, although it does possess superior fishing, daunting rapids, crystalline water, and rugged alpine scenery.

If the running of the Rogue River proved to be another Zane Grey-versus-the-elements tale, it was also the coming of age story of young Romer Grey. Nearing sixteen, Romer was unquestionably, as Zane phrased it, a "second version" of his father. He hunted, fished, bragged, and walked like him. On this adventure, Romer also wanted to be as brave as his father.[10]

Starting at a point about ten miles upriver from Whiskey Creek, the group began their descent of the Rogue in six durable boats. The party encountered seventeen rapids, some treacherous, others tame. Through each chute in the river, Romer challenged his father to outdo him. Zane, perhaps showing his age, could hardly keep up with his son. By the time they reached the campsite at Whiskey Creek, Grey's boat was taking on water. Grey observed the state of the expedition this way:

> Eyes that fell shut as if weighted, and dead slumber, were our reward for that strenuous day.
>
> Morning disclosed a bunch of cripples, several lost articles of baggage, two leaky boats, and various other things that might have been expected.
>
> It also disclosed our campsite, which was an ideal one for a lover of the wilds. A high sandy beach, overgrown with ferns and blooming goldenrod, with several flowering maples and some live oaks, and a single great yellow pine, stood out on the point between the Rogue and its tributary, Whiskey Creek. . . . Directly across from camp roared Rum Creek, tumbling down from a timber-choked gorge. . . . Down the river a little way Booze Creek came in. The Rogue Valley had first been opened by prospectors, and prospectors still worked their claims there. They were responsible for the queer names.[11]

Zane Grey and son Romer ca. 1915. As Romer got older, Grey began taking him on wilderness and fishing excursions within the United States and later to the South Pacific.

They remained at the camp for several days, patching up boats and fishing for steelhead. Grey talked to a prospector who told him that the Forest Service was planning to cut a road through that particular area. Zane shared the prospector's concern for this fragile mountain environment, predicting that if the people of the Northwest did not act soon the Rogue would be endangered by pollution and the arrival of the automobile. "It is difficult to talk to people who are not particulary interested in the value of rivers," Grey wrote with ire. "Nevertheless rivers are as important as land, and infinitely more capable of interesting travelers, tourists, and anglers."[12]

Deep in the evergreen forest, far removed from the pressures of life, Grey eased into the lifestyle that constantly rejuvenated him and allowed him the energy to maintain a hectic writing schedule: "At this camp I experienced a familiar and welcome sensation— the sloughing off of the scales of civilized life, the press of many people, the raucous sounds and vile smells of the city, and the cease- less movement and hurry, the dust and heat, the ever-present rush and honk of automobiles." It took only a few days in nature's realm for his sanity to return. "Dusk fell here sweetly," he wrote, "to the murmur of the river, the babble of the brook, the breaking of the sunset. . . . Something banal oozed out of me, as it were, and I began to feel the encroachment of the strange joys of the wilderness."[13]

After the boats were ready, they broke camp and returned to the river. Romer was feeling particularly confident about taking a series of dangerous rapids, but Grey warned against it. Romer had a burst of anger, muttering he could take the chutes with one hand tied behind him. Takahashi, alone with Romer in one of the boats, de- cided to abandon ship when Grey finally gave in to his son's wishes. "The glow in his face," remarked Grey, "the fire in his eye, the elo- quence of his voice—all so poignantly significant of my own youth —operated against my better judgment." Grey watched from the shore, frozen in fear, as Romer shoved off into the rapids. At first his boat bobbed and spun in the current, then it careened into an exposed rock, sending it helplessly into the air. The boat slammed into the water, but Romer held tightly to the oars. Regaining his wits, Romer righted the boat and took the remaining chutes deftly and confidently. Grey was relieved and impressed, recalling his own boat handling skills on the Santa Rosa River in Mexico more than a decade before.[14]

Grey remarked about the incident:

> Then I felt the need of sitting down suddenly. My frozen feelings thawed out with a vengeance. Presently I was confronted with the realization that a man suffers more poignant fears for his children than himself. Later, when I went to join the others below the rapids I heard Romer declare: "Aw, it'd been apple pie if Bardon [the guide] hadn't yelled. I was going down the side of that rock, and he yelled for me to take the other side."[15]

After many days of rowing and challenging the rapids, they made their way to the Oregon coast. While Zane liked the grit of the journey, Romer quickly tired of the scenery, the exertion, and the drudgery of rowing. Zane recognized that for all Romer's manly war chants, he was still very much a youth. Zane, however, rowed and enjoyed the rugged scenery of the Rogue:

> All around the mountain slopes rose precipitously, so that I received an impression of being surrounded by great green and gray slopes, insurmountable, rising to obliterate half the blue sky. . . . It was good to see such standing virgin timber, untouched by the arch-fiend fire and the destructive, greedy hand of man.
> The Rogue flowed round in a perfect horsehoe bend, and the ridge of land and rock that held the center of this wilderness stage was dwarfed by the lofty peaks above. Yet, in itself it had the dignity of a low mountain. The steep rocky slopes were smooth and amber with heavy moss . . . [and] on top a cluster of pines occupied a level stand. What a place for a cabin! A wanderer in the fields has two griefs—one that he cannot return to each and every one of the lonely beautiful places he has

seen; and secondly; the realization that there are countless numbers of rare wild spots that he will never see. I do not know which is the more poignant.[16]

Downriver, Grey and his party encountered Winkle Bar, the spot where he would later have his cabin. While Captain Mitchell and others fished for steelhead, Grey left the group, tramped a little ways downstream, and discovered the broad curve of the Rogue:

> The river widened to the open valley and spread over a large gravel bar down which it raced in glistening smooth incline to break into white water. . . . I descended from my lofty perch and clambered over the boulder down to the sand. And then, up and down Winkle Bar, I fished all of one of the briefest and happiest days I ever had. I cast and rested and watched the river and the mountains, and listened to the murmur of running water. Then I cast again. Where the hours sped I never knew. Not a sign of a strike or sign of fish did I have! But that did not matter. There was something in the lonely solitude of the great hills, something in the comradeship of the river that sufficed for me.[17]

Several times along the river they interrupted their descent of the rapids to climb the nearby mountains and sightsee in the dense forests. Grey inevitably returned to the arduous rowing:

> Days passed swiftly, glidingly on, like the river. Every morning the mountain slopes across the river from camp flaunted more autumn colors. Every afternoon, when toward evening the breeze came up from the sea and blew for a little while, the yellow leaves of the alders went sailing, fluttering, rustling down to alight on the river and float away. Every night the air grew colder, and every dawn the silver fog hung lower and longer over the peaks.[18]

As the end of their journey to the sea neared, Romer paid his father a supreme compliment: "Dad, I've always noticed how you get a second wind—or spirit—or something—and keep on going at the last when everybody else has quit or is half dead." Romer was referring to Grey's rowing ability, but he could have been talking about any aspect of his father's life.

Hearing such a comment from his first-born son rendered Grey temporarily speechless. When he regained his composure, Grey said to Romer: "So it is in life, my boy. On fishing and hunting trips, on exploring adventures, in baseball and tennis, in your school studies. It will be so in your chosen career. Anyone can start well. You can start with enthusiasm and joy and ambition. But it is the finish that counts. All else is in vain if you do not finish. The great thing is to know that."[19]

Presently, after shooting the rapids and covering thirty miles in nine hours, Grey and his weary party heard "the low distant pounding of surf. Over the bare windswept hills lay the sea. We had indeed trailed the wild Rogue, shot and lined its rapids, rowed its canyon-walled lanes, and glided down its innumerable riffles to its home in the Pacific."[20]

Even as Grey ended his adventure, he continued his plea to save the Rogue River from further environmental damage. He was one of the first writers to popularize the phrase "vanishing America," and warned that the Rogue was particularly vulnerable. "This Rogue River," he remarked, "was named by the French, *Rouge*, because of the red color which it takes on at seasons when the mining is at its height. I expected to find the Rogue . . . the wildest, purest, and most beautiful of rivers. It was certainly one of the most beautiful, but the other attributes failed. . . . There were wild stretches of the river, to be sure; but just when you imagined you were drifting into an untrodden wilderness then your dream would be dispelled." Grey further argued that his concern went beyond the simple musings of "a few sentimental fishermen." Knowing that he had a formidable platform, Grey tried to rally sportsmen to his cause. "Our country is still young," he continued; "its boundless resources are not yet gutted; thousands and millions of men exploit what is not really theirs for their own selfish ends. Coal, oil, timber, and minerals . . .

are all natural products of our vast outdoors. I do not advocate that they should belong to the government, but the government should see to it that the men dealing with these resources should not gut them and not spoil the beauty and health-giving properties of the forests and rivers."[21]

In the 1920s Grey began to realize the power of his name regarding environmental issues. Within a decade, he would become one of the most potent voices in America attempting to protect those disappearing wild places he cherished so much.

From the time they tasted the last morsel of steelhead and doused their Oregon campfires, Zane Grey and Captain Mitchell were planning their next adventure. Zane wished to return to the South Pacific, this time venturing even farther to New Zealand and Tahiti. Mitchell would accompany him. Dolly wished to keep Romer cemented to his schoolwork, nearly demanding he remain at Altadena. R.C. was not available for an extended trip.

Grey was always an active student of angling, despite his strenuous schedule. He read voraciously on the subject, hoping to discover some unspoiled fishing ground or a new invention in tackle. He particularly favored British journals for such information. Since 1900 he had read of the verdant countryside and superior fishing of New Zealand. It was only a matter of time until he would experience the country firsthand.

In 1925 the government of New Zealand offered the famed American writer and angler the opportunity to come "down under" for an extended fishing vacation. Grey enthusiastically accepted. On December 30, 1925, he and Captain Laurie Mitchell sailed out of San Francisco on the Royal Mail Packet S.S. *Makura,* bound for Tahiti and Wellington, New Zealand.

As California faded from view, Grey wistfully remarked: "Every fishing trip is a composite of all other trips; and it holds irresistible promise for the future. The cup cannot be drained. . . . There is always the lure of greater task and achievement, always the inspiration to seek, to endure, to find, always the beauty of the lonely stream and the open sea, always the glory and dream of nature."[22] The next day they encountered "a heavy ridged sea, cold and dark, with sullen whitecaps breaking." According to Grey the *Makura* was "no leviathan, but she certainly was a greyhound of the sea." They made steady progress, heading southwest into open waters. "An old familiar dread of the ocean mounted in me again," he noted. "What a mighty force! It was a cold, wintry, almost invisible sea, not conducive to the thrill and joy of the angler. . . . I leaned over the rail in the darkness, trying to understand its meaning, its mood, trying to be true to the love I bore it in tranquil moments."[23]

On New Year's Eve, 1925, the *Makura* entered rough seas a hundred miles off the California coast, Grey observing that "there was nothing to inspire love, with everything to confound the soul of man. What was the old year to the sea, or the new year soon to dawn with its imagined promise. . . ? Nevertheless, the thought that overbalanced this depression was of the magic isles of the South Seas, set like mosaics in the eternal summer blue."[24]

During these long voyages, Grey worked on his novel manuscripts, sometimes completing the majority of a five-hundred-page manuscript on the outbound leg. Working in pencil, Grey wrote in his stateroom or out on deck. He never really trusted the modern typewriter to get the words right on the page; he also never found the time to learn how to operate one. The pencil flowed in tandem with his fleeting thoughts. To a great degree Grey was running from contemporary life, its conveniences, its moral outrages, its new technologies that instead of making people happier and healthier were actually making them lazier and duller. Because of his strong belief in the traditional, even the primitive, he preferred the simplest of methods to communicate the ideas and impressions that crowded his head.

Days later they crossed the equator and entered the waters of the South Pacific. On January 8, 1926, Grey sighted his first atoll, noting with some pleasure that he saw "with naked eyes what most passengers were using marine glasses to disinguish." Atolls fascinated Zane, reminding him of the Florida Keys. "The great beauty of an atoll cannot be seen from afar," Grey observed. "The ring of coral sand rising just above the sea, the ring of cocoanuts round it, the ring of the turquoise-blue water inside, the ever-famed lagoon . . . with its sands of gold and pearl, its myriads of colored fish, the tremendous thundering of the surf outside—these wonderful features could not be appreciated from the ship."[25]

Upon arrival in Papeete, Tahiti, Grey was not only disappointed but devastated. The land that symbolized the adventurous lives of Melville, Stevenson, and Gauguin was in fact a sordid heap of wasted lives and broken dreams. In town, goods were overpriced and the saloons were crowded with loud, drunken expatriates. Moreover, legions of panhandling beachcombers swarmed along the palm-fringed docks. "The beachcomber," he observed, "always a romantic and pathetic figure, became by actual contact somewhat disconcerting to me, and wholly disgusting." As for the Tahitian women, once celebrated by artists such as Gauguin, he claimed "that photographs do not do them justice. . . . They were strong, well-built, but not voluptuous, rather light skinned with large melting melancholy eyes." He could not resist comparing these women to the free-thinking American women back home: "No scrawny shaved bristled necks, such as the flappers exhibit now, to man's bewildered disgust; no erotic and abnormal signs of wanting to resemble a male! If they could see the backs of these Tahitian girls and their long graceful braids of hair . . . they might have a moment of illumined mind." As a footnote, he concluded: "I spent a full day in this world famous South Sea island port—and it was long enough for me."[26]

Later, Grey would come to love Tahiti and its unique fishing and culture; but in January 1926 he could not muster much affection for it.

After leaving Papeete, the *Makura* steamed six hundred miles toward Raratonga in the Cook Islands, where Grey and Mitchell went ashore and mingled with the villagers. Grey was impressed that liquor was illegal on the British island. In his mind, such a restriction contributed to the orderliness and cleanliness of Raratonga. Here at last was the Utopian vision of paradise he had seen so often advertised, and which had been so conspicuously absent in Papeete. "Absolutely," he concluded of his stay on the island, "this charm would grow on one. . . . I decided that some day I would risk coming for a month or two."

The final leg of their voyage to New Zealand brought two significant events. The first was the crossing of the International Dateline, which inspired some minor celebrations on the *Makura*. The second was Zane's sighting of an albatross that shadowed the ship on the tradewinds. Zane was mesmerized by the solitary bird, recalling the magic of Coleridge's poem "The Rime of the Ancient Mariner." "I had watched condors, eagles, vultures, falcons, hawks, kites, frigate birds, erns, boobies, all the great performers of the air," Grey remarked, "but I doubted that I had ever seen the equal of the albatross. . . . What sailing! What a swoop! What splendid poise and ease, and then incredible speed. . . . The albatross had always haunted me, inspired me, filled me with awe, reverence." He thought it a good omen for his arrival in New Zealand, which occurred shortly thereafter.

Disembarking in Wellington, Grey and Laurie Mitchell headed immediately by train north to Auckland, and then to the remote fishing village of Russell. The beauty, diversity, and friendliness of the people of New Zealand overwhelmed Grey. Villagers, however, were somewhat disappointed that the renowned frontier writer did not arrive in chaps, spurs, and a sombrero. Some even thought that the writer of romances was a woman, a notion that made Grey tremble in his boots.[27]

After shrugging off these popular misconceptions, Grey

immersed himself in traveling and fishing. Like the American West, New Zealand offered a wild and varied landscape. But while Utah and Arizona were fading over Grey's shoulder, the South Pacific was becoming sharper in his focus. Grey and Mitchell began their adventure with saltwater fishing, setting up camp on remote Orupu-kupuku Island, just off the coast of the mainland. Surrounded by beautiful "ty" trees and serenaded by a host of cackling birds—which caused Grey to dub it "The Camp of the Larks"—he often watched the reef before him. Great racks of clouds banded the sky, sailing in a uniform motion that seemed to drag the whole universe with them. Beneath them the sea, wrinkled with white caps, rolled to the horizon. "It was all so beautiful," Zane observed, "and its striking feature was the difference from any other place I had ever seen. Seven thousand miles from California! . . . The very strangeness eluded me. The low sound of surf had a different note. The sun set in the wrong direction for me, because I could not grasp the points of the compass. Nevertheless, I was not slow to appreciate the beauty of the silver-edged clouds and the glory of the golden blaze behind the purple ranges."[28]

Grey and Mitchell wasted no time setting world angling records in their exciting new venue. Captain Mitchell boasted of landing a 976-pound marlin, which was so huge that it had to be cut in three pieces to be weighed. When Mitchell had it hauled up, Grey viewed Cappy's achievement with fierce envy:

> It was considerably larger than Captain Mitchell's 685-pound swordfish, but of a different shape and color; and not anything like the other for symmetry and beauty. In fact, this one hardly seemed beautfiul at all. It was almost round, very fat and full clear down to the tail, and solid as a rock. Faint dark stripes showed through the dark opal hue. The bill was short, and as thick as a spade handle at the point. . . . The length was twelve feet, eight inches; the girth six feet, two inches; the spread of the tail four feet. . . . What an unbelievable monster of the deep! What a fish! I, who have loved fish from earliest boyhood, hung around that Marlin absorbed, obsessed, entranced and

sick with the deferred possiblity of catching one like it myself. How silly such hope. Could I ever expect such marvelous luck? Yet I knew as I gazed upon it that I would keep on trying as long as strength enough was left in me. . . . Oh, the madness of a fisherman![29]

Perhaps inspired by Cappy's luck, Grey landed the first broadbill swordfish caught on a rod and reel in New Zealand. Then came his encounter with a black marlin, the same type of fish with which Mitchell had set a world record.

Grey's entourage consisted of Captain Mitchell, Peter Williams (his New Zealand boatman), Cyril Morton (the photographer of the expedition), Frank Arlidge (who manned the wheel), Leon Warne and Bill Hodgson (who helped Grey look for fish). They soon headed to the North Cape in their launches. Using a 39-thread line, Grey searched the sea for black marlin. Off Bird Rock Grey sighted motion in the water and moved the boat into position. After losing a swordfish that skittered off his line, Grey snagged his huge marlin, which proceeded for the next several hours to drag the boat and its occupants several miles into the open sea. True to his nature, Grey held on. "No child ever desired anything more than I that beautiful black Marlin," he remarked. "It was an obsession. I wanted him, yet I gloried in his size, his power."[30]

For more than three hours Grey grappled with the marlin, which he thought was as monstrous as Cappy's catch earlier. With leaden arms and aching fingers, Grey bobbed back and forth over the gunwhale. "Inch by inch!" Grey wrote. "That old familiar amaze at myself and disgust at such Herculean drudgery took possession of my mind. What emotions were possible that I had not already felt?" As some comic relief, his pilot Peter Williams, stood over his shoulder and muttered: "Well, Mr Grey, you've got a fish here that'll take some landing."

With the eyes of the crew riveted upon him, Grey felt he had "been nailed to his martyrdom." Within the hour he managed to work the Marlin to the surface, then collapsed, exhausted, in his harness. "Never shall I forget the bulk of him," Grey glowed. "the wonderful color, the grand lines. We had to tow him in."[31] Grey immediately wrote Dolly, telling her that he "never had such a whipping by a fish."[32]

Grey's and Mitchell's angling achievements in New Zealand coastal waters were spectacular. According to his personal log, Zane managed to catch over seventeen mako, five yellowtail, one black marlin, and forty-one striped marlin, the latter ranging in size between 168 pounds and 450 pounds. Mitchell's 976-pound black marlin remained a world record for a significant time. Additionally, Cappy landed six mako, three yellowtail, two hammerhead sharks, and twenty-one striped marlin. Both Grey and Mitchell used 36- and 39-thread line with a great deal of success.

After Grey and his party concluded their angling off the North Cape and the nearby islands in the early spring of 1926, Grey and Cappy returned to Auckland to travel into the interior of the North Island. After three months in the searing tropic sun, Grey's face and arms were the color of varnished spars. The always dapper Captain Mitchell was similarly tanned. Grey got a haircut and donned a white shirt, tie, jacket, tweed knickers, and a pair of two-toned Oxford shoes. As a guest of the government of New Zealand, he was reluctant to be anything but a gracious, curious, and famous American tourist.

Sometimes accompanied by a government official, they toured the Waitomo limestone caves on the road to Rotorua, whose cavernous interior Grey compared to Mammoth Cave in Kentucky. But this New Zealand version, with thousands of glowworms hanging from ledges, he claimed was "vastly different, unique, and strangely beautiful in the extreme."[33] Also on their itinerary were Fairy Spring, the Blow Hole, Lake Taupo, and the nearby Waihoro River.

When they got to the river, Grey and Mitchell began preparing their flies for fishing. Zane moved upstream, and the Captain probed some bushes for a good angling spot. On his way Grey encountered a belligerent, long-snouted wild boar. His surprise quickly turned into amusement, as he gently confronted the grunting boar: "Excuse me, Mr. Wild Boar. I have not the slightest intention of disputing your right to this trail." The boar turned downstream and padded into the bushes in the direction of Captain Mitchell. Grey heard Cappy let out a wild yell. Grey hollered back: "Look out, Cap! It's a rhinoceros!"

Grey then observed: "Splashings and crashings acquainted me with the manifest desire of both the Captain and the boar to put distance between them." Grey turned back to camp. Mitchell arrived shortly thereafter, "wetter, dirtier, and angrier" than his companion. "By gad!" exclaimed Cappy. "The ugly beast charged me!" Grey dryly responded: "He made a lot noise getting away from you."[34]

From that time on Zane frequently kidded Mitchell about his way with animals.

That night as he slept in his cot, Grey was awakened by a sinister thundering that seemed to emanate from far out over Western Bay:

> The first part of that sound might have been a waterfall, but the latter was not. Muttering, rumbling, subterranean volcano! I imagined I felt the ground quiver. Voice of the volcano! There was no doubt about it; and the realization was one of great import to me. To read of the quaking of the earth, and to have some one tell of the growl of cataclysmic portent of an eruption were enough to stir excitement and dread; but to feel that the solid ground was unstable as water and to have my ears filled with the terrible rumble were things vastly more agitating. In the silence and blackness of the night the volcano roar seemed unearthly. Indeed it came from under the earth, like storm winds rushing through a vast empty hall! I heard it at intervals for what seemed hours and it worked upon my imagination and emotion as no other single phenomenon of nature ever had.[35]

Although Grey never understood the origin of the rumblings, his surmise that it was a subterranean volcano was probably correct.

In some of his more contemplative moments, Zane relaxed and

absorbed the fascinating animal and plant life of interior New Zealand. Among the many birds that descended on their camp at the Waihoro River were kingfishers, yellow blighties, fantails, and the unique tui, whose distinctive song Grey called "one the sweetest and loveliest of all bird melodies." In the morning shade by the riverbank Grey discovered an often dazzling variety of plant life. Tiny blue forget-me-nots were tucked into lichen-covered ledges, their white and gold centers "too lovely to be forgotten." Farther up the bank was a bewildering array of plants, vines, ferns, moss, and brush, "with color blending like a mosaic inlaid into a cliff wall." Overhanging ti and kowhai trees, now green, would sag under the weight of brilliant red blossoms in December.

Fascinated by Maori culture, Grey hired a six-foot-four native guide named Hoka Down, whose "big heart shone in his ever-ready smile." Hoka Down became one of eleven people (the others included members of Grey's sailing crew) to whom Grey's *Tales of the Angler's El Dorado* was dedicated. The Maori guide led Grey and Mitchell into the wilderness of ferns and ti trees, stopping at a distant, inland pool that interrupted the flow of the famed Tongariro River. This pool—called the Dreadnought Pool because the overhanging bluffs resembled a battleship—was a fisherman's bonanza. The Tongariro, a New Zealand equivalent of Oregon's Rogue River, tumbled out of the mountainous interior and churned through the rocky shallows, much like its American cousin. However, as Grey explained, the Tongariro and the Rogue had significant differences:

> The Rogue, most wonderful of American trout streams, is deep swift cold canyon-walled and rock-rapided, hurrying down to the sea, with but few shallows and bars. The Tongariro appeared to have about the same volume of water, pale blue-green in color and exquisitely clear, too clear for fishing, and though a swift river, still it was not wild in its hurry to escape the confines of its banks. . . . Perhaps the most striking feature of the Tongariro in this section, six to ten miles above the delta, was the number and character of the islands. They were really gravel

bars, under water when the river was in flood, and at low water picturesque green and gray islands around which the channels and rifts ran. . . . The channel that curved westward under our bank was narrow, shallow, and boisterous. The middle channel took most of the river volume, and it roared down, deep and fast. The other channel ran glancing and smooth away to the southward, and dropped out of sight.[36]

The Dreadnought Pool fascinated Grey. "Points of rocks and bars of boulders jutted out from a luxuriantly foliaged island," he noted. "A low bare gravel bar rose to the left, and stretched to where the third channel roared and thundered in a deep curving rapid. Here most of the river rushed on, a deep narrow chute, dropping one foot in every three feet, for over a hundred yards. . . . Green crystal water! I could see the bottom as plainly as if the depth had been ten inches rather than ten feet."[37]

In their waders and khaki fishing garb, Grey and Mitchell probed the river. Grey was ecstatic over the number of huge rainbow trout he counted swimming near him. As Mitchell watched enviously, Grey pulled out at short intervals five rainbows. "The last jump was splendid," Grey bragged, "with a high parabolic curve, and a slick cutting back into the water. This rainbow, too, was big, fast, strong and fierce. . . . I did everything right. Fisherman's luck!" If Grey was shaking with joy, Cappy was glum. On this afternoon, he came up empty-handed. As they carried their bounty back to camp, Grey heard the murmur of the river. "Tongariro!" he remarked. "What a strange beautiful high-sounding name! It suited the noble river and the mountain from which it sprang."[38]

During his stay in New Zealand, Grey was frequently reminded of his international fame. On one occasion, he received a singular honor from the Maoris, superior anglers who had enormous respect for Grey's fishing abilities. In a ceremony near Rotorua, they bestowed on him the name Maui, the legendary great fisherman of the Maoris. Typically, Grey was embarrassed in such situations, but in this case he declared: "Following my surprise came a feeling of genuine pleasure and appreciation. I bowed my acknowledgment to the speaker, and mentally vowed that I must learn the Maori legend of Maui." The ceremony was followed by songs and dances, which impressed Grey deeply. "The Maori love songs," he remarked, "were wild and sad and wonderfully melodious; and when the girls repeated the chorus in English the effect was enhanced. I left there with my mind haunted by those rhythmic chords, and for me to remember a melody is extraordinary."[39]

In another instance near Cape Brett, Grey's boat encountered a fishing sloop named *Desert Gold,* whose owner assured him that he had christened his boat in Grey's honor. "I was touched, proud, tremendously pleased," wrote Grey. "I had met with innumerable instances of kindly recognition from my reading public in the Antipodes, but to discover an old sailboat, under the beetling brow of Cape Brett, named with one of my book titles, was something singularly affecting to me."[40]

If Grey was a lover of New Zealand landscape and culture, he was openly critical of the primitive techniques of the resident fishermen. During his sojourn he wrote several articles for the *Auckland Tribune* in which he addressed these concerns. Among other things Grey protested the use of the gang, or treble hook, which he considered inhumane and unsportsmanlike. Secondly, he asserted that the New Zealanders' tackle was ineffective and outdated.

Grey favored the single hook, considering the gang hook an aberration to the sport: "I have fished with live bait for many years . . . and always with a single hook, always hooked through the lips of the live bait. The reasons for this are too numerous to mention here. This is not merely my idea, but the practice of the best live bait fishermen in the world. Perhaps I should add that the Japanese are the greatest of all fishermen. Well, they hook their live bait on a single hook."

As for tackle, Grey criticized the New Zealanders' method of securing their reels and guides underneath the rod: "I could not

Grey with a prized yellowtail in New Zealand in 1926. The South Pacific offered Zane a new El Dorado to explore.

understand it," he wrote. "I never understood it until I saw these rods used here at Cape Brett. . . . It is impossible to fight a great game fish with reel and guides underneath the rod. I mean *stop* him and *fight* him. In order to do that an angler must have a short, strong rod, one that will bend and spring back, a heavy reel with adequate drag, and powerful line. Reel and guides must be on top, because if they are not the angler cannot brace his feet on the boat and pull with all his might."[41]

Summarizing his argument, Grey made a final plea: "As for the tackle used here by New Zealand and English anglers, it is hopelessly inadequate, and unsportsmanlike in the extreme. The triple hook is an abomination. . . . It behooves the sportsmen here to adopt the finest and fairest methods of angling; and it behooves the government to stop the dynamiting of schooling fish."[42]

Zane received several scathing letters from anglers. Surprised by the extent of the controversy he had started, he canceled the remainder of the articles he was prepared to write and instead spent numerous hours discussing the issue with fishermen on the beaches. As the debate waned and just before his departure for America, Grey returned to being the gracious, friendly tourist.

On April 27, 1926, he and Laurie Mitchell boarded the S.S. *Tahiti* and sailed for home. "Beautiful New Zealand," he remarked as he was leaving. "Faraway Island! Fernland! Land of Long Afternoons! How could I give it the most deserving name?"

After returning to Los Angeles, Grey headed over the channel to Avalon to fish and revise the notes of his New Zealand adventure. That summer, despite his protests, Dolly took her second trip to Europe. From his writing desk at Avalon he could see the watery blue Pacific and the wafers of sun rising through the mist. He was trying to complete four novels a year, plus assorted articles and short stories. The fear that there would not be enough money always stalked Grey, so after returning from New Zealand his work load increased.

Below him in Avalon harbor the *Fisherman* was moored alongside several movie stars' yachts, rivaling their polish and beauty. Also nearby was the *Gladiator*, Zane's fifty-two-foot round-bottom cruiser that he used for swordfishing around Catalina Island and San Clemente Island. Both ships' mastheads carried his personal pennants bearing the initials "Z.G." On the *Gladiator* he rigged a makeshift desk and wicker chair for working on manuscripts such as *The Drift Fence* or *The Shepherd of Guadaloupe*. Wearing a pith helmet in the shadow of a canvas awning, Zane could write for three or four hours before returning to fishing.

Throughout 1926, as Grey worked on various writing projects at Avalon and Altadena, he felt the lure of the South Pacific. He returned to Tahiti and New Zealand in 1927. Realizing that Tahiti would make an excellent sport fishing base, he purchased eight acres of land on the southern cape near Vairao Bay, which became known as the Flower Point fishing camp. Grey and his entourages used the spot throughout the late 1920s and early 1930s. Situated on a palm-studded bluff overlooking the ocean, the camp consisted of several huts and storage sheds for gear and tackle. The camp was outfitted with a shortwave radio and enough supplies to endure a prolonged storm. Additionally, it afforded a safe harbor for the *Fisherman*. When Grey was not in Tahiti, Captain Mitchell administered the camp, making the necessary repairs and preparing for the next fishing excursion. "Captain Mitchell," wrote Grey of his camp, "had cleared off a bluff, except for the large palms, breadfruit, and other trees, and had put up a number of bungalows . . . including a bamboo-and-palm dining house and kitchen. A little stream ran merrily down out of the jungle. . . . The view from my cabin porch was something I was in no hurry to describe."

Below the camp "Vairao Bay reached from the mountains in the east twenty miles across to a lovely point that ran out of the southwest, and all this vast expanse of water was a heaving amber and rose. . . . The green slopes shone exceedingly rich and vivid. Across the bay the huge peaks of Tahiti were lost in cumulus cloud, and the canyons yawning between were choked with deep, dark purple."[43] After exhausting his descriptive words, he admitted that he would "require time to appreciate the splendor of Vairao."

Tahiti soon mesmerized Grey, seducing him with the silence of its lush mountainsides and with the riot of its color and light.

> We walked inland some distance, and up and down the shady lanes. Flowers, foliage, color, perfume, and langorous warmth everywhere, and always in the background golden-skinned, dark-haired Tahitian maidens. The magnolia blossoms fallen from trees covered the grass—large white and yellow flowers, with most exquisite fragrance; bouganvillea flamed its wonderful cerise from the shady green background; great trees, magnificent clumps of bamboo, always the whispering, rustling, moving, graceful, drooping palms. . . . An empire of sun! In the shade it was always cool, always pleasant, always still, dreamy, strange. I began to absorb Tahiti.[44]

Eventually in Tahiti, Zane Grey met Charles Nordhoff and James Norman Hall, the writing team who collaborated on the international best seller, *Mutiny of the Bounty*. Nordhoff and Hall were former American pilots in World War I who fled to Tahiti to escape the terror and destruction of modern warfare. They settled there in the 1920s, beginning a successful partnership that produced several significant works (including *Men Against the Sea* and *Pitcairn's Island*) and lasted for many years. Grey, in particular, was friends with fellow angler Charles Nordhoff. In fact, Zane gave Nordhoff most of the credit for his remaining in Tahiti between 1928 and 1933. A highly respected swordfisherman, Nordhoff personally showed Grey the best fishing waters around Tahiti, even drawing an annotated map for him that revealed the most secretive coves, reefs, and inlets. "Nordhoff welcomed the advent of anglers experienced in pioneering new waters," Grey remarked, "and showed tremendous interest in our tackle."

The more Grey explored Tahiti, the more he was enchanted by it. He discovered much more than abundant fishing, snow-white beaches, and rustling palm trees. He found one of the routes he was seeking to the primitive past. He had caught glimpses of it in places such as Death Valley, Keet Seel, Monument Valley, and the Grand Canyon, but in Tahiti he was reunited with something far older and more elemental: the sea, the great mother, the great womb. In his mind he knew that all life had sprung from the moist and fertile matrix of the sea. Over the years the sea had woven itself into his life so that it was as important as the desert. He attempted a great novel of Tahiti, *The Reef Girl* (discussed later in this chapter), which brought together the themes of natural purity and civilized barbarism.

For various reasons, the South Pacific never again stimulated Grey as a novelist, but it was fertile ground to inspire his exciting personal narrative *Tales of Tahitian Waters*.

The year 1928—a pivotal one for Zane Grey—had a significant impact on his adventuresome life. Herbert Hoover, a self-confessed Grey fan, became president of the United States. The author was elated. Always envious of Owen Wister's relationship with Theodore Roosevelt, Grey wanted similar acknowledgment from a head of state. With Hoover he got it, though not to the degree that he might have wished. Hoover—who would later lend his name to the Boulder Canyon Project—was raised a Westerner in Oklahoma and Oregon. He supported Western issues and loved Western literature, particularly the novels and fishing stories of Zane Grey. Hoover would also accompany America into its worst economic depression ever, a development that would curtail Grey's numerous wanderings and impact his soaring income.

Romer Grey, left, and Zane ca. 1930, poring over maps of Tahiti and South Pacific reefs. By the time he was twenty years of age, Romer was Zane's constant companion on his travels throughout the world.

In the spring of 1928, Zane and Dolly were clashing again. He arrived in Tahiti from San Francisco, bringing with him equipment and tackle to stock his camp at Flower Point. The *Fisherman* carried "a load of lumber, fuel, water, food supplies, eight portable bungalows, several launches . . . and an assortment of tackle that

beggared description." It was a season of promise that ended disas-
trously. In October it rained constantly in paradise. "Drops of water,"
Grey complained in a letter to Dolly, "have begun to wear on the
stone."[45] His crew on the *Fisherman* were breaking into cliques and
squabbling amongst themselves. Some were even pilfering his equipment and selling it on the black market. Moreover, they had begun
to doubt Grey's management abilities. For the first time in four years,
he was ready to unload his ship to the highest bidder. Additionally,
he told Dolly that he had suffered through two months of "wholly
profitless fishing." Nineteen-year-old Romer accompanied him and
was desperately lovesick. A flapper woman back in California had
rejected him ("a gold digging slut," according to Zane) and he was
simply unbearable around camp.[46]

Also upsetting Grey's life in Tahiti was his personal secretary,
Mildred Smith, who accompanied him to Papeete. For many years
Dolly had been concerned about Mildred's influence on Zane's life
and work. Grey would not admit until much later that his relationship with Mildred went beyond business. Dolly in particular was
upset about the manuscript she received for Grey's story "Amber's
Mirage,"which to her clearly showed Mildred's comments and notations in the margin. She accused Zane of rewriting the manuscript to Mildred's instructions. Zane responded by emphasizing
that "if there were pencil marks on "Amber's Mirage" [he] never
saw them." He went on to admit that he "took M's advice about a
little of the rewriting" and that it helped him "to get her point of
view."[47]

Grey actually collaborated with Smith on several unsuccessful
plays, including *Port of Call* and *Three Tight Lines*. Dolly knew of
their partnership, but was not above reminding Zane that his first
duty was to her. Even though Zane told her otherwise, she suspected
a romance between them. Characteristically, she let go of trying to
manipulate Zane's and Mildred's relationship, which ultimately
crumbled on the Tahiti reefs a few years later.

A bright spot in Grey's year was the publication of *Nevada,* one of his all-time best-selling books. Along with the successes of *Tales of Fresh-Water Fishing, Don: The Story of a Lion Dog,* and *Wild Horse Mesa,* sales of *Nevada* helped boost Grey's career, prompting Dolly to call him "the biggest seller in the world."[48]

Financially, Grey was doing splendidly at the close of 1928, raking in close to $400,000 annually. On the horizon, however, was the crucial year of 1929 and a sinister day—Black Friday—when life for Zane Grey would change forever.

As America slipped into economic decline, Grey returned to the Flower Point fishing camp on Tahiti in 1929 and again in 1930. Although the Depression was worsening Grey seemed unaffected by it. He sold the *Fisherman,* "his beautiful white ship with sails like wings," to a wealthy planter in Tahiti. Later, he regretted it, when he felt too far away from the pitch and roll of the sea. To replace his first ship he bought the *Kallisto,* a world-class yacht, and promptly christened her *Fisherman II.* His second ship proved to be an enormous financial drain on Grey's resources. For one thing, *Fisherman II* cost Grey an initial $40,000, plus an additional $300,000 in renovations. Furthermore, it took $5,000 a month to operate the vessel, which quickly worried Grey and forced him to write hastier work to pay for it.

While in Tahiti, Grey explored his new El Dorado. On his third visit to his Flower Point camp, he admitted that he was "quite beside himself with ecstasy. . . . To walk and up down the narrow sandpaths, under an arch of pawpaw and coleus, and to gaze out . . . at the deep dark blue of the sea, was to realize the magic of the tropics." "Tahiti," Grey bluntly concluded, "was the loveliest land I ever saw."[49] In between angling episodes he worked on the journals that eventually became *Tales of Tahitian Waters* (1931), his sixth collection of narrative fishing essays. Notable for their vigorous sketches of Tahitian fishing and the swift pacing of the prose, these tales are among Grey's best efforts. Before arriving in Tahiti, Grey had heard huge fish stories of toothless sharks that sucked the flesh from their victims; tales of forty-pound bonefish; and mammoth yarns of swordfish over thirty feet long. He came and found an undiscovered fishing paradise, quickly landing record-size swordfish and marlin, one weighing 1,200 pounds. Grey never found his phantom bonefish, but he did help create an enduring folklore for Tahitian fishing. *Tales of Tahitian Waters* is both a record of pioneer anglers in the South Pacific and one man's passion for the sea. It remains a thrilling narrative describing one of the world's great habitats for fish and mammals.

Grey found the Tahitian climate uncomfortable and even annoying. "Weather and climate are perfect according to the white men who live in Tahiti . . . [and] for the person who does not exert himself mentally or physically the climate of Tahiti is about as near to Paradise as humans ever find on earth. But it is too hot and too moist . . . for prolonged writing." He even confessed that Tahiti exacerbated his depressions. "Without any reason at all," he wrote, "I find myself going down clear to China. At night I will go to bed in a fine mood, and have the most horrible dreams, or wake up with a leaden weight upon my chest, and an exceedingly dejected, hopeless mood."[50]

The continuous rain of Tahiti gradually wore on Zane, but he could be inspired by its intensity. Storms over the Flower Point fishing camp always seemed striking and riveting for him. Over the spacious inlet, where the sky warred with the sea, he could frequently witness nature's fury.

> At night the continuous roaring seemed the most violent of wind storms. It drowned the lesser contention on the fringing reef beneath the promontory on which my cottage stood precariously. Almost, my bed appeared to hang over the sea. . . . There was no remembered sound to which I could compare this unearthly, solid, thumping thunder of waters thrown with all

the majesty and might of the Pacific upon the coral reefs. . . . Rain? No Californian or Ohioan ever saw it rain! You must come to Tahiti to see a glorious downpour—or to see a hundred waterfalls sliding off the great steep slopes at once—to see the brooks come roaring down out of the canyons, to see the dark swamps, with their huge gnarled and serrated *mape* trees, and the tree-ferns and the clinging vines, dripping a flood down upon the elephant ears, the broad lily pads, the moss.[51]

When rain drenched the coast for days, Grey remained in his Flower Point bungalow and wrote steadily. Nibbling at food, he pushed on through a manuscript. He became accustomed to the interruptions of anglers and boatmen as they ambled through his cottage. R.C. might distract him with a tall fishing story from the previous day. Captain Mitchell might report that he was headed to Papeete in one of the launches to replenish some supplies. For the most part, Grey's concentration on his material drowned out most disturbances.

One evening, as he finished writing, he peered up from his desk overlooking the bay and gazed upon "a high-arched rainbow—the loveliest phenomenon of nature, and here in tropic Tahiti so rare, so pure, so vivid, that the beauty of it made [his] heart ache."[52] The arc of the rainbow stretched from the verdant canyons behind the camp to a point far distant on the sea. He walked outside and stood in the rain. The sea moaned below him. Lightning flashed through the dark trade-wind clouds scudding on the horizon. When the rain stopped and the clouds departed, Zane saw an evening star appear, a star so brilliant and pure that he likened it to the one over Bethlehem. Moved to deep emotion, he noted: "Ruskin wrote that men of any serious turn of mind had a natural love for fair scenery, and those men who loved nature most had most belief in God. It is something to think of these swift, ruthless, modern days, whether one is fishing, or watching the skies, or toiling at his humdrum daily task."[53]

The Flower Point camp in Tahiti became a second home to Grey.

There he found an inspiring place to write, chat about the doings of the day with his crew, and plan for the next adventure on the sea. He also had time to reflect on the other inhabitants of the cottages:

> Tahiti ordinarily appeared to be a very healthy place, outside of Papeete. Flies did not bother us; mosquitoes not enough to be concerned about; fleas were bad, and a nuisance. They came on the rats and their bites were something to conjure with. Household ammonia relieved me, but did R.C. no good whatever. He used poison-oak remedy. Ants were plentiful, and occasionally would bite. Half a dozen kinds of lizards took up their abode with us, under the pandanus roofs of our cottages. At first they annoyed me, but I soon got to like them, and knew several. Early in the evening they came out to catch insects. I wished I could catch swordfish like these lizards catch bugs. A rather large, fat, gray lizard emitted a very queer sound. I heard it often before I connected it with a lizard. The noise resembled somewhat the grating squeal of a rat. In fact, I thought it was made by the rats. But one evening I satisfied myself that the lizard accounted for it.[54]

Before he relinquished the *Fisherman,* Grey and his comrades toured the surrounding islands—Rangiroa, Apataki, Morrea, and Raiatea. On the approach to Rangiroa, Grey's ship entered the dangerous shoals surrounding the island:

> Suddenly I felt a slight jar. I had felt such a thing before. We had hit bottom. In an instant I was paralyzed. We struck again, careened a little, went on, to the hoarse yells of sailors and others, and then stopped dead. The *Fisherman* keeled over and the bow began to swing to starboard. She pivoted back toward the outlet to the sea, and there she stuck. . . . Native boats put out, and then we learned that the natives had seen we were going aground and tried to warn us. The tide was running out—a most fortunate circumstance. . . . The hours that followed were crowded with noise, action, and fraught with anxiety. . . . The skipper put out kedge anchors and with them and the engine endeavored to work her off. The natives came out to help in any way they could. Flood tide came after midnight, and sometime

in the early morning I heard the ship groan and felt her budge. Little by little, inch by inch, they worked her off the reef. By three A.M. she was afloat, and soon we anchored in deep water nearer the shore. . . . I did not sleep much and was up before sunrise.[55]

Later on Raiatea they witnessed the dance of the fire-walkers, which Grey watched with some skepticism. Clad in short grass skirts and "wreaths of purple bougainvillea," the fire-walkers trod bare-foot, two by two, on a long bed of blazing stones. Then they turned and retraced their steps, shouting a wild "huzzah!" "I had expected some sort of trick," Grey admitted, "but there seemed to be none." After the ceremony, one of the interpreters suggested that Zane try it—wearing his shoes. Not one to shun a novel experience, he and the other men did, confessing that the soles of their shoes grew "uncomfortably warm." Afterwards, Grey remarked that he found "nothing supernatural in the feat of the fire-walkers, or their *feet,* either. . . . These natives have broad, heavy, thick feet, with spatu-late toes. The soles of their feet are as tough as leather. I saw na-tives run over sharp coral that would have crippled a white man."[56]

Grey's investigations of the native culture were largely geared to ending the speculations, rumors, and romantic notions of a host of uninformed writers. While he spent time in the villages watching and observing, he reserved whole days and weeks for trolling in the Tahitian bays and inlets. Constantly in pursuit of swordfish, mar-lin, bonito, and tuna, he swung his fishing launch into the most promising and bountiful waters. Once he slipped on his launch, striking his head against the cockpit, spraining his wrist, and injur-ing a few ribs. The next morning, "bandaged and lame," he battled a swordfish for several hours.

Grey insisted on the most modern equipment and tackle for his Tahitian fishing excursions, spending thousands of dollars annually to outfit his camp and ship. Although he considered his own in-ventory of equipment too extensive to enumerate, he provided his readers with a list of items used by R.C. and Captain Mitchell in Tahiti:

> Two new Z.G. Special Coxe reels, holding 600 and 1,000 yards of 39-thread line.
> Two Hardy-Alma reels.
> Two Hardy-Zane Grey reels, 500 and 1,000 yards 36 and 39 thread.
> Two heavy Kavalesky reels of 1,200 yards capacity.
> Two dozen Shafer Dualwood rods, equipped with special bronze reel-locks, and extra-heavy guides and tops.
> Three dozen assorted rods, hickory and split bamboo, of varying weights.
> Lines of the finest Swastika brand, made by Crandall, Nos. 12, 15, 18, 21, 24, 27, and 36, to the number of a dozen spools for each. Twenty spools of 600 and ten of 1,000 yard 39. For the largest reels we had a few 750-yard No. 42 thread, which we wished to try upon these exceptionally heavy fish over 1,000 pounds.
> Perhaps the most formidable and remarkable of all this assortment of tackle was the trunk of leaders. They were of all sizes, from six-foot piano-wire gig leaders, to thirty foot double airplane wire mako-shark leaders. . . . Besides this collection we had a storeroom full of all kinds of other tackle—nets, ropes, cords, leads, hooks, gaffs, toggles flares.[57]

Zane and his party used the Hardy-Alma and Hardy–Zane Grey reels extensively and successfully in the South Pacific. The Alma, produced in 1925, was the smaller of the two. Manufactured in 1928, the Hardy–Zane Grey was a heavy-duty sport fishing reel that boasted of superior performance in all weather and sea conditions. The Hardy Company of Northumberland, England, made the reel to Zane Grey's specifications, which included that it be the best big-game reel in the world.

Using a Hardy–Zane Grey reel and a Hardy cane and hickory rod, Zane landed a blue marlin off the southern cape of Tahiti. At fourteen feet in length and weighing a whopping 1,040 pounds, the marlin battled Grey for seven hours. As Grey panted and lurched in the harness, his crew fought off several sharks that had begun to feast on the quarry. After the sharks dispersed, Grey and his party headed for shore, where a hundred or so cheering natives greeted the author and his world-record catch.

Sometimes, however, the sea yielded little. Weeks could pass without anyone sighting a fin skimming the water or another mast breaking the dark line of the horizon. "Hot sun, glaring eyes, wind, rough water, rain and rain and rain," he wrote, "the seared eyeballs, the ache from the rocking boat, the pangs of sitting all day long— these after any number of unrewarded days lost their zest and charm, lost all but the terrible sameness, and could become insupportable."[58]

Often when the pressures of fishing and writing became too great, he retreated to the Flower Point camp, particularly to the hundred-foot pier jutting from the reef into the lagoon where the launches were moored. This rickety wooden pier happened to run over coral beds teeming with marine life. For hours Grey sat or reclined indolently on the pier, staring into the clear water, watching the slow metabolism of nature unfold. "Gradually," he noted, "I lost my boyish instinct to capture, first because it proved next to impossible to catch any of them, and secondly because I learned to view the reef as a natural aquarium of my own." He studied the weird and grotesque shapes of coral, "the jeweled mansions of the gorgeous fairy-like little fish, the rows of scalloped shelves . . . and the mosaic of floors, beds, nooks, nests, from which everywhere led lanes and subterranean passages, black holes, and blank spaces, down into the labyrinthine maze of the interior."[59] As a naturalist instead of a hunter, Grey patiently stared at the armadas of angelfish, darting and flashing in the watery light, starfish, turbot, and the jerky movements of an octopus. The reef became a window into a world he often overlooked, one of inexpressible fascination and intricate, unseen life.

Grey established many friendships in Tahiti. Among them was his relationship with an affluent American couple, Eastham and Carrie Guild, who kept a vacation house near Papeete, and according to Zane, had "manifested unusual signs of having gone mad over our fishing game." It also helped that the Guilds were avid readers of Grey's fishing books. Grey remarked that he "did not often take novices under [his] piscatorial wing," but in the Guilds' case decided to make an exception. Within weeks they were part of his fishing camp, which also included Laurie Mitchell, R.C. Grey, Mildred Smith, and thirteen native cooks, housekeepers, and guides, as well as a handful of visiting anglers and sportsmen.

For over a year, between late 1928 and early 1930, the Guilds kept a journal of their fishing adventures in Tahitian waters. In their journal the Guilds took playful names: Carrie became "Carrie Finn" and Eastham became "Ham-Fish." Since Grey loved nautical minutia—sea logs, journals, and diaries—he was fascinated by the Guilds' record of their exploits. Grey was so impressed with the import of the Guilds' log that he decided to incorporate it into his *Tales of Tahitian Waters.* Alas, his relationship with the spirited Guilds ended bitterly in 1931, when he also split with Laurie Mitchell and began to grow disenchanted with Tahiti.

Tales of Tahitian Waters was published rather quickly after its writing, but the same cannot be said of Grey's other book of Tahiti, his novel, *The Reef Girl,* published posthumously in 1977. Unique for its frank sexuality, *The Reef Girl* departs from western themes and jargon, and remains one of Grey's best novels written in his later phase (1926–39).

Grey was at first hesitant to write a novel with a Tahitian setting, believing that he could not penetrate the mystique of native culture. A local trader informed him that the average "Polynesian either cannot or will not tell the truth about himself, and will invariably tell you what will please you, without regard to veracity. . . . How hopeless for the novelist to get at the verisimilitude of life in the South Seas! For that reason alone," Grey explained, he would "deliberate long before daring to undertake fiction with this setting."[60] Despite his shyness, the author possessed subtle and effective means of probing other cultures. Before long, he had sketched the characters, plot, and scenic descriptions of *The Reef Girl*.

Set in Papeete and greater Tahiti, the novel is a tale of mischief, lust, and murder. Grey probes Papeete's degenerate underside of the 1930s. The island by then had become a shore on which all sorts of human wreckage seemed to wash up with regularity. Adventurers, soldiers of fortune, malcontents, criminals, Utopians, and "nature men" arrived in the South Pacific to mingle with the natives and enjoy the the easy fruits of paradise.

The "nature men" intrigued Grey. Mainly American and European expatriates, they lived in remote colonies on Tahiti. Of their apparently indolent lifestyle, Grey remarked (in *Tales of Tahitian Waters*):

> What is in their minds? What did they do in their idle hours? Tennyson's lotus-eaters could not have been nature men such as these. Dreamers do not necessarily have twists in their minds or a disgust for contact with humanity or a hatred of achievement. Thoreau was perhaps the most aloof of the naturalists, but then his life was farthest removed from idle.
>
> These nature men let the world slide. Far indeed from the maddening [sic] crowd! . . . It is hard to understand them, probably impossible. . . . I envied them and their solitude, where surf beat its many-toned music on the shore and the waterfall fell from the purple notch of the great mountain slopes. The world is too much with most people. How impossible to see remote Tahiti. . . . And what I could not understand, I dared not condemn.[61]

"Most visitors," remarks one character in the novel, "come in wantonness—and fall to grief." This disparity between what characters expect from Tahiti and what they get forms the basis of the novel, as the American Donald Perth, an unpublished writer, comes to Tahiti to find his muse and discovers the temptress, Faunee, the reef girl.

It is pure romance with tinges of pathos. Grey's description of the lush tropical coastline and forest are evocative and sharp, especially to those readers accustomed to his observations of the Western landscape. The depth of characterization is especially noteworthy. Faunee, half native and half white, rather than being presented as a sterotypical sexual object, emerges as an ambivalent, fragile victim of European exploitation.

The shift in settings, from Arizona to Tahiti, refreshed Grey. By the late 1920s, Grey, for all practical purposes, was divorced from the desert. It had become too easy for him to merely imagine an American West and then devise a plot that would fit neatly into it. Tahiti, at the least, challenged him to write a story that required concentration, sincerity, and close observation.

Grey's encounters with the native peoples, his extensive journeys into the interior, and his numerous fishing voyages provided him an education about Tahiti that few Americans or Europeans ever achieve. As he studied the culture, he came to view Tahiti as a battleground of intellectual versus sensual values, and as a provocative Arcadia rich in native wisdom. He also found that it helped unleash his own hedonistic nature, as evidenced by the scenes of carefree sexuality in *The Reef Girl*. What is disappointing is that Grey never took the opportunity to write more fiction about Tahiti. With his descriptive abilities and his knowledge of the tensions and problems on the island, he might have added significantly to the literature about Tahiti and the South Pacific.

While he poured his knowledge of angling into *Tales of Tahitian Waters* and his heart into *The Reef Girl*, he managed to squeeze out some residual magic for his western novels. Many of these were written either on the voyage to and from Tahiti or at the Flower

Point fishing camp. *The Lost Wagon Train, The Hash Knife Outfit,* and *Boulder Dam* were among these western novels penned on Grey's hiatus from the West. Written through the mind's eye, as it were, these novels, for all their melodramatic intrigue, reveal Grey's remarkable storytelling ability. He had an enormous imaginative reserve. Though he could slip and stumble in some maudlin scene, rarely did he fall. Missing from these later western novels, however, are Grey's heart and soul, which in the early novels are laid bare over the American landscape.

His mind often worked simply in the process of his novel's creation. On the business page of his life in the 1930s were two columns. In the left column were the debts incurred by ship expenses, travel, etc. In the right column were the number of books and articles he would have to write in order to offset them. Once he ascertained the bottom line in the left column, he plunged into work, setting goals for himself that would have daunted, if not killed, most authors.

In the 1930s, however, Grey's westerns began to slip from the best-seller lists. The more they slipped, the harder Zane tried to bolster them with the familiar devices that had worked in the past He failed to understand that it was not simply a question of a writer's exertion or imaginative powers; it was also a problem of a society jaded by the particular artist's voice and dulled by a specific genre. The reader of the 1930s was different from the reader of the 1920s, with different needs, interests, and desires. Although Grey still claimed millions of international readers, he lacked the stamina to attract fresh legions of them through the Depression.

If *Fisherman I* was a model of beauty and grace, *Fisherman II* was an example of power and speed. It was built by Krupp of Germany, the famous arms manufacturer headquartered in Essen. Reportedly built for Kaiser Wilhelm II, *Fisherman II* was a steel-clad, two-masted schooner powered by enormous engines. Her keel was laid in Bremerhaven toward the end of World War I. The vessel was specifically designed as an escort ship for larger naval cruisers and could withstand the vicissitudes of the Atlantic and North Sea. Grey thought it was the perfect ship to fulfill his ambition of sailing around the world.

Grey hired a crew and brought it from the East Coast to San Pedro, California, the port of Los Angeles, where he hired the Los Angeles Ship Company to make the extensive changes he needed. In Grey's often cavalier way, he told the directors of the company to make the changes in *Fisherman II* as quickly as possible and have it ready to sail by December 30, 1930. The costs for overtime and expensive parts mounted, but Grey never saw them.

Meanwhile, Grey planned his world cruise, which plotted a course to Tahiti, west to Fiji, and through the Coral Sea to Port Moresby, New Guinea. He would then steer north of the Great Barrier Reef and head through the Arafura Sea toward Madagascar in the Indian Ocean. After periods of fishing along the way, he would then sail into the Atlantic and continue around the world, eventually dropping anchor in San Pedro.

Grey decided to take his younger son Loren with him. His older son Romer was recently married to "a young, beautiful, and . . . sensible girl," according to Zane, "with nothing of the flapper about her."[62] While Zane was waiting for the changes to the *Fisherman II,* his daughter Betty married Bob Carney, a Scottsdale photographer and avid fisherman. As a wedding present, Grey suggested to Betty that she and her husband join Zane and Loren in Tahiti and sail with them home. Betty and Bob could cruise to Papeete by commercial liner and rendezvous with the family there. Grey's plans seemed perfect. He could take his ambitious journey and include members of his family at the same time.

Zane, Loren, and the crew sailed on the *Fisherman II* at the end of December 1930, heading toward Tahiti. Out of San Pedro harbor, however, Grey realized that the voyage would be treacherous. The *Fisherman II* rolled violently through the waves, causing Grey to anchor at Honolulu for adjustments to the ballast and other repairs. Workers in Hawaii discovered that the balance of gravity in her hull needed better distribution. After her ballast was corrected and other repairs accomplished, the *Fisherman II* left Hawaii for Tahiti.

Between the islands they encountered a violent gale that tossed the boat like a cork. By the time they reached Tahiti in January 1931, Grey regretfully admitted that "the L.A. Ship Co. had gypped [him] plenty."[63] At his Tahiti camp they joined Captain Laurie Mitchell, who had prepared tackle and equipment for their arrival. While they waited for Betty and her husband to arrive, Zane and Loren fished in the cape. Dolly had also sent the numerous bills for the *Fisherman II*'s changes in San Pedro. Grey was so overwhelmed by the cost ($300,000) that he remarked to her in a letter that he "was filled with misery" over his actions and what they meant for the family.[64]

Grey remained in Tahiti from January through April, fretting about his dwindling resources and anticipating the next leg of the voyage to Suva, Fiji. In the meantime his six-and-a-half-year relationship with Cappy Mitchell began to deteriorate. Mitchell had managed the fishing camp on and off since 1928. Grey paid him an additional $450 monthly to take care of the *Fisherman I* and *Fisherman II* while in Tahiti. Grey's agreement with Mitchell was purely verbal, not written. When Grey arrived in Tahiti in January 1931 and began receiving cables from Dolly about mounting expenses, he began threatening pay cuts for his employees.

Although it is unclear what exactly precipitated the ensuing events, Mitchell became aggrieved over something Grey said to him. For his part, Grey maintained that Mitchell walked out of camp after Grey charged him with failing to accomplish his fishing duties.[65] A simple disagreement between the two intensified.

Mitchell went straight to Papeete and got a lawyer, threatening to sue Grey over unpaid and future wages. By Tahiti law an employee could go after anything the employer owned on the island. Such a threat angered Zane, who called Cappy "a liar and a thief. He was drunk that we know of, and evidently drank right along."[66] Although Grey stated in his letter to Dolly that Cappy was stealing from him, he also made the bold proclamation that he was drinking at his camp, without his knowledge. Stealing from Grey was one thing; drinking on his ship or in his camp was tantamount to mutiny.

While intimidating Grey with a lawsuit, Mitchell also threatened to expose Grey's relationship with Mildred Smith. "Mitchell is a stupid, bull-headed, treacherous Englishman," he told Dolly, who "would give the newspapers stuff that would disgrace Mildred and ruin me."[67] Grey's lawyer and Mitchell's lawyer reached a compromise, in which Grey would pay Cappy $300 a month. Cappy, in what amounted to blackmail, wanted more, pressing Grey for additional money or he would blow the whistle on Zane and Mildred. Grey feared the worst. He remarked to Dolly that Mitchell "may publish that sort of thing whether I sue him or not. He is rotten enough. Mildred, like a damned idiot, *told* him her relationship to me so he can prove it. He would not care about ruining her or anybody."[68]

Not willing to risk public exposure, Grey finally settled with Mitchell, handing over an additional $2,685 and his fishing launch, the *Skyblue II*. Nothing of the Grey-Smith affair reached the international press. If it had, Zane would have been publicly embarrassed, particularly because he had worked most of his life chiseling his clean-cut image.

Grey's disagreement with Mitchell ended their personal relationship. Cappy, however, remained in Tahiti and recieved monthy payments from Zane until Mitchell's death the following year. Shortly after the incident with Mitchell, Grey ended his involvement with

Mildred Smith, replacing her as his secretary with Berenice Campbell, the young runaway who inspired the novel *Wyoming*.

Desperately short of money and with Dolly perpetually cabling him that they were overdrawn at the bank, Grey sailed for the Tongas in early May. Betty and Bob had arrived in Papeete sometime before, and joined them on the *Fisherman II*. On the water Grey was overjoyed to be rid of Tahiti and its problems. After leaving the Tongas, they headed to Suva, Fiji, which Grey planned to reach on the tenth of May. On the way, however, Grey's ship was clearly being battered. "Oh, my god, how this boat rolls," he told Dolly. "Betty is green in the face. Some of the men are very sick. I am feeling rotten. . . . I am down to 136 pounds and going down. I have some kind of infection on my left arm. Itches like hell. Hope I haven't leprosy."[69]

He asked Dolly to cable him more money in Suva. Despite his arrogant statements to her, which he characterized as "mostly baloney," he felt "disappointed and discouraged" about continuing his world cruise. "I'd quit but for the kids," he told her. And despite the rocky voyage, Zane remarked: "They're having a great time."[70]

Grey pressed on to Fiji, complaining that the boat rocked so drastically he could hardly sit in a chair. Writing was out of the question, which he found "a great blow . . . because so much time will be wasted." He realized that the *Fishermen II* was incapable of surviving the high seas. The ship might pitch and roll to its ultimate destination, but the passengers would be dead. "There is a good deal radically wrong with this yacht," Grey admitted, as if he was trying slowly to terms with the reality of the situation. However, in the old Grey tradition, his unquenchable spirit would not give in. "Perhaps I can work out things," he reasoned. As an aside to her, he mentioned that "the Mitchells were due in [San Francisco] today. I *think* I'm worried about what that yellow dog will put in the papers."[71]

Arriving at Suva, Fiji, the *Fisherman II* anchored in the harbor.

Grey wanted to refuel and take on fresh water for the next leg to New Caledonia. He went ashore and was greeted with the sobering cable from Dolly telling him that he was out of money and that he would have to return home immediately. After receiving what he later referred to as "the Suva mandate," Grey was furious. When he calmed himself and talked things over with his family on the ship, he finally agreed to turn the *Fisherman II* back to San Pedro. He simmered long after receiving Dolly's cable, calling her "disloyal" for intervening in his decision.[72]

Just over five hundred miles out of San Pedro harbor on the return voyage, Grey scrawled in his diary: "After six months strife in the South Seas, I am nearly home, worn out in body, but still unquenchable in spirit. . . . My financial ruin appears certain. I am facing the crisis of my life. I am prepared for the worst, and know my clear stern resolve. I will not be crushed by this disaster."[73]

After Grey returned to Altadena, President Herbert Hoover invited him and Dolly to the White House. For a long jovial afternoon Grey and Hoover traded fishing stories and reflected on times in the West. Later Grey headed to the offices of the IRS. With his wallet severely pinched, Grey argued with the agency that he should be allowed to deduct traveling expenses while on his research-gathering journeys. The IRS declined his request, annoying Grey further. Convinced that the "robber's roost" was actually in Washington, D.C., Grey claimed for several years thereafter that the IRS was responsible for his near-bankruptcy. "When I am ruined, as seems inevitable," he moaned in his diary, "it will be my government that I hold responsible."[74] Dolly and Zane's creation of the Zane Grey Corporation in 1932 further tightened Grey's belt, restricting most of his frivolous journeys. By 1933 Zane's financial situation improved enough for him to return to the South Pacific. This time he ordered a forty-eight-foot fishing launch, the *Frangipani,* to be built for him in New Zealand. When he realized that no commercial freighter was large enough to carry it, he sailed the launch under its own power from New Zealand to Tahiti, a distance of 2,400 miles. Grey's remarkable and daring journey in the *Frangipani* was one of the first times anyone had guided a gasoline-powered vessel of this size such a distance. Arriving in Papeete, he trolled the Tahitian waters in his new launch and promptly set three new world records—one for mahi mahi, and two for silver marlin.

At sixty-one years of age, the venerable Zane Grey, the iron man of the Tonto Basin and the *Fisherman I* and *II,* seemed to have a renewed burst of energy.

Throughout the 1930s Dolly conducted most of Grey's business affairs with the motion picture industry. Although he was on speaking terms with some Hollywood producers, Zane distrusted them in particular and the entire star-making process in general. Occasionally he drove the short distance from Altadena to Hollywood, where he lunched at the Brown Derby and then saw a Hollywood Stars baseball game.

By the mid-1930s the name Zane Grey on a movie poster ensured big profits for the studio. "Grey was the most bankable author of the time," asserted Twentieth Century Fox producer Harry Joe Brown.[75] With the advent of the talking picture in the late twenties, film companies remade several of the original Zane Grey silent movies. Within a few years the western was enjoying continued success in the "talkies."

Paramount Pictures, which owned the rights to most Zane Grey properties, featured several new actors who became stars, among them Buster Crabbe, Russell Hayden, and Randolph Scott. The Virginia-born Scott, who became the actor most identified with the Grey hero, made twelve films based on Grey's novels, including such titles as *Wild Horse Mesa, Sunset Pass, The Heritage of the*

Desert, and *Man of the Forest* (all released in 1933). Scott migrated to California in the late 1920s. Tall and square-jawed, he originally was hired by Victor Fleming, director of the 1929 production of *The Virginian,* to help Gary Cooper speak with a Virginia accent. Scott played a few minor stage roles in Los Angeles, until a Paramount scout saw him in a local production at the Pasadena Community Theater. Paramount signed him to a seven-year contract.

In *Man of the Forest,* one of his first starring roles, Scott nearly lost an arm when a mountain lion owned by the studio "overacted" a scene. While the doctor was bandaging his wounds, Scott asked the trainer why he hadn't come to his aid. "It was a good take," replied the trainer, "and I didn't want to spoil the scene."[76]

Due to his rigorous schedule, Grey did not see many Zane Grey movies in the 1930s. Grey, however, admired Randolph Scott's depictions of his fictional heroes. Scott personally shared many of Grey's traits: a strong code of ethics, a silent strength, an emphasis on physical health, and a virile appearance. Near the end his life, after starring in more than eighty films, Randolph Scott credited his early work in Zane Grey movies as the turning point in his career.[77]

In the 1930s, with the help of actors like Randolph Scott, Gary Cooper, and John Wayne and directors like John Ford and Henry Hathaway, the western movie finally achieved maturity. Grey's success in films rivaled his preeminence in the previous decade. Although his impact on the western movie is immeasurable, it was Zane Grey who first insisted that the western landscape should have as much a starring role as any of the actors. A few key people in Hollywood, including John Ford, happened to agree with him.

CHAPTER EIGHT

✠ ✠ ✠

King Maverick

> As a boy fishing was a passion with me, but no
> more for the conquest of golden sunfish and
> speckled chubs . . . than for the haunting sound
> of the waterfall and the color and loneliness of
> cliffs. As a man, and as a writer who is forever
> learning, fishing is still a passion, stronger with
> all the years, but tempered by a . . . keen reluc-
> tance to deal pain to any creature.
>
> —ZANE GREY

In the mid-1930s Grey's view of America was largely restricted to the highway running north of Los Angeles, through the San Joaquin Valley and into Grant's Pass, Oregon. Having turned his back on Arizona, he confined his travels to the Pacific Northwest and its abundant steelhead fishing. It was the depths of the Depression. Old rickety jalopies from the Dust Bowl states joined Grey on the highway to Fresno and Bakersfield, their occupants heading for new lives in the West. Grey's lone western novel in 1934, *The Code of the West,* was selling modestly; the once-lucrative serial market was virtually dead. Later he would grudgingly consent to have his name attached to a comic strip. The old fire that seemingly he could once stoke at will was only smoldering occasionally.

But the boy of summer, who once discovered a rascal's heaven down by the banks of the Muskingum River, could not get fresh-water fishing out of his blood. He treasured the time that he spent fighting a twenty-pound steelhead as much as he enjoyed the two-hour struggle with a seven-hundred-pound silver marlin. Virtually from the moment he disembarked his ship in Los Angeles, he was on the road to Oregon.

For over ten years the Rogue was the standard by which Grey measured any western angling river. "The happiest lot of any angler," noted Grey, "would be to live somewhere along the banks of the Rogue River. . . . Then he could be ready on the spot when the run of steelhead began." The study of the steelhead trout became a passion for Grey, not only on the Rogue but throughout the Pacific Northwest. "This peculiar and little-studied trout travels up streams and rivers flowing into the Pacific. . . . But so far as I can learn they will rise to a fly in only two rivers, the Eel and the Rogue, particularly the latter."[1] In Long Key once, Grey heard from an angling friend that the latter "could not hold these steelhead. . . . The big ones got away [and] they smashed tackle."[2]

Venturing north, Grey began to learn their habits. "The singular difference in steelhead," he observed, "is probably a matter of water. Many anglers claim that rainbow trout and steelhead trout are one and the same species. My own theory is that the rainbow is a steelhead which cannot get to the sea. He is landlocked. And a steelhead is a rainbow that lives in salt water and runs up fresh-water streams to spawn." In Grey's day, "the relation of the two fish [had] never satisfactorily been established." But he could say, unequivocally, "the steelhead is the most wonderful of all fish."[3]

Fishing in Oregon waters brought him singular pleasures. At least part of that enjoyment involved the preparation of the tackle and ceremonial selection of the flies for the day's fishing. Grey preferred English reels to American for steelhead, because "they would hold a hundred yards of linen line besides the thirty or forty yards of casting line." As for flies, Grey often chose a number four and six, which included the "Royal Coachman, Professor, and Brown

Hackle." He was also partial to his Kosmic fly-rod, measuring nine and a half feet in length and weighing eight ounces. His fly-rod was much admired by his fellow anglers, who admitted that they "would cheerfully steal it" if Grey did not sleep with it. "All this fuss and care and deliberation over a lot of fishing tackle seems to many people an evidence of narrow, finicky minds," Grey told his readers. "It is nothing of the kind. It is unalloyed joy of anticipation, and half of the pleasure."[4]

Grey and his angling buddies usually rose in the dark, and were breakfasting by five in the morning. At first light, they waded into the ruffled, choppy water—or "riffle." Lone Angler Wiborn or R.C. often accompanied Grey, but the former usually meandered by himself upstream. In the peaceful roar of the riffle, Grey would cast for hours, hoping for a quick strike or sometimes wishing to enjoy the solitude. "If moments could be wholly satisfying," he observed, "with thrills and starts, and dreads and hopes, and a vague, deep, full sense of the wild beauty of environment, and the vain boyish joy in showing my comrades my luck and my skill—if any moments of life could be utterly satisfying, I experience them then."[5]

Grey loved the wildness of the Rogue. In the early 1930s, however, an angling friend named Fred Burnham suggested he try the North Umpqua River, about forty miles due north of the Rogue. Burnham raved about its cutthroat and rainbow trout, and at its lower reaches, the great steelhead trout. When he tried it, Grey was sold. "I am honest and sincere about this noble river," he wrote, "practically unknown to the world, when I confess that I have given up the Rogue, and the fishing lodges I own at Winkle Bar . . . to camp and fish and dream and rest beside the green-rushing, singing Umpqua."[6]

In 1934, with civilization encroaching on the western environment, Grey used his fame as a platform from which to make a plea for the Umpqua River. In an article published as "North Umpqua Steelhead" in *Sports Afield* (September 1935) he addressed the wonders of the wild river. "Besides Canada," he remarked, "there is no stream in the United States that can hold a candle to the Umpqua for wet or dry fly-fishing . . . [but] those people who live on or near the Umpqua are as a whole deaf and dumb and blind to the marvelous good of the river, and if they do not wake up, its virtue and beauty and health will be lost to them."[7]

He leveled his sights at the logging camps and fish hatcheries that proliferated along the upper sections of the Umpqua. He called the hatcheries "mostly rackets. In very few cases do they increase the number of fish, despite the millions of young fry released in the river." Grey suspected that hatchery fish lacked the wildness of their natural kin. In addition to these threats to the Umpqua environment, Grey was also concerned that access roads would ruin the beauty and the remoteness. "The automobile," he maintained, "is the worst foe of forests and rivers." Despite Grey's warnings, roads constructed after his death pushed deep into the virgin territory that he loved upriver around Steamboat Creek. Today, on the Umpqua River, Grey's legacy survives in shaded places like Split Rock Pool, Z.G. Pool, and Takahashi Pool, named for his cheery wilderness cook of over twenty years.

Grey's shrill and often acerbic tone may sound comparatively tame in an age filled with militant environmentalists. But in 1935, he felt as if he were making a final stand at the western edge of civilization. Grey may have known that his America was vanishing, but he certainly was not going to let it slip away without a fight.

Part of Grey's joy in his later years was watching his sons Romer and Loren develop as skilled fly fishermen. Often, however, sibling rivalry on the Umpqua triumphed over their dedication to angling. On one occasion, which Grey sketched beautifully in "North Umpqua Steelhead," Zane, Romer, and Loren were camped along the Oregon river, engaged in their usual combination of serious sport, male bonding, and occasional tomfoolery. From his camp chair, Zane watched his two sons casting in the river. Romer, cheeky and impulsive, was perhaps the more experienced of the brothers. "Romer fishes fine and far away," Grey observed. "He can cast a hundred feet with ease. But he begins on a pool by keeping out of sight and fishing close."[8] Grey was also struck by Romer's stealth, which he compared to an Indian's, and his ability to wade into a fishing ground without frightening his prey. In summer Romer selected the smaller flies, numbers six and eight, while Zane and Loren preferred the larger ones. Generally, it was a race to see who catch the largest fish with the right fly.

Patient and studious, Loren Grey made up in pluck for what he lacked in experience. When the fly patterns Grey and Loren were using did not provoke any bites, Loren designed new ones. He would wait for hours in the same pool. Finally his patience paid off. He eventually caught more than a hundred steelhead in three months of fishing, Zane proudly announcing that he let a third of them go. One night Loren trudged into camp with a twelve-pound steelhead. "Here he is, fellows," Loren exclaimed. "Look him over. Thirty-two and one-half inches! Look at the spread of the tail!" Loren proceeded to tell a ten-minute story of the fury and peril of the catch. "Oh, boy," he stammered, "I'm tellin' you, it was great!"

Grey beamed. "The boy or the man," he wrote, "who can be true to an ideal, stick to a hard task, carry on in the face of failure, exhaustion, seeming hopelessness—he is the one who earns the great reward."[9]

Loren's story of landing a twelve-pound steelhead was not lost on Romer, however, who thought his brother had introduced a few too many histrionics. One afternoon while fishing at Takahashi Pool, Romer hooked the steelhead that he thought might challenge Loren's catch. "Romer stood high with a long line out," Grey noted. "He reeled fast . . . the bag in the line was as tight as a wire. . . . [The steelhead] looked enormous and he caught all the gold of the setting sun." For the next half hour, as a shaving of moon rose in the sky, Romer battled the steelhead. Zane was a good audience, frequently imploring him to reel in, keep the tension, or release some line.

"Don't let him have an inch," cried Zane. "Hold him! Romer, that steelhead is as tired as he will ever get."

"Oh, Lord!" Romer replied.

The steelhead was the gamest fish that Romer had encountered all summer on the Umpqua. Finally as darkness fell, Romer worked the steelhead out of the water and onto a shallow ledge. Zane reached down and "scooped him up out onto the bank, where he flopped once, and then lay still, a grand specimen if [there] ever was one."

"How much?" asked Romer.

"Fourteen—thirteen pounds," said Zane.

"Whew! Is he that big. . . . Gosh what'll Loren say?"

"It'll be tough on the kid. . . . He's so proud of his record. That twelve-pounder!"

"Dad, don't weigh this one. We'll say eleven and three quarters!"[10]

After this essay appeared in *Sports Afield* in 1935, Grey seldom traveled in America. In fact, "North Umqua Steelhead" represents one of the last essays he wrote about the American outdoors.

Grey's output as an angling writer was prodigious. People frequently asked him what fishing book influenced him the most. Most people perhaps guessed that Izaak Walton's *Compleat Angler* would be at the top of the list. But Grey preferred William Radcliffe's *Fishing from the Earliest Times* (1910). Radcliffe, too, was a tireless vagabond, who searched the world for anecdotes of the sport. Educated at Oxford and proficient in several languages including Hebrew and Chinese, Radcliffe seemed an unlikely candidate to write one of the great angling books of all time. Grey felt inadequate to write the American review of the book, which he called "scientific, scholarly, poetic, philosophic," and ultimately,

Grey at Avalon in the late 1920s. Although he traveled frequently to the Pacific Northwest and the South Pacific in his later years, he loved the solace—and swordfishing—of Catalina Island.

"monumental." Claiming that while he did not need a book to remind him of angling's strength-renewing virtues, Grey maintained that he required this book "to invest his favorite outdoor pursuit with the dignity of education, of culture, [and] with the great minds of the past."[11]

Although Grey's interests were not scholarly, he admired writers who communicated ideas with wit, grace, poetry, and conviction. Grey also appreciated the practical aspects of the articles on fishing he found in American and British periodicals. Radcliffe's book, however, appealed deeply to his idealistic nature; he would come to revere it as something akin to the *The Golden Bough* of angling. On fishing trips, talking with ordinary sports fishermen, Grey continually extolled the merits and insights of Radcliffe's work, declaring that "all fathers of youthful Izaak Waltons or angling Rip Van Winkles should read this wonderful book and learn how fortunate they are to have such inspired sons."[12]

Izaak Walton, that most agreeable of fishing companions and author of perhaps the most famous book on angling, resided in second place along with other Grey favorites, both writers of the past and those contemporary with Grey. *The Compleat Angler; or the Contemplative Man's Recreation* was published in 1653, when Walton was sixty years old. Reading it, one imagines a sprightly and kindly gentleman leaving his cottage and embracing the solitude of an English country stream. Walton, however, lived through the strife and turmoil of seventeenth-century England. One gets the impression that the solace of country spaces saved him in the desperate times.

Not a great deal is known of his life. He was born in Staffordshire, apprenticed at a young age to an ironmonger in London, became intimate friends with John Donne and Sir Henry Wotton, Provost of Eton College—both of whom were anglers—and saw his king executed in 1649. Donne had spent time in prison for his political views, which he voiced stridently. While chaos and uncertainty swirled around him, Walton retreated to the countryside to fish. The Lea, Trent, and Itchen were favorite streams mentioned in *The Compleat Angler*. For catching trout on a summer night in these waters, Walton recommended: "Get a grasshopper, put it on your hook, with your line about two yards long, standing behind a bush or tree where a hole is, and make your bait stir up and down on the top of the water." Later, after Walton's death, industrialization and pollution changed the fecundity of the streams and indeed the face of England.

The significant lesson Grey derived from Walton was that fishing induced a unique harmony between the physical, intellectual, and moral aspects of an individual. Izaak Walton's depiction of an angler virtually blooming along with nature in the serene English countryside, inspired Grey throughout his life. In the 1920s Grey contributed articles to the *Izaak Walton's League Monthly* (among them "The Bonefish Brigade" and "Tyee Salmon").

If Radcliffe leaned to the systematic and erudite, and Walton to the pastoral and contemplative, Zane Grey craved the gritty, hands-on aspects of fishing. For more than thirty years, from his first article for *Recreation* in 1902 to his essay on the Umpqua in 1935, he was one of the stellar writers of the American and Canadian outdoors. His geographical range was impressive: Pennsylvania, New York, Utah, Colorado, Arizona, Florida, Oregon, and Washington; in Canada he fished the Campbell River in British Columbia and the seas around Nova Scotia. He wrote for some of the most prestigious outdoor and variety magazines: *Field and Stream, Outdoor Life, Scientific American, Harper's Weekly, Success, Everybody's, Boy's Life, Outdoor America, Sports Afield, Sunset,* and *Ladies' Home Journal.* The Grey signature was an outdoor essay filled with humor, character, and setting, and propelled by a strong narrative voice. That voice, animated by Grey's remarkable human spirit, often shaped a compelling story from an otherwise maudlin fishing tale.

🐟 🐟 🐟

In 1936, at sixty-four years of age, Zane was still very much the worldly gadabout. He was lean as a fence post, with a clipped mane of white hair and eyes that were deep pools of resolve. For many years he thought of traveling to Australia, but often some personal or financial crisis arose to prevent him from going. As early as October 1933, Zane was preparing an expedition to Australia, but it was not until New Year's Eve, 1936, that he arrived in Sydney.

Part of the preparation for fishing in Australia involved the building of a special launch for Grey, the *Avalon*. His designated boatman in New Zealand and Australia was Peter Williams, and he frequently called upon Williams to order supplies and tackle before his arrival in Sydney. Williams also assisted a crew in sailing the *Avalon* to a remote fishing village, Bermagui, in southern Australia.

Grey came to Australia to sample the diverse varieties of fish, to make a movie about sharks, and to witness the wild beauties of the Great Barrier Reef and the rugged outback. His film producer, Ed Bowen, was on the payroll of the Zane Grey Corporation. With Bowen and two cameramen—Emil Morhardt and Gus Bagnard—Grey set up a fishing camp at Bermagui, a lovely harbor in a majestic setting some 275 miles from Sydney.

Before cameras started rolling for Grey's movie, the party fished for marlin and shark in the waters around Bermagui and nearby Bateman's Bay. Grey had experience with marlin, but chasing the elusive great white shark provided him an exciting challenge. Ever since witnessing their ferocity around Cocos Island in 1925, Grey was transfixed by the stealth and power of sharks. For the next eight months, from the alcoves and bays of southern Australia to the splendor of the Great Barrier Reef in the north, Grey demonstrated his piscatorial skills to an often adoring Australian public. Sharks, regarded as loathsome man-killers, were particularly singled out for hunting because of their abundance. However, not everyone in the country admired Grey or his techniques. Among the dissenting voices was the RSPCA (the Royal Society for the

Prevention of Cruelty to Animals), who accused Grey of unnecessarily prolonging his catches. Specifically, the Ssociety charged him with "playing" with the giant fish and that his three- to four-hour battles with sharks were only for photographing trophies.

Although Grey was stung by the criticism, the society's case may have had merit. Grey knew that the standard procedure in Australia for eliminating sharks was to shoot them. Yet in April, Grey struggled for more than two hours with a 1,200-pound tiger shark near Sydney. Using a standard 39-thread line, Grey finally hauled the shark aboard and proudly proclaimed it a world record. "I think I had a feeling of elation over catching the monster," he wrote, "that never attended any of my other catches. After the sense of terrific labor and risk, it was the conviction of having done a really good deed. That Tiger would never kill and eat anyone."[13] To his way of thinking, he was performing a deed that benefited mankind, and he truly could not see what the fuss was about.

Criticism of Grey's actions were rife in Australia. At one point, he threatened to pack up and leave if the society did not quit hounding him. However, the RSPCA had made its point; Grey, on the other hand, never did realize that people's perceptions of the hunting game had changed drastically in the last twenty years. Despite the barking dogs, his caravan passed on.

The Australian trip exacerbated the notion among some anglers that Grey was simply a trophy fisherman who exceeded the bounds of the sport. He attributed this harsh criticism to jealousy. But even people who knew Grey and fished with him had their concerns. Bob Davis, a lifelong friend and editor of *Munsey's,* declared frankly: "When I reflect on his four world records with rod and reel, it is impossible to determine whether Zane achieved them from love of adventure and conquest or from motives of revenge."[14]

Starring in a film about sharks only increased his stature, in his own mind, as one of the most famous of international anglers. *White Death,* filmed on the Great Barrier Reef, told the story of a group of aborigine villages terrorized by a killer white shark. The hero, played by Grey, arrives to rid the seas of the demon fish. The film did poorly in theaters, which bothered Zane, who had expected that a combination of his star name with a movie about fishing would widen his renown. As the Irish writer George Moore once observed, "nothing is more depressing than the realization that one is not a hero."

While in Australia Grey also maintained a journal (which was revised and published as *An American Angler in Australia* in 1937) and began the preliminary work on his Australian novel, *Wilderness Trek.* He stayed on the Great Barrier Reef for more than three months before heading back to California. In his diary he noted with some satisfaction: "On the whole, I won Australia. . . . Outside of the fishing, I saw and learned a great deal."[15]

Although Grey returned to Australia in 1938, his exploits in 1936 marked the culmination of his life as an active saltwater fisherman. More than twenty-five years of grappling with swordfish, sailfish, tuna, and shark had taken an enormous toll on his heart and body. Wrestling with a fifteen-pound steelhead when he was thirty-five years old was an entirely different matter than struggling for two hours with a thousand-pound tiger shark when he was sixty-five. Grey seemed fit and trim when he left Australia in August 1936, but his heart and organs must have been considerably weakened, which may have contributed to his stroke the following year and eventually to his untimely death in 1939.

American authors—even British authors—frequently have had difficulty writing fiction about Australia. Perhaps the vastness and diversity tempts writers, including Grey, to try to cover everything in one book. Australia and India were the British versions of the American West, important and remote dominions that received their fair share of criminals, cutthroats, misfits, and villains. For the British, India was a coveted military outpost. Australia, however, was the Alcatraz of the Pacific, and relatively insignificant to the British empire.

In literature, authors routinely disposed of unwanted characters by sending them from the drawing rooms of London to the sheep stations of Australia, where, with luck, they could hide their identity, remain out of the way, and create new lives for themselves. Sometimes, as in Dickens's *Great Expectations,* these characters amassed fortunes beyond their wildest dreams. They returned to England rich men with fresh identities and greater expectations.

The outback of Australia reminded Grey, like many writers, of the Southwest desert of the United States. He was also amazed by the strange lingo of the Aussies and the rich bounty of animals and plant life. He did most of his research for *Wilderness Trek* (published 1944) while at the Great Barrier Reef, later by interviewing a number of drovers, cattle station owners, and trackers as he briefly traveled in the outback. He absorbed enough of their conversations to simulate the Aussie speech patterns, and studied their facial expressions to capture a suitable Australian "look." He filled in the rest of the research by examining a stack of books on the terrain, the fauna, and the flora.

What he produced was part Australian travelogue, part western novel, and part pilgrimage, as kangaroos, wallabies, and kookaburras try to steal the scenes from the principal characters. *Wilderness Trek* is vintage Zane Grey, with Aussie flair added to western gunbattles, fistfights, cattle drives, and maiden-rescues. The dialogue is clipped and terse, more snarled than spoken. Grey relates how two American cowboys with shadowy pasts, Red Krehl and Sterl Hazelton, arrive in Australia to help drive a "mob" of cattle through three thousand miles of dust and wilderness. They soon get mixed up with a villain, Ash Ormiston, who forms a renegade band of drovers during the cattle drive through the outback. Red falls for Beryl Dann, a spirited woman who also loves Ormiston. Sterl yearns for the proud Australian teenager, Leslie, the two spending most of the novel figuring out if they can bridge their cultural differences.

Grey's unfamiliarity with the Australian "never-never" becomes apparent midway through the novel, as he abandons his customary vivid descriptions for stock settings and some wooden phrases describing dead gum trees and the innumerable barren waterholes that dot the landscape. Replacing accurate descriptions of the bush and outback are Grey's brief verbal sketches and illustrations. These are effective to a point, but they lack the development necessary to make them fully convincing. The characters must feel the atmosphere and wildness of this wild new land. Unfortunately, they do not. As in most of the later Zane Grey novels the storyline is paramount, with depth of characterization and concrete, sensory description running a distant second. In spite of these limitations, the novel is an often illuminating look at the cultural clashes between the English settlers and the aborigines of the interior.

Because *Wilderness Trek* describes life in Australia, a better title might have been *Australian Trek,* to distinguish this unique novel of the outback from the often bewildering number of Grey's other titles set exclusively in the American West. Summer 1999 saw the publication of *The Great Trek,* which was Grey's original manuscript before it was heavily edited during World War II and became *Wilderness Trek.* With additional descriptions and dialogue restored, *The Great Trek* is no doubt closer to what Grey intended.

Grey's stroke and first heart attack occurred in summer 1937 while he and Romer were fishing on the North Umpqua River. Romer and a guide rushed him down the mountain to the nearest hospital. He recovered the capacity for speech the next day, but was completely paralyzed. After being transferred to a hospital in Los Angeles, he slowly regained movement in his limbs.

His doctors warned him that even mild exercise might trigger a setback. But Grey would not, or could not, sit still. Months later he was up and exercising on a rowing machine. Like Theodore Roosevelt, he believed in the strenuous life, which naturally included activity, travel, and perpetual motion. He yearned to return to Australia. Against the advice of his doctors and Dolly, he sailed once again to Sydney in 1938.

For a time it was the same old Zane Grey. He received the adoration of his Australian fans, who were even more appreciative after the 1937 publication of *An American Angler in Australia*. He posed with koala bears and fished in Sydney harbor. Although somewhat feeble, he showed his venerable, rugged self, clearly enjoying his return visit down under. However, he was in no condition to set world records, or for that matter, to battle sharks and marlin.

After his return to California, and in addition to his intense novel-writing schedule, Grey worked on his long-planned autobiography. Titled by Zane *The Living Past,* the typed manuscript documented Grey's early days through his first year at the University of Pennsylvania. It is not only a penetrating record of youth, but it is also remarkable view of late-nineteenth-century Ohio town and country life. Although some of the conversations may be fictionalized, the veracity of the sequence of events and their emotional impact are clearly evident.

Grey recorded the brief, sweet, painful, and often humorous moments of his childhood with the benefit of a razor-sharp memory: his first smell of burning autumn leaves; his first encounters with his father's eccentricities; his meeting of the Dillon's Falls hermit, Old Muddy Miser; his initial encounters with sunfish and chubs; his baseball intrigues; his often obtuse schoolmasters; his girlfriends and raucous boyfriends; and the overt skullduggery of his teenage years. Grey omitted nothing in his attempt to reconstruct his past.

There is no doubt that Grey showered his love on these narrative memories, toiling through most of 1938 in their development.

The manuscript ends on November 10 of that year, with the brief inscription: "Stopped here for the present at the conclusion of the first year in college of Zane Grey. Page 236." Had Zane completed his autobiography, its length would have exceeded two thousand pages, making it rich in narrative delight and all but unsuitable for publication.

🐟 🐟 🐟

As an adventurer, writer, sailor, and vagabond, Grey traveled where he wanted, when he wanted: Canada, Panama, Mexico, the Florida Keys, Cuba, the Galapagos, Tahiti, Bora Bora, Fiji, New Zealand, and Australia. His avowed childhood dream to was "to sail his own beautiful white ship with sails like wings into lonely tropic seas." He realized the dream and much more.

He seemed always to have the time for adventure. His one dilemma may have been whether to seek new horizons or return to the paradises that he knew so well. He observed that "new places to fish and hunt and explore have always had a perennial fascination for me. . . . How many lonely crags where the eagles perch and scream—how many open mountain ridges where the elk bugles his siren whistle to his mate—how many grassy hilltops, high above the sounding sea—how many windy heights of desert—how many miles of cool ocean lanes, full of great marine fishes—how many, how infinite the number of new, strange, wonderful places in the world that I can never see! It is a melancholy thought. Yet it is happiness to know there are such places."[16]

Although he preferred to be a lone rider, he also chose the company of good friends with whom to share his experiences. At various times they included Muddy Miser, Buffalo Jones, Jim Emmett, Al Doyle, John Wetherill, Nas Ta Bega, George Allen, Pepe, Sievert Nielsen, George Takahashi, the Haughts, Cappy Mitchell, and, of course, the ubiquitous Romer Carl Grey. Whether he was helping Zane cut bait on the Rogue River or land a swordfish in Avalon

Zane and Dolly Grey at their pueblo-style house overlooking Avalon harbor in 1930. Dolly remained steadfast in her support of Grey's career throughout her life.

or a shark in the South Pacific, R.C. was Grey's shadow. R.C.'s wit, his earthy nature, and his similar belief in the vigorous life soothed and challenged Zane throughout his life.

At home his greatest companion was Dolly, who saw him through the depths and heights of his career, who virtually molded his public image, and who often disarmed his bullish egotism. After Zane Grey's death of a heart attack in October 1939, Dolly continued to direct the Zane Grey Corporation and edit the stack of manuscripts that her husband had left to her. She repeated her remark that Zane simply would not edit his work. He preferred to hit the bird of inspiration, as it were, on the wing and then get on to something else. As late as 1953, Dolly was still editing and correcting Zane's manuscripts.

In addition to the backlog of novel manuscripts, Dolly also found fishing tales and short stories that Grey had simply shelved. She sold some of these to magazines. She also continued to monitor the film scripts based on Grey material at Paramount Pictures. While she worked busily in her office, she noted in her diary in 1941 that "things are not right around here without Z.G."

The house on Mariposa Street in Altadena was eventually sold in 1970, with most of Grey's personal effects and mementos being donated to the newly-erected Zane Grey/National Road Museum in Norwich, Ohio, just down the highway from Zanesville.

After Zane's death, his body was cremated. Dolly kept his ashes in a box in a special cabinet in the study at Altadena. Upon her death of a heart attack in 1957, she too was cremated. The family then placed Zane's and Dolly's ashes, side by side, in a country cemetery near their first house at Lackawaxen, Pennsylvania, overlooking Grey's beloved Delaware River. Zane Grey, adventurer and angler extraordinaire, the man who once claimed that he knew "every rapid, every eddy, [and] every stone from Callicoon to Port Jervis," came home with his bride.

✙ ✙ ✙

The Desert Sage

I shall never be able to express whence comes
this pleasure men take from aridity, but always
and everywhere I have seen men attach themselves more stubbornly to barren lands than to
any other. Men will die for a calcined, leafless,
stony mountain. . . . And we, my comrades and
I, have loved the desert to the point of feeling
that it was there we had lived the best years of
our lives.

—ANTOINE DE SAINT-EXUPÉRY

WHETHER he turned up in Sydney, Australia, or in New York City,
the essential Zane Grey must be discovered amid the desert, mesa,
and canyon country of the western United States. Here he researched and wrote the stories that made him world famous; here
he also developed a philosophy that informs most of his novels and
some of his short stories.

The philosophy Grey gained through his experiences in the western deserts has two central tenets. First, Grey viewed the desert as
a great shaper of a man's moral and spiritual being. Grey's central
male characters always have enormous potential, but generally arrive in the West with meager means and confused allegiances.
Grey's characters do not simply endure the ordeal of the desert;
they prevail and triumph. Many men have great intentions and
strong potential, but only true heroes have the mettle to subdue
the wasteland.

Secondly, Grey embraced Wordsworth's belief in the sanctity of the natural world. Like Wordsworth, Grey believed that the world of nature contained better moral instruction than books and learning. Over and over, Grey's characters seek sanctuary and deliverance from pain in nature. Grey's astute descriptions issue from this pantheistic view of the western countryside. Grey was not a fervent believer in the Christian God, but he could spend months listening and watching in the cathedral of the forest.

These two viewpoints seep into Grey's fiction and nonfiction. Often, however, when he could not explain why good men are killed and evil men triumph (such as in the Great War), they caused him suffering and anxiety. At first committed to a Darwinian view of the universe, Grey began to retreat from that philosophy as he got older.

At any given time, Zane Grey could have the plots of two to three novels spinning in his head. Of course this was in addition to a couple of magazine articles, a fishing tale, and an assortment of other narratives, all catalogued for future use. From the time he met Old Muddy Miser at Dillon's Falls in Ohio to the day in 1939 that he last signed copies of *Western Union* in Pasadena, California, stories fed Grey's spirit, nourishing him as food, sleep, and relationships could not.

After he completed the Ohio River trilogy (*Betty Zane, Spirit of the Border,* and *The Last Trail*), he turned his focus to the sprawling desert country of the Colorado River Basin. Novels came from his many experiences and observations: *Heritage of the Desert, Riders of the Purple Sage, The Rainbow Trail, The Light of Western Stars,* and *Wildfire.* From 1912 through the 1920s Grey appeared frequently on the best-seller lists. At times, he virtually dominated them. Spinning off from these novels were movies, serializations, reprints, and foreign translations. He was a publisher's dream, accomplishing what today would be called total market penetration.

Grey was fortunate to arrive on the western literary scene when he did. Capitalizing on the influence of Theodore Roosevelt, Owen Wister, Frederic Remington, Buffalo Bill's Wild West Show, the dime novel, the advent of motion pictures, and prevailing nostalgia for the Old West, Zane Grey turned his version of the western novel from a one-night stand into a long-term, productive marriage. Between 1900 and 1960 the western achieved enormous popularity. With his star power and restless energy, Grey created his own niche in publishing, rewriting the script of how a writer rose to the top and remained there.

However, lost somewhere in his publishing performance and the staggering numbers of his book sales is the story of the writer himself, the artist who shaped these narratives into some of the most enduring fables of our time. Grey was no slouch at writing an inspired first draft. Using a pencil, he wrote quickly and intuitively. The portability of his favored mode of composition allowed him to write virtually anywhere: on location in the desert; on the deck of a ship; in the saddle. Despite his crowded schedule, Grey wrote at least two to three hours each day. Sometimes he stretched it to eight to ten hours. He was probably more frustrated by an unsharpened pencil than he was by the difficulty of shaping a scene.

While his western novels receive justifiable attention, his shorter works—the short stories and novelettes—are an impressive and often overlooked dimension of Grey's legacy. A good percentage of these were originally written for magazines. The magazine's tighter format forced him to restrict action, plot, and descriptions of setting, and to emphasize character. For Grey, whose imagination was at times several strides ahead of his good sense, the shorter format helped curb this tendency and encouraged writing that was direct and insightful.

Before he achieved a major success with *The Heritage of the Desert* in 1910, Grey was desperate for money. Without a full-time job he relied on his writing to earn money for his growing family. Short stories filled this particular need. He could write several and circulate them among New York pulp publishers. *Popular, Success,* and *National Post* were included on his list of possibilities. He also approached *Harper's* and *Field and Stream* with short stories, articles, and serialization proposals. His baseball stories were particularly well-received at this time.

As Grey's career as a novelist skyrocketed, his need to write in shorter forms decreased. However, Grey maintained an affection for the novelette and short story after achieving his success as a novelist. Writing short fiction was a pastime he could turn to when the marathon task of authoring novels was wearing him out. He heard some of these shorter tales from guides and outfitters, often when they were out on the trail or hunched over the campfire. He encouraged men like Al Doyle, John Wetherill, and his Mexican guide Pepe to tell him their best yarns. Often these tales found their way into his stories and novelettes.

Frequently Grey's short works blend fiction and nonfiction. In some cases the boundaries are vague. One prime example, *Don, The Story of a Lion Dog* (*Harper's*, August 1925), purports to relate a nonfiction narrative, much like the plethora of tales and essays that Grey sold as true experience. However, it is more fiction than fact. Grey often used himself as the basis for a story, leaving the reader to assume that the events were in fact true and accurate. How much Grey embroidered a tale depended on the emotional impact that he wanted to achieve. When pressed, however, he would never claim that something was true when it clearly was not.

By the 1920s, Grey's short stories were in the premier magazines —*Harper's, McClure's,* and *Ladies' Home Journal.* His appearance in *Ladies' Home Journal,* whose circulation was nearing two million per month, signaled that the appeal of his westerns spanned the gender gap. Moreover, it brought his work into the realm of re-spectability. Seemingly across all segments of the population—rich and poor, young and old, male and female—Grey's work was in-creasing in stature and public acceptance.

Ladies' Home Journal featured several of Grey's best short works: "The Great Slave" (December 1920); *Tappan's Burro* (June 1923);

The Wolf Tracker (November 1924); *Amber's Mirage* (May 1929); *The Ranger* (October 1929); and "Canyon Walls" (October 1930). *McCall's* published "The Camp Robber" (October 1928), and *Harper's* the aforementioned *Don, The Story of a Lion Dog*. Some of Grey's most significant short stories were published earlier in his career, most notably "The Rubber Hunter" (also known as "The Lure of the River," *Popular*, June 15, 1911); and "Tigre" (also known as "Bernardo's Revenge," *Munsey's*, September 1912). Still others were released posthumously, such as "Quaking Asp Cabin" (*American Weekly*, June 27, 1954); and *Blue Feather* (published in book form by Harper and Brothers, October 25, 1961).

Often confounding the collections of Grey's short works are the numerous excerpts from his novels that are often promoted as actual short stories, such as "The Horses of Bostil's Ford" from *Wildfire*, "California Red" from *Forlorn River*, and "The Revenge of Toddy Nokin" from *Wild Horse Mesa*. These excerpts cannot be classified as independent works.

Arguably the best of Grey's short story collections are *Tappan's Burro and Other Stories*, *Blue Feather and Other Stories*, and *The Wolf Tracker*. The first contains the novelette *Tappan's Burro* and the short stories "The Great Slave," "Yaqui," "Tigre," and "The Rubber Hunter." The second is composed of the novelette *Blue Feather* and the stories "The Horse Thief" and "Quaking Asp Cabin." *The Wolf Tracker* (Walter J. Black, 1976) includes the novelette of the same name plus the short stories "Lightning," "Rangle River," "The Kidnapping of Collie Younger," and "Monty Price's Nightingale."

Virtually all of Grey's shorter works have a primitive edge, as men and women struggle with the primal impulses that make them human but also threaten to destroy them. Nearly half the stories include animals in primary or secondary roles. Tigers, horses, wolves, and dogs, Grey reminds us, are to be feared but also revered. In understanding animals, we learn significant truths about ourselves.

Grey's characters in the short stories are generally lonely and isolated. Either by choice or through circumstance, they wrestle alone with the elements of nature. Often they find themselves in perilous situations of their own making. At times they simply try to survive in a hostile environment. But even on the brink of their own destruction, they still have a reverence and a deep respect for nature.

Two memorable stories that emerged from Grey's 1909 trek down the Santa Rosa River in Mexico are "Tigre" and "The Rubber Hunter." "Tigre," perhaps inspired by a local folktale that Grey learned in the Tampico area, relates the story of a man named Bernardo who, suspecting his wife of infidelity, releases an old blind jaguar in hopes of tracking down her lover. "He never loses," proclaims Bernardo. "He trails slowly . . . but he never stops, never sleeps, till he kills." It is a diabolical scheme. Afraid for her lover, Bernardo's wife Muella flees into the jungle to warn Augustine, pursued by the fearsome, crafty jaguar.

Adding to the suspense is that the reader never really sees the jaguar. The jungle, trailing with creepy vines and punctuated by animal and bird noises, becomes a fearful place for the fleeing lovers, as they imagine the cat lurking behind every tree and bush. Muella and Augustine wait, almost panic-stricken, for an attack that never comes.

Toward the end of the story the irony of Muella's and Augustine's escape becomes evident: they have not traveled deep into the jungle but rather in a circle, arriving where they started—near Bernardo's village. And "Tigre," whose "large, yellow, pale, cruel" eyes are sightless, has chosen someone else as his prey. In a story that evokes associations with William Blake's "The Tiger," Grey crafts a tale of eerie suspense.

In "The Rubber Hunter," a story with a similar atmosphere, Grey tells of how the Peruvian boatman Manuel attempts to become rich by acquiring quantities of rubber. A sly, derelict figure, Manuel is accused by Valdez, a Spanish captain and boat owner, of making money in the slave trade, a charge Manuel shrugs off. "I never hunted slaves," he growls at Valdez. "I never needed to sell slaves. I always found cowcha [rubber] more than any man on the river."

Before he begins his mission into the jungle, Manuel meets a stranger, called simply "Señor," who agrees to accompany him to look for rubber. Over several days Manuel and the mysterious Spaniard pole their way up the Pachitea River into a region occupied by cannibals. Gradually, the two become friends. Later, Manuel learns of the secret that binds their murderous pasts.

As they prepare to harvest the rubber from a great forest of trees, they are attacked by cannibals. Manuel resists bravely, but Señor is killed. Pursued into the jungle by the cannibals, Manuel flees back to civilization. Half-starved and bitten by sand flies, Manuel stumbles back to the place he began his journey. On the way he encounters two orphaned cannibal children. Deciding not to leave them to the jaguars, he takes them back with him. With no rubber to boast of, Manuel returns to the company of boatmen downriver, his two young charges in tow. Captain Valdez, thinking that Manuel has been slave-trading, barks at him, "Your choice, Manuel—the chain gang or the river." Sensing his ironic end, Manuel turns his canoe upriver for one more chance at the bonanza of rubber trees in the high, dark jungles.

"The Rubber Hunter" is among Zane Grey's best short stories. Beyond its romantic sweep, it has elegant pacing, sinister atmospheric effects, and trenchant irony. Grey's exploits with Pepe and George Allen on the Santa Rosa River in Mexico supplied him with the grittiness of these two short stories; the journey also showed him that the jungle hid as much malice and treachery as the desert.

Zane Grey may not have been the first major author to write in a complimentary way about Native American culture, but his voice certainly was the loudest. One of his major concerns was that

Zane Grey, looking resolute and defiant, dressed in a buffalo coat on
the lawn at Altadena, in 1935, a few years before his death.

Indians were being herded onto reservations, where they could not flourish and would surely die. He was afraid that well-meaning white educators, unaccustomed to Indian mysticism and religion, would irreversibly damage their lifestyle, folklore, and culture. In his famous novel *The Vanishing American,* he voiced most of those concerns.

Grey's perennial favorite among places to study Native American life was the Navajo-Hopi reservation surrounding Kayenta, Arizona. There he had many Indian acquaintances, who told him of their history and their tales. He also researched other tribes, the Crows in the North and the Yaquis in Mexico. He singled out the Yaquis as a tribe who suffered unusual and persistent oppression by the Mexicans. Although he tried to establish an affinity with all Indian peoples, he thought that the Yaquis were among the most victimized and brutalized tribes on earth.

In the story "Yaqui," which unfortunately suffers from excessive length, Grey traces the sordid history of the Sonoran tribe. The Yaquis were a peace-loving people before gold was discovered on their land, Grey reminds us. "Like eagles," Grey wrote, "the Indian tribe had lived for centuries in the mountain fastness of the Sierra Madre, free, happy, self-sufficient." Following the discovery of gold, the Yaquis were attacked, subjugated, and virtually sold into slavery. On the Yucatan Pensinsula they toiled harvesting henequen, a fiber used to make rope and twine, while the rich Mexican planters profited from their labor. The story relates how one Yaqui takes his revenge on his Mexican oppressors.

In this often brutal tale, Grey describes the large henequen plantations and debilitating labor of a captive warrior named Yaqui. "As far as he could see," Grey noted, "stretched a vast, hot, green wilderness with its never-ending lines and lanes, its labyrinthine maze of intersecting aisles, its hazy, copper-hued horizons speared and spiked by the great bayonet-like leaves." The living conditions for Yaqui were appalling: "Here he was chained in the thick, hot moist night, where the air was foul, and driven out in a long day under a fiery sun, where the henequen reeked and his breath clogged in his throat and his eyes were burning balls and his bare feet were like rotting hoofs."

Gradually, Yaqui is promoted to working in the plant where the henequen fiber is extracted from the leaves. He becomes proficient in the iron press, which takes the raw henequen and forms it into bales for shipment. Grey makes it clear that Yaqui has many opportunities to escape but for some reason prefers the routines of the henequen factory and his special knowledge of the iron press.

In contrast to the drudgery of the Yaqui workers, the Mexican families on the Yucatan lead lives of idle luxury. They attend the bullfights; the young maidens plan their weddings. In one instance, Señorita Dolores is about to wed the dashing scoundrel Lieutenant Perez in a grand ceremony. Yaqui is asked to fashion the most exquisite bale of henequen for the wedding. Inside the bale will be placed an expensive jewel box for the bride Dolores. During the ceremony, however, the bridegroom is nowhere to be found. The family implores Dolores to open her gift anyway. "With a swift flash of his huge black hands," Yaqui sweeps the strands away. The aghast group stares down upon the contents: "Instead of the jewels, there, crushed and ghastly, [lies] the bridegroom Perez."

For Grey, such a tale was small recompense for centuries of the Yaqui's humiliation. In "The Great Slave" he further probes the Indian's difficult existence on the North American continent before the arrival of the Europeans, as tribes fight for territory and supremacy. In language more reminiscent of a folk tale than of a short story, Grey relates the saga of the Crow warrior Siena, "a hunter of the leafy trails . . . the remnant of a once powerful tribe, beautiful as a bronzed autumn god, silent, proud, and forever listening to the voices of the wind."

If "Yaqui" is too long, "The Great Slave" lacks the tension and narrative energy common to other Grey stories. Siena's life in the woods is related in often stereotypical terms, as Grey recounts his abduction and enslavement by the Crees. Siena, however, carries with him a new weapon—a white man's rifle. A bitter winter descends on the Crees and hunger is rampant. The Cree leader, Baroma, pleads with Siena to help them hunt for game. "Siena waits," comes the reply. Baroma asks: "What does Siena wait for?" "Freedom," says Siena. He hunts successfully with his rifle, and the Crees are saved. However, as the reader learns, Siena's freedom is not near at hand. He must first use one more virtue—his extreme patience—before he can lead his liberated people out of the land of the Crees.

Grey sympathized with the plight of dying races, and frequently he chose a strong, proud warrior to symbolize their struggle. In *Blue Feather* Grey recounts the decline of the Anasazi—called Sheboyas in the story—in the drought-stricken Southwest of the thirteenth century. Grey had long been fascinated by the ancient cliff-dwellers and the fierce combats between warring rock citadels. In the story, Blue Feather, a Nopah spy, travels to the land of the cliff-people, the Sheboyas, whose high kingdom is shriveling under an unremitting sun. Promising to bring them rain, Blue Feather insinuates himself into their culture, engaging in foot races, pleasing the women, and winning at gambling. After securing the Sheboyas' trust, he meets the chief's daughter, the mysterious, reclusive Nashta, whose spell he falls under. Blue Feather's original mission was to spy for the Nopahs on the Sheboyas. However, Blue Feather's love for Nashta places him in the desperate position of being torn between two cultures.

Like "Yaqui," *Blue Feather* is a frequently bloody tale of conquest, plunder, and revenge, punctuated by moments of romance and hasty courtship. Although the frequent asides, sub-plots, and excessive descriptions are distracting and even annoying, the story crackles with Grey's matchless energy.

🐟 🐟 🐟

"The Horse Thief" (published in *Country Gentleman* as "The Out-laws of Palouse") was the sole story Grey sold to a magazine in 1934 and one of the last serials that appeared before his death. It is a standard oater of the kind that Grey virtually patented. Despite his extensive writings in other areas, and despite his desire to write more respectable material, Grey's name, in most people's minds, will probably forever be associated with the drawling, gunslinging cow-boy. By the 1930s the label of western writer was one he grudgingly accepted.

After cowpoke Dale Brittenham stumbles upon horse rustlers in the Salmon River Mountains of Idaho, his life—and theirs—would never be the same. Subduing the hombres, Dale leads the stolen horses back to their rightful owners at the Watrous ranch. The overjoyed Edith Watrous thanks him profusely for his courage and for bringing back her beloved horse, Prince. Dale soon becomes embroiled in the chicanery at the ranch: Edith is bethrothed to the horse thief Hildrith Leale in an arranged marriage but secretly loves Dale; the sheriff accuses Dale of being part of a local horse-thieving gang. The methods Dale uses to free himself from this tangled mess form the basis of the story, which, unfortunately, is rife with clichés and trite situations. Grey's writing is not entirely at fault. Decades of the Hollywood western have tarnished for read-ers of the present day Zane Grey's work of the 1930s. Some of his more shallow and melodramatic work of this decade has found de-served obscurity, but other, better crafted, stories await rediscovery.

Of the stories collected in *Blue Feather*, "Quaking Asp Cabin" has the strongest sense of authenticity. Beginning with the disarm-ing and provocative assertion that "log cabins have played a great part in the history of the West," this tale, spun around one of Grey's treks in the Tonto Basin, is pure adventure and mystery. Using the story-within-a-story technique of Joseph Conrad, Grey traces the intriguing history of a log cabin deep in heart of the quaking aspen country of eastern Arizona. Grey relates the first story in typical narrative essay fashion, as he seeks to uncover the history of Quaking Asp Cabin, at which he happened to sojourn. During that stay in the cabin, Grey noticed a faint, bloody handprint on the stone fireplace. He asked several people, including Richard Haught, about the former inhabitants of the cabin. They told him several stories about the region (which can be found in *To the Last Man, The Hash Knife Outfit,* and *Tappan's Burro*). However, these tales did not satisfy Grey' s curiosity. Three years later in Arizona he finally met a man who could relate the true history of Quaking Asp Cabin. Thus begins the second story, told in the third person, which originates in the 1870s.

The mystery of Quaking Asp Cabin is a tale of courage, deceit, lust, murder, hatred, and forgiveness—the perfect ingredients for a Grey story. According to Grey's narrative, Richard Starke, his wife Blue, and Richard's brother Len arrived in Arizona from the east, anticipating building a cabin and living off the land. They erected the cabin in the aspens, finding much happiness and freedom in their new home. One summer, however, Richard catches his wife in Len's arms, which causes him silent anguish. Later, Len tries to kill Richard. As Richard, shot in the chest staggers into the cabin, he leaves a bloody handprint on the fireplace stone. Recuperating from the gunshot wound, Richard hears Len and Blue planning their life together. Len confesses to Blue his own anguish about their predicament. "This wilderness cabin is accursed," Len admits. "If it were not cursed by nature . . . then I cursed it—my crooked rotten selfish self—and you cursed it—with your pretense of wifehood and motherhood . . . with the female in you that couldn't be satisfied."

Len flees the Quaking Asp Cabin, leaving Richard and Blue to work through their barbed feelings. As the years pass, Richard grows to be an old man consumed by his hatred for his brother and Blue. He rarely speaks to his wife. But then tragedy forces Richard to surrender his hatred and to seek the whereabouts of his brother. He asks a friend to bring Len to the Quaking Asp Cabin. Many years after the brothers' separation, Richard waits at the cabin, hoping that Len's return will erase the bloody handprint on the fireplace—the persistent reminder of the depth of Richard's hatred. As Richard listens for Len's arrival, his sudden joy is accompanied by a heart attack. In a moment of perfect happiness and fulfillment, Richard hears "the sound of hoof-beats coming—faintly—fainter—lost."

Unfortunately, the strength of Grey's novelette *The Wolf Tracker* is diluted by the uneven quality of the other stories in the collection. Weakest among them are "Rangle River" and "The Kidnapping of Collie Younger." On the surface "Rangle River" appears to be standard Grey formula fiction: an attractive, effete Londoner named Marian Hastings arrives in rough Australia to claim her inheritance —a sprawling, arid cattle station in the outback called Rangle River. What follows, however, hardly resembles Zane Grey at his best or even at his mediocre. Intended as a kind of postcard of Australia, the story is flimsy, the characters tissuey, and the setting unconvincing. Moreover, the storyline reads like a synopsis. Some scenes are feebly sketched and the dialogue often is wooden and contrived. One contributing factor to the weakness of this story may have been Grey's stroke in 1937, which, according to Dolly's secretary, Eleanora Evans, left him with a very shaky hand. In a later interview, Evans reported that when Dolly brought her the story "untyped . . . it was not quite as legible as the other ones."[1]

If "Rangle River" suffers from a complete lack of sincerity, "The Kidnapping of Collie Younger" is crippled by other problems. Set in the 1930, contemporary with the time of writing, the story relates how two brothers, John and Roddy Brecken, conspire to kidnap a college coed named Collie Younger. John's plan calls for Roddy to drive the spirited and flirtatious Collie Younger into the mountains, "rough her up," and wait there until John arrives on the scene to rescue her. Once the bothers act on their plan, however, a real set of kidnappers intrudes on the scene, intent on demanding ransom for both Roddy and Collie.

The story is actually better than this brief synopsis would suggest. Unfortunately, the plot has to compete with frequent references to sadism, emotional abuse, and misogyny. Such distractions mar the effort, and in some cases, might lead modern readers to dismiss the entire work as sexist, misguided, and perverse. "The Kidnapping of Collie Younger" might be sound in technique and characterization, but its major flaws may deter readers in the future.

The additional stories "Lightning" (first published in *Outing*, April 1910) and "Monty Price's Nightingale" (*Popular*, May 1915) are breezy vignettes of frontier life. Written as early as summer 1909, "Lightning" is an exuberant short story that reveals how two Mormon cowboys attempt to capture the renegade stallion Lightning. Like most of Grey's equines—from Sage King and Wildfire to Silvermane and Don Carlos—Lightning is strong, intelligent, and elusive. Lured by a bounty on the mustang, Lee and Cuth Stewart track the horse from Arizona into Utah, accompanied by a hound named Dash. Frequently, they see Lightning on nearby mesas, standing nobly— and defiantly—against the gnarled cedars and sky. Only through stealth and cunning are the two cowboys finally able to capture the mighty stallion, and then it is a hollow victory. As the lassos gather around Lightning's neck, Lee admits with lack of enthusiasm: "I reckon that reward, an' then some, can't buy him."

In the latter story Grey focuses on the brief fame of a footloose, misunderstood Arizona cowpoke named Monty Price. Written with the same jaunty zest as his "Rube" baseball stories, "Monty Price's Nightingale" is an arresting character study of a rather peculiar drover. "He was a magnificent rider," wrote Grey. "He possessed the Indian's instinct for direction; he never failed on the trail of lost stock; he could ride an outlaw and shoe a vicious mustang." However, Monty Price could not keep a job. After six months of roping and branding cattle, Monty, without any particular reason, slips away in the middle of the night. Later, while traveling on the range, he meets his former boss, Bart Muncie. Muncie claims that Monty has a "streak of yellow" and challenges Price to a gunfight to prove his theory. Monty refuses. To his pals Monty seems "a silent, morose, greedy cowboy, a demon for work, with no desire for friendship, no thought of home or kin."

Monty seems destined for a bitter, lonely life. But Monty has a nightingale singing inside him that tells him otherwise. Its song grows "rosier and mellower and richer" day by day, as he travels to his own rhythm. During a hot arid spell, he is out riding on the prairie when he sights smoke billowing from the ranch house of his old nemesis, Bart Muncie. Rushing to the scene, Monty rescues Bart's little daughter Del and escapes through a wall of flames.

Monty barely survives the ordeal: "he could never ride a horse again. Monty's legs were warped, his feet hobbled. . . . His face was dark, almost black, with terrible scars." And so Monty lives out the rest of his days as "a burned-out, hobble-footed wreck of a cowboy," his only real distinction in life being his ability to listen to his own song.

Two of Grey's best novelettes were published within a year of each other—*The Wolf Tracker* (November 1924) and *Don, The Story of a Lion Dog* (August 1925). Both represent, along with *Tappan's Burro*, the height of Grey's shorter fiction. The impact of *The Wolf Tracker* may be different for modern readers than for those in 1924. For one thing, wolf populations have actually decreased drastically since 1930, with or without the help of wolf hunters. For another, wolves have recently been reintroduced into areas such as Yellowstone Park, where their absence over time has caused more harm than good. In some instances, the modern reader might sympathize more with the wolf than with the tracker. But in Grey's day, it was assumed that his readership took the point of view of the hunter and central character.

The story reveals the methods of an aging wolf hunter named Brink as he tracks the phantom wolf Old Gray. Early in the narrative Brink meets a group of discouraged cattlemen who relate the savage exploits of Old Gray. Promised a handsome reward, Brink sets out to bring down the wolf. Brink seems fairly typical of a Grey protagonist. "All his early boyhood," Grey relates, "he had been a haunter of the woods and hills, driven to the silent places and abodes of the wild . . . from the cold borders of the Yukon to the desert-walled Yaqui. . . . Women had never drawn him, much less men."

The strength of *The Wolf Tracker* is in Grey's ability as a writer to establish the close relationship of Brink and the natural world. With patience and determination, Brink endures thunderstorm and blizzard in his pursuit of Old Gray from the forests of Arizona to the plateaus of New Mexico. Often Brink wonders if his will and stamina are equal to the wolf's. When the pain in his body becomes too great, Brink thinks of giving up the chase. But the "strange, sustaining, unutterable, ineradicable" power drives him on. While the reader might wonder what precise motivation keeps Brink in the hunt, the tracker will not admit defeat.

The major weakness of *The Wolf Tracker* is that it focuses too narrowly on the hunter and rarely describes the actions of the wolf-antagonist. For a story such as this to succeed fully it must be something more than simply a revenge pursuit. After all, Old Gray's actions killing cattle are the result of his nature. He is not a villian, because he is not responsible for his acts. In this story, several shifts in focus between the hunter and Old Gray would give the narrative more interest beyond the mere stalking of a menacing wolf. Animal characters in fiction must have at least a shred of dignity. Otherwise the narrative results in an imbalance detrimental to the novel or novelette.

Given Grey's emphasis on the main character, the end becomes predictable. Human triumphs over animal. Brink's dedication, craft, and guile pay off. When it comes, however, to surrendering Old Gray's hide, Brink will not even give the idea a second thought. No one but Brink, not even the ranchers who put up the reward, would ever have the trophy of the wolf's hide. "Keep your money," Brink tells them. "Old Gray is mine."

Zane Grey published his first dog story, "Tige's Lion," in 1908, during that remarkable trip with Buffalo Jones and Jim Emmett to the rim of the Grand Canyon. Grey always had a special affection for the dogs that pulled the dangerous duties of flushing mountain lions from their lairs. Some were homely and bedraggled. Others were tenacious and rowdy. He wrote about these dogs in *The Last of the Plainsmen*, "Roping Lions in the Grand Canyon," and in one of his best novelettes, *Don, The Story of a Lion Dog*. In the dogs' often fearless and unaffected manner, he recognized the heroic virtues commonly lacking in humans.

Among Jones's "motley assembly of canines" Grey spies the hound named Don, who seems "out of place because of his superb proportions, his sleek, dark smooth skin, his noble head, and great, solemn black eyes." During their trek through the Painted Desert, Grey witnesses how Jones frequently uses his blunderbuss to remind the dogs they are after lions, not jackrabbits. "Wal, it looks worse than it is," Jones explains, to no one's real satisfaction. "I'm usin' fine birdshot an' it can't do no more than sting." Grey watches as the crusty Jones fires a volley in front of Don. "See hyar," Jones bellows at Don. "I knowed you was a deer-chaser. Wal, now you're a lion dog." Angered by Jones's drastic training measures, Grey tries to make friends with the recalcitrant hound. "His tragic eyes haunted me," muses Grey. "There was a story in them I could not read." Thus begins a relationship that would forever affect how Zane Grey viewed the animal world.

Like a father following his favorite son—but not admitting he is doing so—Grey watches Don chase and tree several lions for

capture. With the other dogs—Ranger, Moze, Sounder, and Tiger
—Don develops a fearless attitude around ferocious cougars. This,
of course, makes him valuable in camp, but places him in constant
danger. Although Grey traveled with a dog named Don, the canine
figure is really a composite. The narrative *Don, The Story of a Lion
Dog,* although based on actual events, is a fictionalized version that
incorporates exploits of both the 1907 and 1908 journeys with Buffalo
Jones. The clue to why Grey chose to fictionalize Don's story oc-
curs in the opening paragraph. Grey writes that it took him "years
to realize the greatness of a dog." Despite his many accounts of the
story of Don ("Last of the Plainsmen," "Roping Lions," etc.), Grey
needed the flexibility of fiction to give the story scope, intensity,
and focus. After all, Don was the hero, not Zane.

By the time *Don* appeared in *Harper's* magazine in 1925, Grey
had achieved some mastery in the animal story. Although he never
attained the widespread popularity or recognition of an Ernest
Thompson Seton or a Jack London, Grey did carve his own niche
in 1920s publishing. With *Tappan's Burro, The Thundering Herd,*
and *Don, The Story of a Lion Dog,* Grey voiced his own opinions
about the often unsung heroes of the animal world. Whether he
was discussing the plight of the bison, the dog, or the burro, he discovered, quite to his delight, that not all the heroes of the West
wore guns or rode horses.

Unlike what happened to the real Don, the story ends tragically.
After chasing a lion through virtually impassable territory, most of
the dogs limp back to camp—except Don. Deeply troubled, Grey
maintains a "vigil on the lofty rim" where he "could peer down the
yellow-green slope and beyond to the sinister depths." He hears
Don's lonely baying in the distance, and then silence. "How lonely,"
cries Grey, "how terrifying that stupendous rent in the earth. . . .
What did they mean—this exquisite hued and monstrous canyon
—the setting sun—the wildness of a lion, the grand spirit of a
dog—and the wondering sadness of a man?"

⚞ ⚞ ⚞

Throughout his life Zane Grey played many roles, assuming various masks. Often these roles were in contrast to the famous writer of western novels: freshwater fisherman, baseball pitcher, explorer, nature lover, sailor, adventurer, saltwater angler, short story writer, essayist, tale-spinner extraordinaire. Frequently, the real Zane Grey can be found, not in his novels, but in one of these pursuits and avocations.

From the time he discovered the fishing holes and baseball diamonds around Zanesville, Grey never stopped pursuing life to the hilt. Blazing like a meteor, he soared through life. He found an early mentor in Old Muddy Miser. He perfected a curve-ball, and stories to accompany it, that served him up to his college days at the University of Pennsylvania.

Arriving in New York City, he discovered the effervescence and disappointment of urban life. Here also he found his muse, and went on to write some of his early outdoor essays for *Recreation* and *Field and Stream.* Writing not only offered him an outlet for his talent, but it also provided him a serious alternative to his dental practice. While he established himself as a writer of westerns such as *The Heritage of the Desert* and *Riders of the Purple Sage,* he continually indulged his love of freshwater and saltwater fishing.

During his struggle to the top he met an extraordinary woman named Lina Elise Roth, later known as Dolly Grey, who maintained an unflagging belief in him both as a person and as a writer. While their children were maturing, the couple had their moments of turmoil and happiness. And even after Zane became a gypsy traipsing about the world, Dolly still anchored his writing business and his emotional life. How much of his success he owed to Dolly can only be conjectured. Quite simply, without her, his rough-cut talent might have foundered very quickly.

Certainly one of the most prolific of authors, Grey was also one of the great writers of the outdoors in the twentieth century. In terms of geographical range and breadth of subject matter, few writers could compete with him. This was quite a remarkable accomplishment for a writer who was not published until he was thirty years old. Between 1902 and Grey's death in 1939, a span of thirty-seven years, Grey produced a staggering output of western novels, short stories, and novelettes, as well as a sizeable body of outdoor nonfiction. And yet there was still enough time for to him to roam and enjoy the wild regions of the earth, a legacy he shared with his readers.

Behind all of Grey's exploits was the voice of the raconteur. Fishing, playing baseball, hiking, riding a horse, and sailing a ship became subjects for great storytelling. Perhaps the best story Grey ever wrote was the life he led. In such works as "The Living Past," *Tales of Lonely Trails, Tales of Fishes, The Short Stop, Tales of Fishing Virgin Seas,* and *Tales of Tahitian Waters,* Zane Grey offered the reader the very best of himself. Even without the weight of his western novels, these adventurous books would give him a prominence in American literature. Judged on their own merits, the nonfiction works give his career an important new scope, for they allow us to see the complex sides of one of the most underrated writers of this century. This other person—the vagabond Zane Grey— was someone readers came to know perhaps more intimately than a relative or a friend. Through his tales, essays, stories, and letters, Grey provided a fascinating glimpse into the American character, and in the process, he revealed his own.

APPENDIX

❧ ❧ ❧

Zane Grey's All-Tackle, World Deep-Sea Fishing Records

Zane Grey followed his passion for angling around the world. Below are the world records he held. Although they have since been broken, his accomplishments in deep-sea fishing are still recognized by fishing enthusiasts.

1. Bluefin tuna, 758 pounds; Nova Scotia, Canada, 1924.
2. Yellowfin tuna, 318 pounds; Cabo San Lucas, Mexico, 1925.
3. Pacific sailfish, 132 pounds; Cabo San Lucas, Mexico, 1925.
4. Pacific sailfish, 135 pounds; Zihuatanejo, Mexico, 1925.
5. Yellowtail, 111 pounds; Bay of Islands, New Zealand, 1926.
6. Broadbill swordfish, 582 pounds; Santa Catalina Island, 1926.
7. Pacific dolphin (mahi mahi), 53 pounds; Vairao, Tahiti, 1930.
8. Giant Tahitian striped marlin (blue marlin), 1,040 pounds; Vairao, Tahiti, 1930.
9. Pacific sailfish, 170 pounds; Vavau, Tonga Islands, 1931.
10. Pacific dolphin (mahi mahi), 64 pounds; Vairao, Tahiti, 1933.
11. Silver marlin, 618 pounds; Vairao, Tahiti, 1933.
12. Silver marlin, 710 pounds; Vairao, Tahiti, 1933.
13. Striped marlin, 450 pounds; Bora Bora, Tahiti, 1933.
14. Tiger shark, 1036 pounds; Sydney, Australia, 1936.

I often find traditional bibliographies unhelpful, because I find it difficult to tell which sources were important to the writing and which were
secondary. In view of this, I have provided the reader all the information
of a standard bibliography. I have also provided commentary on those
sources I found particularly helpful and why.

1: The Boy of Summer

Zane Grey is a biographer's dream. Besides being a highly reliable observer, he records his experiences in his partial autobiography "The Living Past" in painstaking detail, right down to the shape and color of
things. "The Living Past" was published in the *Zane Grey Reporter* (Zane
Grey's West Society former official publication) between April 1986 and
March 1988. It is a bonanza of early information on Zane's fishing and
baseball days. My own book *Zane Grey: Romancing the West* (Athens:
Ohio University Press, 1997) provided some background information of
Grey's college baseball experiences. I also relied on parts of Frank Gruber's *Zane Grey* (Cleveland: World Publishing, 1970), although I found it
unreliable in certain circumstances. (The late G. M. Farley once showed
me twelve pages, single-spaced, of errors he had identified in Gruber's
biography; since then I've tried to corroborate all information in Gruber's book from other sources.) Grey's baseball books were helpful: *The
Short Stop* (New York: A. C. McClure, 1909); *The Young Pitcher* (New
York: Harper, 1911); and *The Red-Headed Outfield* (New York: Harper,
1922). Grey's *Tales of Fresh-Water Fishing* (New York: Harper, 1927) is an
endless source of wisdom and knowledge. Readers might more readily
find some of the essays in *Tales* in *The Best of Zane Grey, Outdoorsman*,
edited by George Reiger (Harrisburg: Stackpole Books, 1972). Also for
this chapter I used H. V. Brands's biography of Theodore Roosevelt,
T.R.: The Last Romantic (New York: Basic Books, 1997), an excellent resource that incorporates much of T.R.'s unpublished correspondence. A

helpful resource was *The Best of Field and Stream,* edited by J. I. Merritt (New York: Lyons and Burford, 1995). Ohio town newspapers of the 1890s, especially the *Delphos Herald,* were extremely helpful in documenting Grey's semiprofessional baseball career. Excerpts in this section are taken from *The Red-Headed Outfield and other Stories* (New York: Walter J. Black, 1976) and Reiger's *The Best of Zane Grey Outdoorsman.*

Notes

1. Z.G., "The Living Past," chapter 3.
2. Ibid., chapter 7.
3. Ibid.
4. Ibid.
5. Ibid.
6. *Delphos Weekly Herald,* August 9, 1894.
7. Z.G., "The Living Past," chapter 8. Grey never mentioned the outcome of the crime or whether he in fact reported it to the police. His partial autobiography resumes a discussion of his financial difficulties at the time.
8. See *Romancing the West,* 9–16.
9. Brands, 281–82.
10. Z.G., *The Red-Headed Outfield,* 19.
11. Ibid., 23.
12. Ibid., 42.
13. Z.G., "The Living Past," chapter 2.
14. Ibid., chapter 3.
15. Ibid., chapter 6.
16. Z.G., *Tales of Fresh-Water Fishing,* 1.
17. Reiger, 15
18. Ibid., 2–4.
19. Ibid., 8–9.
20. Ibid., 15–18.
21. Reiger, 286–91.
22. Z.G., *Tales of Fresh-Water Fishing,* 26–34.
23. Reiger, 51.
24. Ibid., 52.
25. Ibid., 54.

2: Those Damned Cowboys

This section was helped immeasurably by three important works on Theodore Roosevelt: David McCollough's *Mornings on Horseback* (New York: Harper, 1983); H. V. Brands's *T.R.: The Last Romantic* (New York: Basic Books, 1997); and one of the great biographies of T.R., *The Rise of Theodore Roosevelt* (New York: Coward, McCann, 1979) by Edmund Morris. These sources not only discussed Roosevelt's contribution to the frontier era, but helped me place Grey in the context of turn-of-the-century America. Roosevelt's letters in the Roosevelt Papers at Harvard University were extremely helpful in getting a feel for the language and attitudes of the Gilded Age. One of the most accessible sources for readers is the Time-Life series on the West. Specifically, *The Chroniclers* (New York: Time-Life, 1977) discusses the relationship of T.R., Wister, and Remington in some depth and offers interesting anecdotes on their relationship. Owen Wister's *The Virginian* (New York: Harper, 1902) is a study all on its own in the popular novel. Also Ben Merchant Vorpahl's essay on Roosevelt, Remington, Wister, and Frederick Jackson Turner in *A Literary History of the American West* (Fort Worth: Texas Christian University Press, 1987) assisted this chapter greatly, as did his book *My Dear Wister: The Frederic Remington–Owen Wister Letters* (Palo Alto: American West, 1972). Philip Knightley's *The First Casualty* (New York: Harcourt, Brace, 1972) was helpful in describing the role of the correspondent during the Spanish-American War.

Notes

1. Morris, 737.
2. Ibid., 41.
3. Ibid., 60.
4. Ibid., 60–61.
5. Ibid., 102.
6. Ibid., 126.
7. Brands, 162.
8. Morris, 283.
9. Ibid., 282.
10. Ibid.
11. Ibid., 283.

12. Ibid., 283.

13. Ibid.

14. Ibid.

15. Ibid., 326.

16. Morris, 329.

17. Ibid.

18. Ibid.

19. Ibid., 330.

20. Ibid., 331.

21. *Chroniclers*, 123.

22. Ibid., 204.

23. Letter, Remington to Wister, September 1894, Owen Wister Papers, Library of Congress.

24. Vorpahl, quoted in *Literary History of the American West*, 289.

25. Brands, 337.

26. Ibid., 338.

27. Ibid., 338–39.

28. Ibid., 339.

29. Ibid.

30. Morris, 622.

31. Knightley, 56.

32. Brands, 356.

33. Ibid., 357.

34. Ibid.

35. Morris, 664.

3: The Strong Brown God

Two indispensable works for this section, especially for understanding the importance of the Colorado River to the West, were Marc Reisner's brilliant *Cadillac Desert* (New York: Viking, 1987) and Wallace Stegner's classic *Beyond the Hundredth Meridian* (Boston: Houghton Mifflin, 1954). Reisner's work is particularly good in establishing a historical and modern perspective on the Colorado. Also helpful were William Fradkin's *A River No More: The Colorado River and the West* (New York: Knopf, 1981) and Frank Waters's *The Colorado* (1946; Athens: Swallow Press, 1985). Zane Grey's works on the Colorado River are, of course, central to his thinking on Western issues. Although I prefer the original Harper editions because, among other reasons, they contain the wonderful illustrations, I've listed the titles under their reprint editions: *Roping Lions in the Grand Canyon* and *The Rainbow Trail* (Roslyn, N.Y.: Walter J. Black, 1976); *The Last of the Plainsmen; Wildfire;* the essay "Nonnezoshe," from *Tales of Lonely Trails* (New York: Harper and Brothers, 1922); and *Boulder Dam* (New York: Harper, 1963). The geographical knowledge of Dr. Charles Pheiffer helped enormously, particularly his booklets "Conestogas to Kanab" and "The Surprise Valleys of Zane Grey."

Notes

1. Z.G., *The Last of the Plainsmen,* 22–24.
2. Z.G., "Roping Lions in the Grand Canyon," 43.
3. Reiger, 21.
4. Ibid., 22.
5. Ibid., 30.
6. Ibid., 32.
7. Ibid., 33.
8. Ibid., 48.
9. Z.G., "Nonnezoshe," p. 7 in *Tales of Lonely Trails.*
10. Theodore Roosevelt, "Across the Navajo Desert," *Outlook,* 105, October 11, 1913.
11. Reisner, 30.
12. Z.G., *The Rainbow Trail,* 358–65.
13. See *Romancing the West,* chapter 12 for Grey's association with Hollywood.
14. Reisner, 58.
15. Z.G., letter to Dolly Grey, September 30, no year.
16. Ibid.
17. Z.G., *Boulder Dam,* 123.
18. Ibid., 15.
19. Ibid., 47.
20. Ibid., 88.
21. Ibid., 228.
22. Z.G., *Wildfire,* 3.

4: My Dear Dolly

Since, for various reasons, Dolly Grey has been overlooked in most biographies of Zane Grey, this part required extensive research into the letters and diaries of the couple. The best collections are part of the G. M. Farley Papers in the Cline Library, University of Northern Arizona in Flagstaff, and the Zane Grey collection at the Ohio Historical Society. These were essential to this section, as well as to some of the later parts of the book. Richard S. Van Wagoner's *Mormon Polygamy: A History* (Salt Lake City: Signature Books, 1989) discusses Grey's uneasy relationship with Mormonism. I also consulted two biographies by G. M. Farley: *Zane Grey: A Documented Portrait* (New York: Portal Press, 1986) and *The Many Faces of Zane Grey* (New York: Silver Spruce Publishing, 1993). G. M. tackled the reasons behind Zane's recurring depressions—something I did not feel qualified to do. Farley's documentation is sound, his research exhaustive. Other books cited in this part include Jean Karr's biography *Man of the West* (New York: Greenburg Publishing, 1949) and the primary work *The Rainbow Trail*.

Notes

1. Karr, 31.
2. Dolly to Z.G., January 7, 1904.
3. Z.G. to Dolly, April 8, 1907.
4. Dolly to Z.G., no date or month, 1909, Mss 1262 The Zane Grey Papers, Ohio Historical Society.
5. Dolly to Z.G., February 23, 1922.
6. Dolly to Z.G., September 21, 1916.
7. Van Wagoner, 89.
8. Ibid., 89–90.
9. Ibid., 91.
10. Ibid., 89–90.
11. Z.G., *The Rainbow Trail,* 72.
12. Dolly to Z.G., February 18, 1913.
13. Ibid.
14. Dolly to Z.G., April 11, 1913.
15. Dolly to Z.G., September 17, 1916.

16. Ibid.

17. Z.G. to Dolly, September 21, 1916.

18. Ibid.

19. Ibid.

20. Dolly to Z.G., August 1, 1916.

21. Dolly to Z.G., October 26, 1920.

22. Z.G. to Dolly, February 28, 1918.

23. Dolly to Z.G., February 23, 1922.

24. Dolly to Z.G., January 18, 1924.

25. Dolly to Z.G., April 28, 1922.

26. Z.G. to Dolly, May 30, 1922.

27. Z.G., *Tales of Fresh Water Fishing,* 103.

28. Ibid., 105–6.

29. Dolly to Z.G., June 20, 1925.

30. Dolly to Z.G., June 24, 1926.

31. Dolly to Z.G., November 25, 1926.

32. Dolly to Z.G., March 22, 1927.

33. Z.G., diary, June 20, 1928.

34. Dolly to Z.G., March 22, 1927.

35. Dolly to Z.G., May 6, 1933.

36. *Better Homes and Gardens,* March 1931, 15–18.

37. Dolly to Z.G., August 20, 1932.

38. Dolly to Z.G., March 13, 1933.

39. Ibid.

40. Ibid.

41. Ibid.

42. Dolly to Z.G., May 6, 1933.

43. Dolly to Z.G., June 9, 1932.

5: The Pathfinder

Zane Grey's essays have long been admired but, except among aficionados, they have been overlooked. Hence, this section relies heavily on the primary sources: *Tales of Southern Rivers* (New York: Harper and Brothers, 1924) *Tales of Lonely Trails* (Harper, 1922) and *Tales of Fresh-Water Fishing* (Harper, 1928). In these narrative essays I was struck by

Grey's gift for storytelling. They ring closer to real experience than most of his novels. Also for this chapter I relied on *A Treasury of Outdoor Life* (New York: Harper and Row, 1975), edited by William E. Rae, which compiles the best of the magazine from more than a hundred years and offers insights into Z.G.'s relationship with the editors.

Notes

1. Z.G., letter to George Allen, October 27, 1911.
2. Z.G., letter to George Allen, February 27, 1912.
3. Reiger, 120.
4. Ibid., 127.
5. Ibid., 129.
6. Ibid., 129–30.
7. Ibid., 132.
8. Ibid.
9. Z.G., *Tales of Lonely Trails,* 19.
10. Reiger, 215–16.
11. Z.G., *Tales of Lonely Trails,* 41.
12. Ibid., 48–49.
13. Ibid., 185.
14. Ibid., 198–99.
15. Ibid., 224.
16. Ibid., 224–25.
17. Ibid., 225.
18. Ibid., 248.
19. Ibid., 250.
20. Ibid., 252.
21. Ibid., 48.
22. Ibid., 358.
23. Ibid., 374.
24. Ibid., 375–76.
25. Ibid., 388.
26. Ibid., 387.
27. Ibid., 394.

6: The Sea Gypsy

For this chapter I relied on Grey's first book of angling essays *Tales of Fishes* (Harper, 1919), and his exuberant *Tales of Fresh-Water Fishing* (Harper, 1928), as well as two books on Hemingway: *Twentieth Century Interpretations of* The Old Man and the Sea, edited by Katharine Jobes (Englewood, N.J.: Prentice Hall, 1968), and *Ernest Hemingway* by Carlos Baker (New York: Charles Scribner's Sons 1969). In this section I sought to establish connections between Grey and Hemingway. Baker in his book mentions that the young Hemingway was so impressed with Grey's fishing books that he frequently gave them away as Christmas gifts.

Notes

1. Z.G., *Tales of Fishes,* 11.
2. Ibid., 12.
3. Ibid., 13.
4. Ibid., 85.
5. Ibid., 127.
6. Baker, 194–95.
7. Jobes, ed., 4.
8. Z.G., *Tales of Fishes,* 142.
9. Baker, 244.
10. Z.G., *Tales of Fishes,* 107.
11. Ibid., 109.
12. Ibid., 110.
13. Ibid., 113.
14. Ibid., 122.
15. Reiger, 136.
16. Ibid., 137.
17. Ibid., 138.
18. Ibid., 138.
19. Ibid., 139.
20. Z.G., *Tales of Fishes,* 144.
21. Ibid., 138.
22. Ibid., 141.
23. Reiger, 84.

24. Z.G., *Tales of Fishes*, 242.

25. Ibid., 246.

26. Ibid., 248.

27. Ibid., 27.

28. Ibid., 35.

29. Ibid., 41.

30. Ibid., 47–48.

31. Ibid., 47.

32. Ibid., 50.

33. Ibid., 188.

34. Ibid., 172–73.

35. Ibid., 267.

36. Ibid., 263.

37. Ibid., 267.

38. Ibid., 198–99.

39. Ibid., 200–201.

40. Z.G., *Tales of Fresh-Water Fishing*, 87.

41. Ibid., 90–91.

42. Ibid., 59.

43. Ibid., 63.

44. Ibid., 64.

45. Ibid., 66.

7: The Barefoot Adventurer

This chapter, which deals mainly with Grey's adventures in the South Pacific and Oregon between 1924 and 1933, features Zane's primary sources *Tales of Fishing Virgin Seas* (New York: Harper, 1925); *Tales of the Angler's El Dorado, New Zealand* (Harper, 1926); *Tales of Swordfish and Tuna* (Harper, 1927); *Tales of Tahitian Waters* (Harper, 1931) and *Tales of Fresh-Water Fishing* (Harper, 1928). Another helpful text was George Reiger's *The Best of Zane Grey, Outdoorsman* (previously cited), as well as the letters and diary of Zane Grey. Among the pleasures of these original Harper editions are the abundant photographs taken by Zane and his group. In *Tales of Tahitian Waters*, there are priceless shots of Tahiti in the 1920s, and an especially good one of the twenty-two-member

Zane Grey "outfit" at the Flower Point fishing camp. In *Tales of Fresh-Water Fishing*, Zane photographed the "shooting of the Rogue River" in a series of interesting shots. Also in the same volume, there are some candid photos of Dolly landing a fish in Oregon. Also helpful in this part was Jean Karr's account of Grey's adventures titled *Zane Grey: Man of the West* (New York: Greenburg Publishing, 1949), and for Grey's role in the western movie, Frank Gruber, *Zane Grey* (Cleveland: World Publishing Company, 1970).

Notes

1. Reiger, 169.
2. Ibid., 171.
3. Ibid., 172.
4. Ibid., 174.
5. Ibid., 174–75.
6. Ibid., 176–77.
7. Karr, 178.
8. Ibid., 181.
9. Reiger, 185.
10. Z.G., *Tales of Fresh-Water Fishing*, 180–90.
11. Ibid., 190.
12. Reiger, 269.
13. Z.G., *Tales of Fresh-Water Fishing*, 167.
14. Ibid., 190–95.
15. Ibid., 199.
16. Ibid., 201.
17. Ibid., 208.
18. Ibid., 236.
19. Ibid., 255.
20. Ibid., 256.
21. Ibid., 211.
22. Z.G., *Tales of the Angler's El Dorado, New Zealand*, 1–2.
23. Ibid., 3.
24. Ibid., 4.
25. Ibid., 12.
26. Ibid., 14–15.

27. Ibid., 25.

28. Ibid., 30.

29. Ibid., 99.

30. Ibid., 117–18.

31. Ibid., 128.

32. Z.G., letter to Dolly, March 14, 1926.

33. Z.G., *Tales of the Angler's El Dorado, New Zealand*, 142.

34. Ibid., 156.

35. Ibid., 158–59.

36. Ibid., 179.

37. Ibid., 191.

38 Ibid., 204.

39. Ibid., 145.

40. Ibid., 48–49.

41. Ibid., 211.

42. Ibid., 214.

43. Z.G., *Tales of Tahitian Waters*, 88.

44. Ibid., 89.

45. Z.G., letter to Dolly, October 14, 1928.

46. Ibid.

47. Ibid.

48. Dolly, letter to Z.G., December 23, 1928.

49. Z.G., *Tales of Tahitian Waters*, 213.

50. Ibid., 238.

51. Ibid., 267.

52. Ibid., 135.

53. Ibid., 135–36.

54. Ibid., 159.

55. Ibid., 18.

56. Ibid., 121–22.

57. Ibid., 91–92.

58. Ibid., 139.

59. Ibid., 241–42.

60. Ibid., 5.

61. Ibid., 152.

62. Z.G., diary, August 21, 1930.

63. Z.G., letter to Dolly, February 6, 1931.
64. Ibid.
65. Z.G., letter to Dolly, March 15, 1931.
66. Ibid.
67. Ibid.
68. Ibid.
69. Z.G., letter to Dolly, May 8, 1931.
70. Ibid.
71. Ibid.
72. Dolly, letter to Z.G., March 13, 1933.
73. Z.G., diary, July 10, 1933.
74. Z.G., diary, November 17, 1933.
75. Gruber, 210.
76. Ibid., 206.
77. Ibid., 207.

8: King Maverick

For the years between 1934 and 1938, I've emphasized the article "North Umpqua Steelhead" in the September 1935 issue of *Sports Afield*, an article also found in Reiger's *The Best of Zane Grey: Outdoorsman*. Several primary works also figure in the section, including *Tales of Fresh-Water Fishing, An American Angler in Australia* (Harper, 1937), and *Wilderness Trek* (Harper and Brothers, 1944). For a different perspective on Zane Grey's fishing I used an unpublished memoir of angling friend Bob Davis, who also served as editor of *Munsey's Magazine,* and an article Grey wrote for the *Catalina Islander* concerning his Australian trip.

Notes

1. Z.G., *Tales of Fresh-Water Fishing,* 107–9.
2. Ibid. 111.
3. Ibid., 108–9.
4. Ibid., 109–10.
5. Ibid., 122.
6. Reiger, 269.
7. Ibid.

8. Ibid., 272.

9. Ibid., 276.

10. Ibid., 280.

11. Z.G., *Tales of Fresh-Water Fishing,* 154–55.

12. Ibid.

13. Z.G., *Catalina Islander,* July 20, 1936.

14. Bob Davis, unpublished memoir, 1928.

15. Z.G., diary, October 17, 1936.

16. Z.G., *Tales of Fresh-Water Fishing,* p. 92.

9: The Desert Sage

For this section I relied solely on the primary short works: *Tappan's Burro and Other Stories* (Harper, 1923; *Tappan's Burro,* one of Grey's best novelettes, is discussed in *Romancing the West,* pp. 132–33) and *Blue Feather and Other Stories* (Harper, 1961). *The Ranger and Other Stories* (Harper, 1960) is slightly inferior to the first two, but noteworthy. *The Zane Grey Review* supplied additional information.

Notes

1. *Zane Grey Review,* February 1997, p. 4.

INDEX

Also by Stephen J. May